34-94 BK Bud April 94

National

Rifle

Association

National Rifle Association

Money, Firepower & Fear

Josh Sugarmann

National
Press
Books

Washington, D.C.

First Edition

Library of Congress Cataloging-in-Publication Data

Sugarmann, Josh, 1960-
National Rifle Association: money, firepower & fear
Josh Sugarmann
268 pp. 15.25 cm x 22.85 cm
Includes index
ISBN 0-915765-88-8: $19.95
1. National Rifle Association of America--History.
2. Gun control--United States--History.
3. Lobbying--United States--History.
I. Title HV7436.S84   1992
363.3'3'06073--dc 20   91-29926
CIP

PRINTED IN THE UNITED STATES OF AMERICA

Acknowledgments

Everyone thinks they are an expert on gun control. After all, we all have televisions, and the accepted "solutions" have been around since the 1920s. Yet unlike most public policy debates, gun control is unique because few of those involved in the issue have a true understanding of it. I have been fortunate to have the friendship and advice of two of the most insightful of that limited number. My sincere thanks and gratitude go to Kristen Rand, not only for her help with this book, but for her unyielding efforts over the past three years on behalf of the Firearms Policy Project of the Violence Policy Center. The insight and advice of Paul Lavrakas, chair of the Violence Policy Center, has also been crucial in the writing of this book.

Others that I would like to thank include Michael Beard and the staff of the Coalition to Stop Gun Violence, Ted and Françoise Gianoutsos, Michael Ambrose, Gerald Arenberg, Glenn Baker, Cornelius Behan, Joe Casey, Dennis Ciccone, Dr. Beverly Coleman-Miller, David Conover, Rex Davis, Vinnie DeMarco, Linda Farmer of the National Firearms Association, Marlene Lynch Ford, Peter Franchot, Gill Genn, E. Jay Miller, Dan Moldea, the Police Executive Research Forum, Daniel Ruth, John Snyder of the Citizens Committee for the Right to Keep and Bear Arms, Eric Sterling of the Criminal Justice Policy Foundation, Jesse Sugarmann, Liz Sugarmann, Jerald Vaughn, Robert Wadman, David Wallace of the National Security Archive and Willie Williams. My sincere thanks and gratitude go to Karen Lehrman for editing the original manuscript and additional editing provided by Leona Hiraoka. In addition I would like to thank Rebekah Greenwald and Rebeccah Kingsley. I would also like to thank Rich Taylor, who provided primary research assistance for this book. Further assistance was provided by Jonathan Kales, Heather McCulloch and Kris Quandt.

Contents

Introduction

Guns R Us

The National Rifle Association of America has for more than 120 years stood as the most visible defender of "the right to keep and bear arms." From its meager beginnings—$485 and a handful of volunteers toiling out of a cramped New York City office—the NRA has grown to an $88 million-dollar-a-year, corporate non-profit with nearly 2.6 million members, 400 employees and assets of $128 million. Today's NRA is more than an organization—it is an American institution. Yet who is the NRA?

The news media and a large segment of the American public often stereotype the NRA as a fraternity of drunken, fatigue-clad rednecks who, when they aren't stumbling through the woods in search of Bambi, are home in their bunkers mimeographing tracts on the coming Apocalypse. New York Governor Mario Cuomo once characterized its members as men who "drink beer, don't vote, and lie to their wives about where they were all weekend." And although this stereotype is popular with editorial-page cartoonists, it oversimplifies the NRA.

The NRA views itself as occupying a far loftier niche in society. Since its establishment, it has single-mindedly devoted itself to an ideal that found its genesis in the Revolutionary War: the American rifleman tradition. Its embodiment is the hero of the Revolution, the citizen-soldier. In its

1967 official history, *Americans and Their Guns*, the NRA reminds us:

> Freedom from Great Britain was not won by supermen using superweapons; it was won by ordinary citizens whose will to fight for liberty was backed by an intimate knowledge of firearms gained through the use of personal weapons.

The coonskin-capped legacy of the rifleman tradition is one of rugged individuals whose freedom, and that of their nation, is guaranteed solely by the unlimited availability of firearms.

When challenged, the NRA offers as validation of its views the Second Amendment of the Bill of Rights—"A well regulated militia, being necessary to the security of a free state, the right of the people to keep and bear arms, shall not be infringed." As NRA field representative Fred Romero warned in 1990:

> The Second Amendment is not there to protect the interests of hunters, sports shooters and casual plinkers, although those are convenient spinoffs. The Second Amendment is there as a balance of power. It is literally a loaded gun in the hands of the people held to the heads of government.[1]

It is this Second Amendment fundamentalism that inspires and drives the leadership of the NRA and an activist core of its membership. An absolutist—if truncated—interpretation is spelled out in four-inch metal letters on the granite exterior wall of its Washington, D.C., headquarters: "The Right of the People to Keep and Bear Arms Shall Not Be Infringed."

The NRA views its role as transcending mere public policy. "You would get a far better understanding if you approached us as if you were approaching one of the great religions of the world," explained former Executive Vice President J. Warren Cassidy in 1990.[2] Cassidy is right. Like any religion, the NRA has its gods, commandments and hierarchy. The faith is passed down by the leadership to the laity, and, like all good fundamentalists, both are unswayed by the complexities of modern life.

The gods of the NRA—living and dead—bask before the membership in sepia-toned images of Western folklore and frontier individualism. The members' worldview is summed up by Louis L'Amour in his novel *Radigan*:

> There are times in life when the fancy words and pretty actions don't count for much, when it's blood and dust and death and a cold wind blowing and a gun in the hand and you know suddenly that you're just an animal with guts and blood that wants to live, love and mate, and die in your own good time.

The pantheon of modern-day dieties who symbolize the NRA's ideals includes John Wayne, Roy Rogers, Charlton Heston and Chuck Yeager. Both Wayne and Rogers have been honored with NRA members sweepstakes in their name, while Heston and Yeager have lent their faces to various NRA advertising campaigns.

In full-page magazine ads Heston promises:

> The NRA defends your freedoms, but that's just the beginning. The NRA is the National Governing Body for America's Olympic shooting team. . . . More than 18 million Americans . . . have turned to courses supported by the NRA to learn safe hunting skills and outdoor ethics. The NRA teaches America's youth firearms safety through more than 1,800 NRA-affiliated Junior Clubs, where over 35,000 citizens of tomorrow learn responsible gun ownership today. Add it all up and you have the real NRA. A strong voice and responsible friend of mainstream America.[3]

Without doubt, the NRA's vision appeals to many Americans. There are more than 200 million guns in America, 70 million gun owners and 20 million hunters. Virtually half of all households own a gun, and one out of four American homes has a handgun. The NRA counts among its friends and supporters celebrities such as Kevin Costner and Susan Howard, congressional leaders and U.S. presidents. Congressional supporters include the majority of those in leadership positions from both sides of the aisle. Recent U.S. presidents who have accepted NRA membership include Dwight Eisenhower, John Kennedy, Richard Nixon, Ronald Reagan and George Bush. A notable exception to this list is lifelong hunter Jimmy Carter. Life Members Ronald Reagan and George Bush have both addressed the NRA's annual meetings, Reagan being the first sitting president to do so.

Yet contrary to Heston's hearty assurances, mainstream America is not the NRA's best friend, nor are mainstream gun owners. According to 1988 and 1989 Gallup polls, more than 70 percent of all Americans favor banning Saturday Night Special handguns—inexpensive, shoddily made, short-barreled handguns best suited for crime. Three-quarters of all Americans favor the 1988 federal ban on plastic firearms undetectable to airport X-ray machines and metal detectors. Seventy-two percent of Americans favor banning semi-automatic assault weapons.[4] And an imposing 91 percent support a seven-day waiting period for handgun sales.[5]

The NRA typifies these polls as knee-jerk responses to crime and violence by an ill-informed public that has developed an anti-gun bias from the slanted reporting of network news and urban newspapers. Yet support for such measures *among gun owners* is virtually the same. Sixty-six percent favor banning Saturday Night Specials. Sixty-eight percent favor banning assault weapons. Support for banning plastic guns holds at 74 percent.[6] And 90 percent of all gun owners favor a waiting period with background check for handgun sales—just a percentage point less than the general public.[7]

Despite the vagaries of polling, these figures represent general support for gun control in America, including banning specific categories of firearms. At the very least, this broad support, occurring against a backdrop of 12,000 suicides, 9,000 murders and 1,000 fatal accidents involving handguns alone each year, should allow for a rational dialogue regarding the role of firearms in America and the possible controls that could be placed over their distribution and use. The NRA is the primary reason this has not happened, and this is because the manifestation of the NRA's beliefs is its unyielding stance against gun controls. In the words of former NRA President Joe Foss: "I say all guns are good guns. There are no bad guns. I say the whole nation should be an armed nation. Period."[8] In their self-described "NATO Strategy," gun advocates view an attack on any one type of firearm as an attack on all firearms.

The hard-line views of the NRA are crafted not from the majority of gun owners, or even its members, but from its leadership and an activist core of 600,000 members. Although throughout its history the NRA has expressed little faith in gun controls, its absolutist views did not harden until 1977, when Harlon Bronson Carter seized power in a membership coup that later became known in NRA lore as the Cincinnati Revolt. Under Carter, the man who ran the NRA was no longer merely its chief executive officer, but leader of its anti-gun control "Cause." In a 1980s direct-mail solicitation Carter warned:

> We all know their Master Plan. First, outlaw all handguns. Then register all rifles and shotguns. Finally, confiscate and destroy all rifles and shotguns. Make no mistake, these anti-gun and anti-hunting forces are working feverishly for the day when they can gather up your rifles, handguns, and shotguns and ship them off to gun-melting furnaces.

Carter transformed the NRA. Through the magic of direct mail the NRA grew from 940,000 members in 1977 to three million members in 1986. With the promise of magazines, belt buckles and baseball caps, he created a funding mill that ensured the replenishment of its coffers. Yet each year the NRA loses hundreds of thousands of members. There are far more ex-NRA members in America than members. Since 1977—contrary to the promise on which Carter was elected head—the role of the NRA rank and file has not been participation, but funding for the gun control battles of the Second Amendment fundamentalists.

Since Carter's resignation as executive vice president in 1985, no leader since has been able to carry on his legacy. Instead, there have been a series of failures, whose exits from the organization have been shrouded in scandal and intrigue. While the NRA is often perceived as a seamless monolith, it has at times been held hostage to the weaknesses of those who lead it.

The NRA is often equated in the public mind with the "gun lobby," but they are not quite one and the same. The NRA has its lovers, friends and fellow travelers. If its first love is its own ideology, its second is the firearms industry. The NRA has successfully forged a partnership with the industry—shielding it from criticism while protecting its product—to the point where it is has become nothing less than a manufacturers' trade association. The NRA's "slippery slope" argument against gun control dovetails perfectly with the needs of an unregulated firearms industry searching for new markets. Both the NRA and the industry share a common goal: to increase gun sales and expand the universe of those who buy them. For the industry it means dollars. For the NRA it means new members to finance its battles.

And although the NRA's primary bond is with those who manufacture guns, it has many close acquaintances. The most notable is the federal government. In its early years, the NRA's success was guaranteed by government programs that aided in membership recruitment. To this day it enjoys a relationship with the White House, federal legislators and government agencies that is unique among non-profits. When the issue is guns, the federal government comes to the NRA not for advice, but approval. And operating in the NRA's shadow are other pro-gun organizations, such as the Citizens Committee for the Right to Keep and Bear Arms, the Second Amendment Foundation and the Gun Owners of

America. Unlike the NRA, these organizations focus solely on the politics of gun control. Not only are they the NRA's competitors, they are its conscience—quick to attack the NRA any time they feel it wavers from an uncompromising pro-gun stance.

Although the NRA usually attempts to portray itself to the public as a gun-wielding happy-face, its most effective tools in achieving its agenda are fear and intimidation. In newspaper and magazine ads, Americans are warned of the need for an armed civilian population as a check against the tyranny of a strong federal government. Other ads paint a world in which unarmed victims are easy prey for criminals and the police are never there when you need them. The only reliable form of self-defense, readers are assured, comes from the barrel of a gun.

On Capitol Hill and in state legislatures the NRA relishes its reputation for brass knuckle political power. Its political approach is not sophisticated: reward your friends and punish your enemies. But it works. Its activities are carried out by its lobbying arm, the Institute for Legislative Action (ILA), and its political action committee, the Political Victory Fund (PVF). In 1990 ILA received the largest piece of the $88 million NRA budget pie—nearly $18 million—to battle federal and state gun controls and motivate the membership. In addition, ILA's anti-gun-control message permeates virtually all other NRA programs: publications, fundraising, public affairs and member services. For the 1987-88 election cycle, PVF spending topped $4.6 million, with $1.5 million targeted to defeat Democratic presidential nominee Michael Dukakis.

ILA "legislative alerts," mailed to members to inform them of proposed local, state and federal laws, ensure that when the issue is gun control, the NRA will be heard—en masse. Steeped in emotional direct-mail rhetoric, NRA mailings portray every gun control measure as a personal attack threatening the very life of each NRA member and his family. As a result, congressional offices measure NRA mail by the bag. At the local level, whenever the issue of gun control is broached, the overwhelming presence of irate, orange-capped NRA members at public hearings is guaranteed. The level of emotion is so high that intimidation from NRA members, from vandalism to death threats, is not uncommon.

Not surprisingly, many NRA members are devoted single-issue voters who never forgive those who betray their "rights." To most Americans gun control—which pierces the public consciousness only when something truly horrible happens—is only one of many issues a candidate is judged on. NRA members, however, stay focused.

The key aspect of the NRA's political power, however, is the *threat* of injecting the issue of gun control into a campaign. With its ability to dominate a political campaign and quickly derail any politician's packaged message, gun control is an issue most candidates hasten to avoid.

NRA retribution is not limited to lawmakers. As the result of its federal legislative battles over the past decade—opposition to laws restricting armor-piercing bullets, plastic handguns and assault weapons, and the successful passage in 1986 of its McClure-Volkmer firearms decontrol bill—America's police organizations, formerly one of the NRA's oldest allies, have abandoned it. Never good at accepting criticism, when law enforcement leaders questioned the NRA it followed its natural instinct—and attacked them.

The NRA's success has come at a price. Easy weapons availability coupled with an unfettered firearms industry has resulted in record high death rates—as well as increased public support for gun controls and shifts in the dynamics of the debate. The key beneficiary of this shift has been the organized gun control movement. The movement began in the mid-1970s with the founding of Handgun Control, Inc. (HCI) and the National Coalition to Ban Handguns (NCBH). Fifteen years later, HCI has come to dominate the movement. It is now headed by Sarah Brady, the wife of former White House Press Secretary James Brady, who was shot and critically wounded in John Hinckley's 1981 assassination attempt on Ronald Reagan. HCI has become adept at motivating public sympathy and crafting modest, "common-sense" legislation that enjoys broad public support and highlights the NRA's extremist dogma. An example of this is HCI's flagship legislation, the Brady bill, which proposes a national seven-day waiting period with optional local background check.

Until now, reality has rarely intruded on the NRA's dreamy view of guns. While the Prohibition-era violence of the 1930s and the urban unrest of the 1960s resulted in limited firearms laws, they did little to stem the flow of weaponry or place limits on the industry. The NRA's ability to dismiss the outside world, however, may be coming to an end.

Today the guns are bigger, the victims and killers are younger, and the bodies stacked a little higher. The new generation of firearms is defined by firepower and menacing good looks. Or as an urban trauma surgeon remarked when asked to describe the changes he's seen in gunshot victims, "Well, they have more holes in them now. And the holes are a lot bigger."

In America's cities a culture of violence spawned by drugs has taken hold. In a world in which kids are killed over scuffed sneakers, perceived slights and girls' honor, drugs are no longer necessary—just wounded pride and a gun. Young black males, for whom murder is the leading cause of death, are disproportionately the victims and perpetrators. And while the NRA calls for strict laws to punish these urban teens, it fails to recognize any link between the bloodshed and its own ideology.

In America's inner cities, violence has transformed the culture to the point that getting shot—and living—is, as one former drug dealer says, "like a badge of honor." In Washington, D.C., after fatal shootings drug dealers sometimes drop off money at the funeral home to pay for the victim's services. Murder is no longer personal, it's just business. Youth funerals are so commonplace that the dilemma is not facing the question of death, but what to wear. At a friend's funeral, a young black teen comes in eating a McDonald's hamburger. Without missing a step he wraps the burger and puts it in his back pocket as he goes to view the body. As he walks back down the aisle he takes the hamburger out of his pocket, unwraps it and continues eating. At another funeral, a woman gets up to leave before the service has ended. A teenage girl behind her taps her on the shoulder. "You can't leave," she says. "The 'presser' hasn't come yet." The woman, puzzled, sits back down and asks her friend what "the presser" is. He's the murderer, she's told.

Murder has become so institutionalized in some areas that to send a message you have to torture and then kill your victim. An increasing number of young black men coming into the District of Columbia's morgue have bullet holes in their genitals. "When we first saw it," says Dr. Beverly Coleman-Miller of the city's Public Health Commission, "we thought they were just bad shots. But then we kept seeing it."

Coleman-Miller adds, "One of the most profound things is that when you talk to these young people about firearms, they start talking about their Second Amendment rights. 'I have a right to own this gun for my protection and to protect my family,' they say. They sound just like the members of the NRA." The American rifleman tradition isn't what it used to be.

Endnotes

1. "California Gun Control Law Runs Into Rebellion," *New York Times,* (December 24, 1990).
2. "Under Fire," *Time,* (January 29, 1990) at 16.
3. *American Rifleman,* (January 1991) at back cover.
4. *Sourcebook of Criminal Justice Statistics,* U.S. Department of Justice, Washington, D.C. (1989) at 174.
5. *Ibid.* at 180.
6. *Ibid.* at 174.
7. *Ibid.* at 180.
8. "Under Fire," *supra.*

Part I

Who is the NRA?

Chapter One

Soldiers to Lobbyists

An accepted truism of the firearms debate is that until the 1960s the National Rifle Association was merely a boys club for woods-frolicking hunters. In fact, the early members of the NRA—ex-military men, National Guardsmen and elected officials—had little use for hunters. Their primary concern was marksmanship—on the field of battle and in competition. And while in its early years the NRA endorsed, and even drafted, gun controls it opposes today, a disdain for such measures and a belief in the right of law-abiding citizens to own virtually all categories of firearms has remained constant throughout its history.

The founding fathers of the NRA, William Conant Church and George Wood Wingate, were both Union veterans of the Civil War. In 1863 Church became editor of the newly founded *United States Army and Navy Journal and Gazette of the Regular and Volunteer Services.* In its pages, he championed the need for military marksmanship, as evidenced by the limited shooting skills of Union troops during the war. Church found a kindred soul in Wingate, by this time a captain in the New York State National Guard.

In August 1871 Church wrote, "An association should be organized . . . to promote and encourage rifle shooting on a scientific basis. The National Guard is today too slow in getting about this reform. Private enterprise must take up the matter and push it into life."[1]

Church envisioned an association modeled on the National Rifle Association of Great Britain, which had been established in 1859 by officers of the country's volunteer militia. Clubs had been formed and ranges built throughout England to improve marksmanship and encourage participation by "citizen-soldiers."

On November 17, 1871, New York state granted the National Rifle Association a charter "to promote rifle practice, and for this purpose to provide a suitable range or ranges in the vicinity of New York . . . and to promote the introduction of a system of aiming drill and target firing among the National Guard of New York and the militia of other states."[2]

To raise money for range construction, the NRA turned to the New York Assembly. A friendly legislator introduced a bill requiring the state to allot $25,000 for the purchase of land for the NRA. The NRA agreed to contribute $5,000 as well as develop and manage the facility. To ensure the bill's passage, the NRA began a process it would perfect throughout the next century. Church publicized the measure in the *Journal* and encouraged that letters be written in support. With the state's money in hand, the organization purchased 70 acres of land in Long Island and christened the new range "Creedmoor."

By January 1873 the future looked bright: revenue from the previous year had totaled more than $37,000, most coming from National Guard members. But the NRA's quick rise came to an abrupt halt with the election of Alonzo Cornell as governor of New York.

As recalled in *Americans and Their Guns*, in a meeting with Wingate Cornell made it clear that the NRA's admiration for the "citizen-soldier" was not universal. "The only need for a National Guard," said Cornell, "is to show itself in parades and ceremonies. I see no reason for them to learn to shoot if their only function will be to march a little through the streets." When Wingate argued the need for marksmanship training, Cornell "roared" back, "then we should take their rifles away from them and sell them to benefit the Treasury. It would be more practical and far less expensive to arm them with clubs which require no instruction in their use." The victim of poor economic times and an unsympathetic state government, by June 1892 the NRA had deeded Creedmoor to the state and suspended operations. Its records were put in storage and its shooting competitions exiled across the river and placed under the auspices of the New Jersey State Rifle Association. Yet by December 1900, in the wake of increased national interest in competitive shooting, the NRA was reactivated. The new NRA swore to fulfill its mandate to be a truly national organization, never again depending on the whims of a single state for its survival.

The Lost Opportunity

The passage of New York state's Sullivan Law in 1911, enacted after an assassination attempt on New York Mayor William Gaynor, prompted the NRA's first written criticism of gun control. A key component of the Sullivan Law was the issuance of a police permit before an individual could purchase a handgun. An editorial in the May 1911 edition of *Arms and the Man* (predecessor to the NRA's *American Rifleman* magazine) criticized the law, stating:

> A warning should be sounded to legislators against passing laws which . . . seem to make it impossible for a criminal to get a pistol, if the same laws would make it very difficult for an honest man and a good citizen to obtain them. Such laws have the effect of arming the bad man and disarming the good one. . . .[3]

In its early battles against gun control, the NRA was quick to blame another, more recent, technological innovation— the automobile. The auto had resulted in a new breed of armed criminal: mobile and able to evade capture by crossing jurisdictional lines. An April 1926 article in the *American*

27

Rifleman cited the experiences of "veteran New York police instructor" John Dietz. Said Dietz:

> It's the automobile that's making the going tough for the police—not the one-hand gun. A little job of bank-robbery with maybe a killing or two never bothered a crook. What worried him was the get-away. He couldn't make it in the horse and buggy days. But he can make it now with the fast auto.[4]

These views were echoed in the article by bank robber Emmett Dalton of the horse-bound Dalton gang, who stated:

> A bunch of drug-store cowboys, hopheads and lounge lizards with automobiles can get away with something the hardest-boiled men of twenty years ago fell down on. Why, if our crowd had been supplied with automobiles we'd have moved the Capitol at Washington over across the river and carried the treasury building home with us. But in our day you had to depend on horses.

Reporter Wilbur Cooper, the article's author, dismissed gun control as an anachronistic approach favored by old-time cops more likely to rely on their fists than their guns. Wrote Cooper:

> This is the day of bobbed hair, fast autos, flappers, bathing beauties, synthetic gin, easy money and beau brummel crooks. The old-time, two-fisted copper is as out of place as a hoop-skirt. The cops who will finally put the bee on crime will be hard-driving autoists with a shooting skill that will make robbery, hold-up and crime in general a precarious occupation. But it's easier—and cheaper for the present—to pass fool laws.[5]

Some found the NRA's logic more than a little difficult to follow. Testifying before Congress in 1934, NRA President Karl Frederick noted that "automobile owners are . . . as a class, a much more criminal body, from the standpoint of percentage, than pistol licensees."

"Do you make that statement seriously?" asked Democrat Robert Doughton of North Carolina.

"Yes, sir," replied Frederick.

"That the ordinary man who owns and operates an automobile is more likely to be a criminal than the man who arms himself?" asked Doughton.

"You have not kept the sharp lines of distinction," replied Frederick.

"They are too sharp for me to grasp," countered Doughton.[6]

The 1934 hearings stemmed from the wave of violence that had accompanied Prohibition as well as the interstate bank robbery sprees of such criminals as John Dillinger. This, coupled with an assassination attempt on President-elect Franklin Roosevelt in Miami the year before, increased pressure for federal gun controls. Testifying before the House Ways and Means Committee, Attorney General Homer Cummings warned:

> There are more people in the underworld today armed with deadly weapons, in fact, twice as many, as there are in the Army and the Navy of the United States combined.... [T]here are at least 500,000 of these people who are warring against society and who are carrying about with them or have available at hand, weapons of the most deadly character.[7]

Thus the Justice Department proposed a plan: the buyer of any machine gun, sawed-off shotgun or handgun would go through an application process that included fingerprinting, photographing, criminal background check and a tax on the weapon. To limit the availability of specific categories of firearms, while avoiding any perceived Second Amendment conflicts, the plan relied on the taxing powers of the Internal Revenue Service. For machine guns, sawed-off shotguns, silencers and other "specialty weapons," the tax would be $200. For handguns, which were not to be restricted, the tax was a dollar. If the licensed weapon was resold, the purchaser would have to go through a similar process. Hunting rifles and shotguns were exempted from regulation.

"Frankness compels me to say right at the outset," said Cummings, "that it is a drastic bill."[8] The NRA agreed. Frederick warned that "in our opinion, little of value can be accomplished by Federal legislation at this point."[9] In spite of this, NRA Executive Vice President Milton Reckord told the House Ways and Means Committee, "We believe that the machine gun, submachine gun, sawed-off shotgun, and dangerous and deadly weapons could all be included in any kind of a bill, and no matter how drastic, we will support it."[10] Reckord had promised that "the association I represent is absolutely favorable to reasonable legislation." As proof, he cited the NRA's involvement in developing a previous law, the Uniform Firearms Act. The bill established a set of firearms laws for the District of Columbia and had been offered by the NRA as a model for other states. The D.C. law established a 48-hour waiting period for handgun sales; required a license to carry a concealed handgun; required the licensing of firearms dealers; banned the sale of machine guns, silencers and sawed-off shotguns; authorized additional penalties for criminals armed with firearms; banned the possession of handguns by persons convicted of a violent crime; and forbade handgun sales to minors, drug addicts or those "not of sound mind."

In reiterating his endorsement of the Uniform Firearms Act, Frederick made it clear that although the NRA had helped draft the law, it had little faith in its effectiveness. Its citation at the hearing was primarily to prove that the NRA officers were reasonable men and that their criticism of the proposed federal law should be viewed in this light.

During the hearings, the NRA applied the lessons it had learned in New York state to the federal legislators. Representative John McCormack, Democrat of Massachusetts, questioned Reckord about a telegram the congressman had received that morning from the West Coast urging him "to give all possible consideration to recommendations proposed by [the] National Rifle Association." Regarding the

stream of letters received by the committee, Reckord acknowledged that "in each State, or practically every State, we
have a State rifle association, and we advised a number of
those people that the hearing would be held today."

"Did you ask them to wire in here?" asked McCormack.

Replied Reckord, "I would say yes, probably we did. . . ."

"Did you wire the people telling them what the [NRA]
recommendations were going to be to the committee?" Mc-
Cormack continued.

"No, except that the legislation is bad," said Reckord.

"And they blindly followed it?" asked McCormack.

"I would not say blindly," replied Reckord.

"They did not know when they sent the wires in what the
association was going to recommend?" McCormack continued.

"Except that we were going to recommend legislation,"
Reckord replied.[11]

Reckord's moderate tone bore little resemblance to that of
NRA publications regarding the bill. The May 1934 *Rifleman*
warned that the measure's

> viciousness . . . lies not in what appears on the surface of
> the bill, but in the *intent*. . . . Its viciousness lies in the
> opportunity for disarmament by subterfuge. It is, there-
> fore, of vital importance that those of our citizens who
> object to . . . [the bill] unless it be modified as requested
> by The National Rifle Association, or who would object
> to the bill even if so modified, communicate at once by
> telegram and special-delivery letter with both their Rep-
> resentatives and their Senators in Washington.[12]

The measure was eventually passed out of committee, but
without the handgun provisions. This action outraged the
gun control movement of the day—women's groups. At its
convention, representatives of the two-million-member
General Federation of Women's Clubs listened as Assistant
Attorney General Joseph Keenan attacked the committee
version of the bill. They then passed a resolution demanding
passage of the bill in its original form. The NRA was angrily

denounced by the convention's participants, and a telegram was sent to the committee members and congressional leaders expressing the "outrage" of the conventioneers over handguns being stripped from the bill. "Such deletion," read the telegram, "emasculates [the] bill and makes it a joke. We hold that the security and safety of the homes and families of all the people of this country and the protection of life and property for all the 120,000,000 of people in this land transcends the selfish interest of any organized small minority."[13] It didn't work. In June 1934 the watered-down version of the bill, the National Firearms Act (NFA), was signed into law by President Franklin Roosevelt.

Déjà Vu

The 1934 hearings stand not only as the great lost opportunity in the history of gun control, but as a reminder of how little has changed. Although licensing and registration schemes are of little value today, in 1934 America's handgun population was a fraction of today's 50 million to 70 million weapons. Cummings' regulation package would have allowed police to use licensing as a tool against illegally obtained handguns. In addition, as new hazardous weapons appeared on the market, taxes levied against them could have been increased to restrict availability.

Many of the controls proposed in 1934 might well have hindered the availability of the more powerful firearms found on American streets today. Discussions included the need to regulate high-capacity ammunition magazines and bulletproof vests. The committee considered, and abandoned, machine gun definitions that would have had a tremendous impact on today's firearms violence. Under the National Firearms Act, a machine gun is defined as "any weapon which shoots . . . automatically more than one shot without manual reloading, by a single function of the trigger." The committee had weighed other, more restrictive, definitions that would have capped civilian firepower. One would have classified "any weapon designed to shoot automatically or semiautomatically twelve or more shots without reloading" as a machine gun. A second would have classified as a machine gun "any weapon which shoots . . . automatically or semiautomatically, more than one shot, without manual reloading, by a single function of the trigger." The first definition would have limited the public to weapons capable of holding only twelve rounds or less, the second would have limited it to single-shot weapons.

Other federal firearms legislation introduced that year, but not acted on, seems innovative even today: ammunition fired from the barrel of all handguns and machine guns sold would be kept on file, the weapon's "signature" available to aid in the tracing of guns used in crime; ammunition could be sold only to a licensed handgun owner, and then only in the caliber appropriate to the gun; and ammunition would have markings distinctive to specific regions of the country to aid police in criminal investigations.

Although the proposals themselves were innovative, the arguments in their favor have a familiar ring. Control advocates pointed to the licensing and regulation of cars and drivers as a useful analogy. Comparisons to the low murder and crime rates of European nations with strict handgun controls were also cited. A memorandum released at the hearings comparing the firearms laws and murder rates of Great Britain with those of the United States concluded that "it is unnecessary to discuss the infrequency of crimes committed with firearms in England, for repeated comparisons between such conditions there and in this country are becoming much too unpleasant for the law-abiding American citizen."[14] Nearly 60 years later little has changed.

In 1937 Attorney General Cummings again attempted to win support on Capitol Hill to bring handguns under the National Firearms Act umbrella. Said Cummings, "While the National Firearms Act has been of great assistance in the work of law enforcement, it is far too limited in scope. In some respects, small weapons are even a greater menace than machine guns, since they can be concealed with greater facility."[15] The next year Congress moved to enact a new federal gun bill. It wasn't Cummings' handgun bill, but a compromise measure—drafted by the NRA. The Federal Firearms Act (FFA) of 1938 was the first attempt to regulate interstate and foreign commerce in firearms and ammunition. Manufacturers, importers and dealers were required to obtain annual licenses from the Internal Revenue Service (the annual dealer's fee was a dollar). The shipment of weapons to other than a licensed dealer or manufacturer in states that required a permit to purchase was banned. It also outlawed shipping firearms and ammunition to persons convicted or under indictment for a crime punishable by more than a year in prison, or a fugitive from justice. The law was, unfortunately, easy to circumvent—those in proscribed categories merely lied. In the 30 years following enactment of the FFA there was only one conviction of a purchaser for violating his state's permit law.

Although the FFA represented the final triumph of the NRA over the Justice Department, the organization failed in its attempts to repeal the 1934 machine gun law. As the result of complaints from the Justice Department, a section of the FFA overturning the 1934 law—which the NRA now described as a "very drastic act" with "many bad features"—was removed.

Although the '40s and '50s were mostly uneventful as far as federal gun control was concerned, it was boom time at the NRA. After World War II NRA membership tripled, exceeding 250,000 in 1947. Starting in 1946 the organization finally began to expand beyond its historic base of military and civilian target shooters to include hunters. This new focus rose in part from the large number of World War II veterans who, having been exposed to firearms, had taken up hunting upon their return home. Shooting etiquette learned on the battlefield was, however, viewed less fondly on the homefront by the general public. As a result, the NRA instituted a hunter training program and began lobbying for mandatory hunter safety training in states.

The Assassination Years

This 30-year gun control lull came to an abrupt end on November 22, 1963, with the assassination of President John F. Kennedy. Lee Harvey Oswald had purchased his rifle, a Mannlicher-Carcano, through an ad placed in the NRA's *American Rifleman* magazine. The ad read:

> LATE ISSUE! 6.5 ITALIAN CARBINE. Only 36" overall, weighs only 5 1/2 pounds. Shows only slight use, lightly oiled, test fired and head spaced, ready for shooting. Turned down bolt, thumb safety, 6-shot, clip fed. Rear down sight. Fast loading and fast firing.

On March 12, 1963, Oswald mailed the ad's coupon and a postal money order for $21.45 ($19.95 plus $1.50 postage and handling) to Klein's Sporting Goods Co. in Chicago. The gun was shipped via parcel post the same month.

According to journalist Robert Sherrill in his 1973 book, *The Saturday Night Special,* the NRA not only facilitated Oswald's gun purchase, but also aided in the development of the ammunition that would make this notoriously inaccurate gun more effective. During World War II the United States seized huge numbers of the rifles. When the government later decided to give a quantity of the guns to Greek anti-Communists, it worked with the NRA at Maryland's Aberdeen Proving Grounds to develop higher-quality ammunition that would improve the gun's accuracy. Some of the ammo eventually made its way onto the U.S. market and into Oswald's hands. When NRA Executive Vice President Franklin Orth told this story to a Senate staffer in the 1960s, he added, "Please don't tell anybody because we don't want to be hung with having been involved in producing the ammunition that killed the President."[16]

Even before the Kennedy assassination, Connecticut Democrat Thomas Dodd, chair of the Senate Judiciary Juvenile Delinquency Subcommittee, had begun investigating the role of mail-order firearms in crime. Although a 1927 law banned the mailing of concealable weapons, handguns and ammunition could still be shipped via common carrier. No restrictions existed regarding the shipment through the U.S. mail of rifles, shotguns and larger weapons. Mail-order sales had increased dramatically since the late 1950s and were an easy way for people in proscribed categories to get weapons. The committee also found that the import of foreign surplus weapons, including bazookas and anti-tank guns, had also ballooned and that the weapons were easily available through mail-order houses. A 1960s advertisement for a 60mm mortar labeled it

> an ideal item for your den or front lawn . . . this is the perfect tool for getting even with those neighbors you don't like. Perfect for demolishing houses or for backyard plinking on Sunday afternoons.

After two and a half years of subcommittee investigation, Dodd introduced his bill, S. 1975, in August 1963. The bill banned the interstate sale of firearms to those under the age of 18 and required anyone purchasing a handgun interstate by mail to include with the order a signed affidavit attesting to their fitness to possess the weapon and identifying the purchaser's local law enforcement official. Prior to shipping, the dealer or manufacturer had to send a copy of the affidavit and a description of the weapon to the named officer. The bill, a limited measure, received the endorsement of both the NRA and the industry. Following the Kennedy assassination, Dodd, with the NRA's blessing, expanded the scope of the bill to include rifles and shotguns.

Although congressional mail initially ran eight to one in favor of the bill, the tide began to shift. Dodd and others pointed to the NRA as the source of the opposition. Testifying before Congress in January 1964, NRA President Bartlett Rummel denied any involvement:

> We have not drummed up people from all over the country to contact you . . . we have made no concerted

effort to bring pressure on Congress . . . these communications to you have more or less arisen spontaneously.

But while the NRA leadership voiced grudging support of the bill on Capitol Hill, it sent a different message to its 600,000 members. Although the NRA did not officially lobby, it spent $144,000 in 1963 alerting its members to proposed "anti-gun laws" so that they could "act quickly and decisively, in a well-organized manner, to defeat such threats" to the rights of "loyal Americans." S. 1975 died in committee. Dodd threatened an investigation "to identify and expose the activities of the powerful lobbyists who have successfully stopped gun legislation from being passed in every Congress."[18] Nothing came of it.

On March 8, 1965, President Lyndon B. Johnson, linking "the ease with which any person can acquire firearms" to the country's rising violent crime rate, called for increased gun controls. The Johnson proposal would: ban mail-order firearms sales by requiring that interstate shipment of weapons occur only between licensed dealers, manufacturers and importers; increase the dealer licensing fee from a dollar to $100; ban the dealer sale of long guns to those under 18 and handguns to those under 21; and ban the import of surplus military weapons.[19] Dodd introduced the president's bill, blaming prior defeats on "the blind, almost mindless, efforts of a segment of the gun enthusiasts, with their shabby, time-worn slogans."[20] The next month the NRA urged its members to oppose the bill, warning that it could eventually ban "the private ownership of all guns" and would grant Treasury "unlimited power to surround all sales of guns by dealers with arbitrary and burdensome regulations . . . if the battle is lost, it will be your loss, and that of all who follow."[21] Responding to Dodd's charges that the letter mischaracterized the bill, the NRA's Orth asserted to Dodd that any errors were unintentional. Replied Dodd: "I don't think it was a mistake. Your readers apparently got an impression the writer intended."[22] Testifying before Congress, James Bennett, former director of the Federal Bureau of Prisons, labeled the NRA leader's statement "sheer hypocrisy." And he said of Orth, "How can he come here with a straight face and try to disclaim this as unintentional, or weasel out of it...."[23] Nonetheless, Dodd's bill once again died.

In fighting gun controls, the NRA was—and is—quick to portray the battle as one between true Americans, i.e., gun owners, and those who are either misguided or have some sinister intent. The most obvious beneficiary of an unarmed America, the NRA argued, would be Communists. The October 1967 *Rifleman* featured an article by NRA member John Persakis. Soon after arriving in New York as a Greek seaman in 1943, Persakis inadvertently found himself at a Communist cell meeting. A key component of the lecture, he recalled, was that all Communists should support gun control. When Persakis questioned the man next to him as to why he shouldn't own a gun, the man replied with a sinister undertone, "Oh, but *we* will have guns."[24] This argument was expanded the next month with an NRA editorial titled "The Faces of the Opposition." The article featured caricatures of those who supported gun control: the do-gooder, the politician, the fanatic and the extremist. Said the NRA:

> The anti-gun element wears several faces. There are the sincere faces of do-gooders, some of whom literally would not harm even a germ-laden fly. There are the cynical faces of politicians who would traffic in emotionalism to get votes. There are the over-tensed faces of fanatics ready to doom whatever they dislike—in this instance, firearms—and the calculating faces of extremists determined to destroy what we know and treasure as the American way of life. All of these people would like to bury our guns. Some of them would like to bury us, also.[25]

The NRA's ability to stop any gun control measure ended in 1968. On April 4, Martin Luther King was gunned down on the balcony of the Lorraine Motel in Memphis. The next day the Omnibus Crime Control and Safe Streets Act of

1968—which was amended to include a ban on the interstate sale and shipment of handguns—became the first firearms control bill to pass out of committee since 1938. On June 5, against a backdrop of urban rioting, New York Democratic Senator Robert Kennedy—who had just won the California presidential primary—was gunned down in Los Angeles by Sirhan Sirhan with a .22 handgun. He died the next day. That same day, the crime bill cleared Congress. It was signed into law on June 19. Although the public supported stricter gun controls (a January 1967 Gallup poll found that 70 percent believed that "laws concerning handguns should be more strict"), most Americans had never been motivated to act. Now they were. As historian Richard Hofstadter noted in 1970, after the killings "there was an almost touching national revulsion against our own gun culture."[26] Letters poured into Capitol Hill while enraged citizens picketed the NRA's headquarters. "Can Three Assassins Kill a Civil Right?" asked the NRA in the July *Rifleman*. A besieged Orth promised that Kennedy's assassination could not have been prevented by any law "now in existence or proposed."[27]

After the Kennedy shooting, President Johnson called for extending the mail-order ban to include rifles and shotguns, the licensing of gun owners and the registration of firearms. Said Johnson, "Our citizens must get licenses to fish, to hunt and to drive. Certainly no less should be required for the possession of lethal weapons that have caused so much horror and heartbreak in this country."[28] Testifying before Dodd's Senate subcommittee, NRA President Harold Glassen labeled the measure part of a conspiracy to "foist upon an unsuspecting and aroused public a law that would, through its operation, sound the death knell for the shooting sport and eventually disarm the American public."[29] In a letter described by Maryland Democratic Senator Joseph Tydings as "calculated hysteria," the NRA warned its 900,000 members that "the right of sportsmen in the United States to obtain, own and use firearms for proper lawful purposes is in the greatest jeopardy in the history of our country. . . . [T]heir goal is complete abolition of civilian ownership of firearms. The situation demands immediate action by every law-abiding firearms owner in the United States."[30]

- Both houses rejected LBJ's call for registration, due in large part to an NRA mail blitz. On October 10 Congress did extend the ban on interstate sales and shipment of handguns to include rifles, shotguns and ammunition. Over-the-counter sales of long guns were permitted to residents of contiguous states as long as the sale did not violate the firearms laws of either state. Other components of the bill included: banning the importation of military surplus weapons; setting 18 as the minimum age for the purchase of a long gun; and setting new licensing and recordkeeping standards and fees for dealers, manufacturers and importers. Senate debate on the bill had begun with Dodd urging that the NRA—with its record of "blackmail, intimidation and unscrupulous propaganda"—be stripped of its tax-exempt status and its leaders forced to register as lobbyists.[31] Johnson signed the legislation, the Gun Control Act of 1968, on October 22.

Besides banning the importation of surplus military weapons, the 1968 laws also outlawed the importation of Saturday Night Specials—inexpensive, short-barreled handguns with no sporting purpose made from inferior materials. A Saturday Night Special ban had received a surprising endorsement in the February 1968 *Rifleman*, with the NRA stating:

> Shoddily manufactured by a few foreign makers, hundreds of thousands of these have been peddled in recent years by a handful of U.S. dealers. Prices as low as $8 or $10 have placed concealable handguns within reach of multitudes who never before could afford them. Most figure in "crimes of passion" or amateurish holdups, which form the bulk of the increase in violence. The Administration . . . possesses sufficient authority to bar by Executive direction these miserably-made, potentially defective arms that contribute so much to rising violence.[32]

In a March *Rifleman* editorial noting the favor with which this stance had been greeted by the membership, the NRA reassured readers that the organization

> does not necessarily approve of everything that goes "Bang!" Viewed realistically, junky .22 handguns that retail for as little as $7.98 . . . aren't suited for target shooting, handgun hunting, or police or protection purposes. Most honest-to-goodness gun owners wouldn't have one around. Yet the reckless use of such junk has harmed legitimate firearms ownership.[33]

Federal law, however, did not forbid the importation of the handguns' parts, which could then be assembled onto U.S.-made frames. Domestic production and assembly of the weapons soon jumped from 60,000 in 1968 to a million in 1970. The fact that the import of these handguns was banned while their domestic manufacture was allowed to continue (coupled with Dodd's hailing from the gun-producing state of Connecticut) led many in the industry to label the 1968 law a trade protection act for domestic handgun manufacturers, which, in effect, it was.

As a result of the continued importation of the handguns' parts, Indiana Democrat Birch Bayh introduced a Senate bill to end the domestic production and sale of handguns that failed to meet a "sporting purposes" test as defined by the Secretary of the Treasury.

Support for the bill grew dramatically following the May 15, 1972, assassination attempt on Alabama Governor George Wallace. Wallace had been shot by 21-year-old Arthur Bremer in a Laurel, Maryland, shopping center with a short-barreled, .38 revolver. Following the shooting, Chicago Mayor Richard Daley commented, "I would hope this would be the opportunity to do some soul searching by the Congress to pass legislation to outlaw handguns."[34]

Building on the organization's 1968 endorsement of a Saturday Night Special ban, NRA Executive Vice President

Maxwell Rich testified that "the National Rifle Association concurs in principle with the desirability of removing from the market crudely made and unsafe handguns." He noted that NRA publications did not accept advertising for such "junk guns" because "they have no sporting purpose, they are frequently poorly made, and they do not represent value received to any purchaser."[35] When pressed by Bayh as to the NRA's willingness to support a ban on Saturday Night Specials, Rich responded, "On the Saturday Night Special, we are for it [banning] 100 percent. We would like to get rid of these guns."[36] The measure was passed by the Senate 68 to 25 on August 9, 1972 but never came to a vote in the House. Rich's endorsement of, at least, the concept of banning Saturday Night Specials set forces in motion that would eventually lead to his ouster—and to the creation of the NRA we know today.

Endnotes

1. Trefethen, James, *Americans and Their Guns*, Stackpole Books, Harrisburg , PA (1967) at 34.
2. *Ibid.* at 10.
3. Leddy, Edward, *Magnum Force Lobby*, University Press of America, Lanham, MD (1987) at 83.
4. Cooper, Wilbur, "The Evolution of the Cop," *American Rifleman*, (April 1926) at 9.
5. *Ibid.* at 11.
6. House Hearings on National Firearms Act, (April/May 1934) at 54.
7. *Ibid.* at 4.
8. *Ibid.* at 5.
9. *Ibid.* at 59.
10. *Ibid.* at 81.
11. *Ibid.* at 63.
12. "Disarmament by Subterfuge," *American Rifleman*, (May 1934) at 4.
13. "Clubwomen Insist on Anti-Pistol Bill," *New York Times*, (May 25, 1934).
14. House Hearings on National Firearms Act, *supra*, at 28.
15. "Urges Firearms Act to Include All Kinds," *New York Times*, (May 5, 1937).
16. Sherrill, Robert, *The Saturday Night Special*, Charterhouse, New York (1973) at 168.

17. "No Action Taken to Regulate Firearms Shipments," *Congressional Quarterly Almanac*, (1967) at 272.
18. *Ibid.* at 273.
19. "Gun Control Bills Stalled by Stiff Opposition," *Congressional Quarterly Almanac*, (1965) at 861.
20. *Ibid.* at 641.
21. "Hearings Held on Administration Gun Bill," *Congressional Quarterly Almanac*, (1965) at 641.
22. *Ibid.* at 643.
23. *Ibid.* at 644.
24. "Oh, But We Will Have Guns," *American Rifleman*, (October 1967) at 53.
25. "The Faces of the Opposition," *American Rifleman*, (November 1967) at 18.
26. Hofstadter, Richard, "America as a Gun Culture," *American Heritage*, (October 1970) at 6.
27. "Shootings, Mail, Lobbying, Push Congress to Act," *Congressional Quarterly Almanac*, (1968) at 563.
28. "Gun Controls Extended to Long Guns, Ammunition," *Congressional Quarterly Almanac*, (1968) at 553.
29. *Ibid.* at 558.
30. "Shootings, Mail," *supra*, at 564.
31. "Gun Controls Extended," *supra*, at 560.
32. "Are We Really So Violent?" *American Rifleman*, (February 1968) at 16.
33. "Restraint on TV, Cheap Handguns Wins Favor," *American Rifleman*, (March 1968) at 15.
34. "Daley Asks Handgun Curb," *New York Times*, (May 17, 1972).
35. Senate Hearings on Saturday Night Special Ban, (September 13, 1971) at 315.
36. *Ibid.* at 323.

Chapter Two

The Cincinnati Revolt

During the turbulence of the 1960s, the two contrasting faces of the NRA came into focus: the smiling, benevolent sportsman and the fevered, angry Second Amendment fundamentalist. NRA Executive Vice President Maxwell Rich represented the first face. The second belonged to a large, imposing man with a shaved head who looked like a cross between Mr. Clean and a .45 slug—Harlon Bronson Carter. Carter was unyielding in his opposition to gun controls. In 1975, as head of the NRA's newly formed lobbying arm, the Institute for Legislative Action (ILA), he was asked if he would "rather allow those convicted violent felons, mentally deranged people, violently addicted to narcotics people to have guns, rather than to have the screening process for the honest people like yourselves?" Such a sacrifice, Carter responded, was "a price we pay for freedom."[1] And it is Carter who defined the modern-day NRA.

The NRA had been a part of Carter's life since he joined it in 1930 at the age of 16. In 1951, he was elected to the board of directors, served as its vice president from 1963 to 1965, president from 1965 to 1967 and became a member of the executive council (a lifetime position) in 1967. For most of this time Carter served in the U.S. Border Patrol, eventually rising to its head in 1950 at the age of 37. In 1961 he was named commissioner of the Southwest Region for the Immigration and Naturalization Service (INS). Carter retired from government in 1970. Three years later, agents investigating corruption in the INS confronted him with various allegations, including the charge that when he left his position, 40,000 to 50,000 rounds of government ammunition had left with him. Carter eventually testified before a federal grand jury in San Diego, where he denied any knowledge of the missing government ammo. No charges were filed.

At NRA headquarters, when Harlon Carter spoke, people listened. In a July 1972 address to the NRA's executive committee—held during debate over the Bayh Saturday Night Special bill—Carter voiced his fears that the NRA was losing sight of its true mission. In outlining his concerns, he spelled out the political philosophy that would eventually dominate the organization.

Carter's speech centered on NRA Executive Vice President Rich's endorsement of a Saturday Night Special ban. "My Lord," said Carter, "he has been Pilated and crucified repeatedly on an unfortunate choice of words, and I sympathize with his position."[2] (These "unfortunate" words had also been part of an NRA press release that had supported the Bayh bill in principle.) Continued Carter:

> Now someone says to me . . . , "Yes, but we took positions back five or six years ago, and we made statements some years ago," and he pointed out to me that I had made a statement one time relating to pot metal pistols. I did. But these people now have introduced confiscatory gun bills; they confirm a belated conviction that some of us have held for some time which are what this ultimate goal is, which is to prohibit the private ownership of firearms in this country. [As a result] . . . any position we took back at that time is no good, it is not valid, and it is simply not relevant to the problem that we face today. The latest news release from NRA embraces a disastrous concept... that evil is imputed to the sale and delivery, the possession of a certain kind of firearm, entirely apart from the good or evil intent of the man who uses it and / or (2) that

the legitimate use of a handgun is limited to sporting use.[3]

The same characteristics that made Saturday Night Specials easy targets for restriction—their low quality and ease of concealment—were, according to Carter, positive attributes. Said Carter: "I can produce actual cases that the cheap handgun that snaps in . . . [a police] officer's face instead of firing has saved many, many lives, and the question arises: What are we trying to do? Upgrade the quality of handguns in the hands of our criminals?"[4]

Palm-sized Derringer handguns, which would also come under the Bayh bill, he argued, were uniquely suited to the small hands of children for self-defense. Said Carter:

> There was a little boy . . . and it was real cold and he had his hands in his overcoat. He had one of these little old derringers, and four bushy guys ambled up in an arrogant manner. He stopped them, and three of them were very nice and decent, and one of them said, "What would you do if I told you I had a pistol and I was going to kill you?" And he says, "I would kill you, you son-of-a-bunch." These little guns have a very noble and a very important place and we should make our position clear.[5]

The seeds of discontent planted by Carter in 1972 bore fruit in 1977 at the annual meeting in Cincinnati, Ohio. Prior to Cincinnati, friction had grown between two segments in the NRA: the Old Guard and the New Guard. The Old Guard consisted of the then-current NRA leadership and their supporters. Although they defended and promoted handguns for self-defense (the "homely old shotgun," however, was touted as the best home-defense firearm), their primary firearms interest was recreational: marksmanship, hunting and safety training. Their concerns over gun control were limited to its effects on traditional sporting activities. To the Second Amendment fundamentalists of the New Guard, stopping gun control was paramount. To this vocal minority, gun ownership was no longer a recreational issue, but a political one. They viewed the NRA as the last bulwark

against a government and newly formed gun control movement that wanted nothing less than the banning of all guns.
The events at Cincinnati have an almost legendary quality
among NRA true believers. In battles over the NRA's direction, combatants are quick to lay claim to the true spirit of
Cincinnati, which has come to mean member empowerment
and a fierce dedication to absolute gun rights. In the same
way that politicians of both parties evoke the legacy of JFK,
so it is with NRA factions and the Cincinnati Revolt. The only
complete history of the event is *Revolt at Cincinnati,* a 52-page
tract by *Gun Week* editor Joseph Tartaro. Cincinnati, says
Tartaro, was

> a classic confrontational situation . . . not unlike the
> schism between the American colonists and the Crown in
> 1775. . . . [T]he alienated members were fully aware that
> conflict within the pro-gun movement could be
> dangerous. But they saw the prospect of an NRA increas-
> ingly concerned and spending money on conservation as
> even more dangerous.[6]

The New Guard accused the incumbent leadership of
abandoning its dedication to the Second Amendment for a
newfound devotion to conservation and environmentalism.
Although the Institute for Legislative Action had been
founded in 1975 at the behest of Representative (and NRA
board member) John Dingell, Democrat of Michigan, the
leaders of the New Guard felt that the leadership had placed
severe financial and political restraints on it. Other examples
of weakness and betrayal cited by the New Guard included
the unwillingness of the NRA to participate in the 1970
Citizens Against Tydings (CAT) campaign to defeat pro-
control Senator Joseph Tydings, Democrat of Maryland, and
a statement in the *NRA Fact Book on Firearms Control* characterizing the Second Amendment as being "of limited practical utility" as an argument against gun controls.
Events that occurred in 1976 led the New Guard to con-
clude that the organization was actively being destroyed

from within by the Old Guard leadership. Chief among these was a decision by the Old Guard to move the NRA's headquarters from Washington, D.C., to Colorado Springs, Colorado, where the NRA would build a "World Sports Center" to house itself and other organizations involved in sports and the outdoors. The New Guard viewed the decision to sell the NRA's eight-story granite and marble office building at 1600 Rhode Island Avenue not as an escape from Washington's crime and high cost of living, but as an abandonment of politics.

These concerns were bolstered when a copy of the NRA-commissioned *ORAM Report* was leaked. The report was a private fund-raising study for a planned 37,000-acre NRA recreational center in New Mexico. The project had been approved by the board in 1973 and originally named the National Shooting Center. Initially portrayed as a hunter's Xanadu, by 1976 it had been renamed the National Outdoor Center amid cries from the New Guard that its shooting focus had been diminished.

The report concluded that to obtain the $30 million needed for the center the "NRA must attract to its cause powerful leadership and financial support that is today either repelled or put off by NRA's image as the leader in the fight against gun control."[7] The study found that "the current media image of the NRA destroys its ability to raise money from foundations, especially the large ones such as Rockefeller, Ford and Mellon."[8] The very mention of the name Rockefeller raised the hackles of Trilateral Commission conspiracy theorists always on the lookout for One-Worlders.

Fears of an imploding NRA were magnified when approximately 80 staff members were fired or given early retirement in November 1976 in preparation for the move to Colorado. Leadership characterized the move as "streamlining," but it soon became known as "The Weekend Massacre." Among those whose departure was announced was Institute for Legislative Action head Harlon Carter.

As a result of these events and others, the Federation for NRA was born—an independent, ad hoc committee of disgruntled NRA members and staff. Its leader was NRA Life Member Neal Knox, a tobacco-chewing ex-newspaperman and editor of *Rifle* and *Handloader* magazines. Others involved in the initial planning stages included: Carter; his replacement, Robert Kukla; and *Gun Week's* Tartaro. Their goal was nothing less than a coup that would oust the Old Guard leadership and place control of the organization in the hands of the members. The months leading up to the May 1977 convention were filled with attacks on the NRA in various segments of the gun press, many of them written by Knox.

In a May 1977 *Rifleman* editorial titled "Our Strength is In Unity," Rich responded to the "half-truths, innuendo, and statements out of context" being levied by the Federation. The controversy, he promised, stemmed from

> a few writers in the gun press . . . pushing a shallow, biased and unfounded attack on the National Rifle Association. Our highest priority is safeguarding the right of gun ownership and the future of shooting sports. This is the single fiber that binds us together—and to give it muscle, we need the unity and strength of our members—all members.[9]

Rich's plea was too little too late. On the night of May 21, 1977, more than 2,000 NRA members met in the Cincinnati Convention-Exposition Center in a session that lasted until nearly 4 a.m. "Perspiration," wrote Tartaro, "flowed like wine."[10]

Armed with walkie-talkies and bull horns, the orange-capped members of the Federation were "loaded for parliamentary bear." By the end of the evening the Old Guard was ousted and bylaw changes were enacted empowering the membership to elect the NRA executive vice president, who previously had been chosen by the board. To the cheers of the crowd, Carter was elected the new leader of the NRA. Other bylaw changes included: making defense of the Second Amendment paramount; increasing funding power for the Institute for Legislative Action, which was placed under the control of the executive vice president; greater member participation in the board nomination process; a moratorium on development of the New Mexico property; a reversal of the decision to move to Colorado; and a requirement that all future bylaw changes be approved by membership vote. As the NRA's new leader, Carter promised:

> Beginning in this place and at this hour, this period in NRA history is finished. There will be no more civil war in the National Rifle Association. . . .You, the membership, are entitled to have an NRA that is responsive to your wishes. You cannot be denied, my beloved friends; you are the NRA, not I. . . . [Y]ou are all we have. . . .You're America's greatest people, my friends, don't ever forget that you are.[11]

Carter soon appointed co-conspirator Neal Knox the new head of ILA. Knox personified the new NRA's "no-compromise" approach. Knox's vision was that of an NRA that would go on the offensive and roll back the Gun Control Act of 1968, crushing those who got in its way. As Knox often paraphrased: it was good to be loved, it was better to be feared. Knox moved quickly to fulfill his mandate. Idaho Republican Senator Jim McClure and Missouri Democratic Representative Harold Volkmer soon filed a bill that would in effect gut the Gun Control Act of 1968. The McClure-Volkmer firearms decontrol bill would be the NRA's flagship piece of legislation until its passage in 1986. At the same time Knox launched a concerted campaign to discredit the federal Bureau of Alcohol, Tobacco and Firearms (ATF), the government agency charged with enforcing federal firearms laws.

Carter too knew what he wanted—members and money. He envisioned an NRA army so large and strong that no politician would dare defy it. Under his reign, the NRA began a merchandising program, which continues to this day, that needed only Ed McMahon to make it complete. Special insurance, contests, member-get-a-member giveaways, and an avalanche of belt buckles, hats, key chains, patches and coffee mugs gave the NRA's direct mail the feel of a carnival huckster run amok. Carter beckoned Americans to join what he called "The New NRA," an organization that "gives you so many valuable new shooter and hunter benefits that old-timers like myself can hardly recognize it!"

NRA membership was no longer a patriotic duty. It was a bargain. For $15 a year members got not only a year-long subscription to *American Hunter* or *American Rifleman* magazines, but free gun liability insurance, theft insurance and, in an offer rather unique in non-profits, accidental death and dismemberment insurance. And that wasn't all.

There was cancer insurance. In a letter promoting the NRA's insurance program, Carter warned that "in the five minutes it might take you to read this letter, more than 6 new cases of Cancer will be diagnosed!" A listing of cancer's seven warning signals included changes "in bowel or bladder habits" and "nagging cough or hoarseness." (Not everyone shared Carter's enthusiasm. A 1980 congressional study characterized most cancer insurance, riddled with fine print and low benefit-to-premium ratios, as a "ripoff." *Consumer Reports* labels such dread disease insurance one of the two worst buys in health insurance.)

There was group hospital insurance. "Exclusive NRA Features" in the program included paying double for hospital confinement due to a firearms injury and the "Special Added Benefit" that if a firearm accident resulted in the death of an insured NRA member an additional $1,000 payment would be made to the estate of the deceased.

Finally, there was supplemental accidental death insurance. Warning that "an Accidental Death occurs every five minutes in the United States!" the American Sportsman Accidental Death & Dismemberment Group Insurance Plan offered NRA members "Double Death Benefits" while hunting, trapping or fishing.

Carter's insurance programs continue to this day. A 1991 cancer mailing warns:

> If you are reading my letter in a room with two other people . . . odds are one of you will get cancer sooner or later. What if it's you? Sure, thanks to the success of advanced cancer treatment far more lives are being saved than ever before. But treatment can be *so* expensive, sometimes you can sooner make full recovery from cancer than recover your financial independence. NRA people are proud, grassroots Americans who have trouble imagining themselves a burden to others.

Carter's member-get-a-member mailings heaped lavish praise on recipients and promised prizes for those willing to bring new members into the fold. The NRA's Member Honor Roll offered "really sharp looking caps that . . . may become real collectors [sic] items some day" for those who enlisted new inductees. Along with the special commemorative cap, which featured a patch announcing "NRA, Proud, Strong, United," came gold stars in recognition of the number of members recruited, the top honor being five stars.

In its "Champion of the Second Amendment" promo, Carter promised members:

> You are truly a Champion of our Second Amendment Rights. I want to acknowledge your Championship status and I would like every gunowner, non-gunowner, member and non-member of NRA to know just how important and respected you are by the Board of Directors and staff of your National Rifle Association of America. Webster's dictionary describes a Champion as . . . "a person who fights for a cause . . . winning . . . excelling over all others." That is you!

New-member prizes included window decals, key chains and a custom 24-ounce NRA beer stein. Those who signed up 20 members received all these prizes, plus a wall plaque with the champion's name engraved in brass.

And it worked. NRA membership skyrocketed to the point where it was gaining 30,000 new members a month. The only problem was that many of Carter's new army were devoted more to the NRA's trinkets than to the organization itself. Many joined merely for the window decal and the prized hunter-orange baseball cap—and then left. These one-shot, "orange-hat" members, as they were known to the NRA staff, numbered in the hundreds of thousands each year. Says former NRA lobbyist David Conover, "They're like the guys who buy the Oakland Raiders jackets. They buy it for the image."

In spite of its growing numbers, it was an embattled NRA that met in Denver for its annual meeting in 1981. The 1980 murder of John Lennon and the assassination attempt on Ronald Reagan earlier in the year had once again brought calls for increased gun controls.

Addressing the membership, Carter extolled the organization's success and warned of the dangers ahead:

> Almost four years ago today, I was elected . . . to set a firm legislative course . . . to resist ominous gun law proposals [aimed] at those who commit no crime. Four years ago there were 940,000 members. Now there are 1,900,000. The budget has increased 50 percent. There must be membership. There must be millions like you. We must trip our enemies and help our friends in the political arena. We must build the NRA into such a strong force, no politician in America will dare intrude on our rights. You know, sadly, why President Reagan isn't here. But you heard President Reagan himself advocate no restriction on those who commit no crimes. . . . [He] rejected the maudlin enticements of the press to say something in favor of gun control while he lay wounded by one little man's bullet.[12]

Knox's analysis of the assassination attempt was less subtle. He warned the meeting attendees:

Once again we meet when the wolves of the press are howling for the blood of the National Rifle Association. What was the motive of the man who shot President Reagan. . . his motive was to commit a heinous act which the press would play up and bring him to the attention of a pretty little girl. Now that pretty little girl was in a movie in which a person was wanting to assassinate a President. But that pretty little girl, in the movie, prevented it from happening. . . . Look at what the press provided. They provided the motive.[13]

The Denver meeting marked the last real attempt by the Old Guard to regain control of the organization. Since 1977, the ousted faction, which still had strong representation on the board, had launched various assaults on Carter. Eager to protect its victory, no conspiracy theory was too bizarre for the Federation for NRA, which reappeared locust-like at each annual meeting to defend its reforms. A rumor at the 1978 Salt Lake meeting was that NRA Mormons—bitter over the ouster of fellow Mormon Maxwell Rich—were going to unite to defeat Carter. Federation newspapers and samizdats warning of board maneuvers and power plays by the Old Guard were standard ingredients of post-1977 meetings.

In Denver the Old Guard hoped to enact a bylaws change that would return election of the executive vice president to the board. They lost the vote by a nearly two-to-one margin. Then, in a surprise move that would seal their fate, Carter demanded that his annual term be expanded to five years. The membership, recognizing that such a demand contradicted the spirit of the Cincinnati reforms, refused. Carter threatened to quit, and the extended term was approved unanimously. Yet it wasn't job security that drove Carter to make his power grab, but a violent episode from his adolescence that he had no interest in rehashing each year.

On March 3, 1931, in Laredo, Texas, the 17-year-old Carter shot and killed 15-year-old Ramón Casiano. Carter arrived home from school that day to find his mother upset. Three Hispanic youths had been loitering outside the family home, and Carter's mother felt that the trio might have knowledge about the theft of the family car three weeks earlier. Carter told his mother that he would find the boys and see if they would come back to talk to her. When he left, he took a shotgun with him. According to the testimony of 12-year-old Salvador Peña, he, Casiano and two other Hispanic youths were returning from swimming when they ran into Carter, who asked them to follow him up to his house.

Casiano, the oldest of the boys, told Carter he couldn't make them go with him. He then took out a knife and asked Carter if he wanted to fight him. The two argued, and Carter aimed the shotgun at Casiano's chest. Casiano told Carter not to do it, and pushed the shotgun aside with his hand. He then took a step back and began laughing. Carter then shot and killed him.

In court, Carter's lawyers pleaded self-defense, arguing that he had merely meant to disable the arm that held the knife. At the trial, the judge—recognizing that by demanding that the youths come with him at gunpoint Carter had essentially attempted to kidnap them—instructed the jury:

> There is no evidence that defendant had any lawful authority to require deceased to go to his house for questioning, and if defendant was trying to make deceased go there for that purpose at the time of the killing, he was acting without authority of law, and the law of self-defense does not apply.[14]

Carter was convicted of murder without malice aforethought and sentenced to serve a maximum of three years in prison. Carter's lawyers appealed, and a higher court reversed the conviction, citing the failure of the judge "to submit to the jury appropriate instructions upon the law of self-defense."[15] The charges were eventually dropped. The story was reported during the 1981 convention by Carter's hometown paper, the *Laredo Times*. When confronted by one newspaper with the story, Carter initially denied that he was the same man. He then alleged that the prosecutor was the judge's son (he wasn't) and that the shooting had taken place on the Carter family's property (it hadn't).[16] Five years after the shooting, Carter joined the U.S. Border Patrol. As a result, some of his enemies snidely noted years later, he could now shoot Mexicans legally.

To fulfill his vision of a powerful, respected NRA composed of tens of millions of members, Carter needed to expand beyond the organization's historic base of white, male gun owners. This could not be done, however, until he counteracted the popular image of the organization as an army of gun-toting rednecks. Carter wanted a warmer, fuzzier NRA that would win the hearts, minds and pocketbooks of middle America. So in early 1982 the "I'm the NRA" "image correction campaign" was launched. The goal of the campaign (the original theme of which was "I am the Gun Lobby") was to present firearms in a non-threatening manner and portray gun owners as a diverse group that reflected the best of America. The ads, which appeared in such high-profile magazines as *Time, Better Homes and Gardens, Business Week, Esquire, Life, McCall's, Boys' Life* and *Sports Illustrated*, featured blacks, whites, men, women, children, the handicapped and celebrities. Among the celebrities were such NRA stalwarts as Chuck Yeager. For any who doubted Yeager's dedication to firearms, his self-titled autobiography quickly settled the question. Recounting the death of his two-year-old sister Doris Ann, Yeager wrote:

> Shortly before Christmas, when I was four-and-a-half and [brother] Roy was six, we were sitting on the floor in the family room playing with Dad's 12-gauge shotgun. Roy found some shells and loaded the gun; he accidentally fired and the baby was killed. I suppose some parents would've locked away any guns following such a tragedy, but Dad didn't. Shortly after the funeral, he sat down with Roy and me. "Boys," he said, "I want to show you how to safely handle firearms."[17]

Other celebrities who would proclaim "I'm the NRA" included Tennessee Ernie Ford, Roy Rogers and Washington Redskins running back John Riggins. (Riggins' involvement with the NRA came to an abrupt end in 1985, when, at a gala dinner, he admonished Supreme Court Justice Sandra Day O'Connor, telling her, "Come on, Sandy baby, loosen up. You're too tight." Riggins then passed out on the floor.)

Gun Control Resurgent

Following the 1981 meetings in Denver, the NRA found itself battling a newly resurgent gun control movement. In June that year Morton Grove, Illinois, became the first American municipality to ban the sale and private possession of handguns. Exceptions to the law included police, military personnel while on active duty, private security guards, licensed gun collectors and target shooters who kept and used their handguns at licensed gun clubs. San Francisco, site of the 1978 assassinations of Mayor George Moscone and City Supervisor Harvey Milk, enacted a ban the next year. (The San Francisco ban was later overturned on the grounds that because of the comprehensive nature of California's handgun laws, the state had occupied the field of handgun regulation, preempting any local ordinances.)

Soon after the Morton Grove ban, the NRA filed suit in federal court arguing that the law violated the Second Amendment. In 1982 a U.S. appeals court found that "because the Second Amendment is not applicable to Morton Grove and because the possession of handguns by individuals is not part of the right to keep and bear arms, [the Morton Grove ordinance] does not violate the Second Amendment." The U.S. Supreme Court refused to hear the case, letting the decision stand. And although the Illinois state constitution guarantees the individual right to keep and bear arms, the Illinois Supreme Court found that the ban was a proper use of police power to protect the public safety.

Morton Grove offered a new direction for the handgun control movement. NRA money and intimidation could bottle up federal gun control laws, but its influence was limited in local communities. NRA efforts to influence local city politics would be seen as a David and Goliath situation, the

Washington monolith beating up on the small town. This led to a key shift in the NRA's political strategy. The organization soon began a concerted effort to enact statewide firearms preemptions that would forbid local communities from passing firearms laws stricter than state regulations. In moving to deny local communities the right to pass gun control laws, the NRA made it clear, local officials charged, that "freedom" was a relative term. Utilizing its field staff, affiliated gun clubs and members, the NRA was remarkably successful. Before enactment of the Morton Grove law, only three states had passed or confirmed through litigation total preemptions. By 1991 the number had reached 41.

After an initial flurry of activity, local bans never seemed to catch fire beyond the Chicago suburbs. In California, however, the groundwork was being laid for what gun control advocates envisioned as the decisive battle that would change the course of gun control in America. And it did—but not the way the movement had expected.

California's Proposition 15 was a complicated statewide referendum that would in essence ban the sale and possession of new handguns while allowing previously owned handguns to be registered and kept by their owners. This handgun "freeze" resembled a similar law passed in the District of Columbia in 1976. After its announcement, supporters quickly gathered nearly 600,000 signatures, assuring that the measure would be on the ballot in November. Initial public opinion polls showed that the measure had a substantial edge of support. They also revealed that the public did not support banning handguns. Prop 15's success depended on the ability of its supporters to differentiate between a "freeze" and a "ban." The NRA's goal was to make sure that there was no difference in the public's mind.

The NRA recognized that if a handgun freeze passed in the bellwether state of California it could set the pattern for similar laws across the country. Faced with Armageddon, the NRA brought in Republican political consultant George Young to run the campaign and whip the squabbling tribe of pro-gun organizations into shape. Non-NRA pro-gun groups pushed to frame the debate in terms of Second Amendment freedoms and the need for a heavily armed civilian population to protect against government oppression. Young read them the riot act: the focus of the campaign was to be self-defense and fear of crime.

Millions of firearms industry and NRA dollars and a series of brilliant Young ads assured that by election day the race was a done deal. One of the most successful TV spots was a commercial featuring an elderly women—someone's grandmother, perhaps *your* grandmother—in bed. The sound of breaking glass is heard off screen. She phones the police, but the line is busy. The commercial ended with the doorknob to her bedroom door slowly turning.

On November 2, 1982, Prop 15 was overwhelmingly rejected 63 percent to 37 percent. Addressing a victory celebration in Los Angeles, Carter promised that the loss would set back gun control across the nation. "We haven't talked them out of it, but if they try we'll beat them. This is a message, the kind of message that legislators all over the United States will understand, because the people have spoken."[18] One of those who received the message was losing Democratic gubernatorial candidate Tom Bradley. For Prop 15 the NRA had registered more than 300,000 new voters through California gun stores. Few of them were Bradley fans. Bradley lost by little more than 93,000 votes to his opponent, George Deukmejian. Bradley learned his lesson. On a subsequent failed campaign for governor in 1986 he abandoned his anti-handgun stance.

Carter's estimation of Prop 15 was right. The public and press perception was that the gun control movement had had its chance, and blown it. For the next two years the press was loath to cover an issue that had been put before the public— and settled. And for many in the movement "ban" had become a four-letter word.

Et Tu, Harlon?

One face notably missing from the Prop 15 victory celebration was ILA head Neal Knox. Knox had been fired after the organization's annual meeting in Philadelphia earlier in the year. The only speaker to be greeted by a standing ovation in Philadelphia, Knox had welcomed the membership with a raised fist, shouting, "Good afternoon, Gun Lobby." Like Carter, Knox was developing his own following.

According to Knox, he was asked to resign by Carter "in the interests of harmony, loyalty and unity."[19] The lobbyist's unyielding stance had offended too many on Capitol Hill. Knox viewed himself as the very embodiment of the "no-compromise" edict of Cincinnati. His fear was that Carter, now secure in his five-year term, had become corrupted by power. Knox felt that his ouster sealed Carter's betrayal of the Cincinnati reforms. The New Guard had become the Old Guard. Knox's dismissal marked a shift in the NRA's civil war. No longer would Carter be battling the forces of moderation. The new attacks, led by Knox, would be from those whose views were even more extreme than Carter's own.

Knox's worst fears for the NRA came true with the appointment of his successor, J. Warren Cassidy. Board member Cassidy, 51, was a former Lynn, Massachusetts, mayor and insurance salesman who had led the successful statewide effort to defeat Massachusetts' 1976 handgun ban referendum. Cassidy disdained the blood and guts demeanor of Knox, stating, "There have been lobbyists at the NRA whose zeal has occasionally gotten in the way of their common sense."[20] Said Cassidy:

> Harlon's dream, and mine, is for the NRA to extend its influence on public officials and society beyond the gun issue, to make the NRA an even more prominent force in American life. We're an organization of decent, responsible, intelligent citizens, but we weren't respected, and

we certainly weren't liked. We suffered from a very poor public image.[21]

Whereas Knox knew only power and punishment, Cassidy favored gentler forms of coercion. "You don't swagger into an office and bluster and threaten retribution. . . . [W]e work with . . . [the elected official to] try to bring him along. If that doesn't work, eventually we would try to defeat him."[22] Initially, Cassidy spent much of his time on Capitol Hill apologizing for Knox's past behavior.

Under the Federation for NRA banner, Knox quickly launched his second campaign to save the NRA. In attacking Carter, Federation publications charged that he had

> amassed all power within NRA, then removed himself from the control of the members through his five year term. He then interfered with NRA Institute's legislative activities in ways that he had promised never to do. Now he uses the resources of NRA to defend his *monarchy*— through mailings to members and unsigned articles in the magazines—claiming that he is preserving *democracy* in the NRA!

Knox and his supporters cited a laundry list of events to support their charges that Carter, living off the fat of the membership, had grown weak and flabby. Carter had refused to fire the Washington lobbying firm of Timmons & Co. after it was revealed that the firm not only worked for one of the NRA's primary enemies—the American Trial Lawyers Association—but had apparently lobbied against a product liability bill that the NRA endorsed. (Timmons & Co. remains a consultant to the NRA to this day, and still counts among its clients the American Trial Lawyers Association.) In addition, Carter had told Knox to abandon a $700,000 lobbying campaign to block Senate confirmation of NRA antagonist Representative Abner Mikva, Democrat of Illinois, to the U.S. Court of Appeals for the District of Columbia. And in March 1982, charged Knox, Carter had told him that the McClure-Volkmer firearms decontrol bill had "no chance" and that Knox should "quit holding our friends' feet to the fire by making them vote on a bill that isn't going anywhere."[23]

To once again "democratize" the NRA, the Federation proposed bylaw changes at the 1983 annual meeting in Phoenix that included the return of a one-year term for the executive vice president. Most important to Knox was an amendment that would allow members to elect the head of the Institute for Legislative Action. Few doubted who Knox envisioned in the job.

Carter countered this attack with his own ad hoc group, the Committee to Protect the Cincinnati Reforms, and with editorials in the NRA's magazines. At the annual meeting, Committee publications warned of "dissidents" out to "destroy the NRA" and, in turn, cited Carter's achievements: a membership of more than 2.6 million; the California victory; and the "I'm the NRA" campaign. Knox's efforts were easily crushed.

Carter's trump card was the NRA's new best friend, Ronald Reagan. Reagan's willingness to address the NRA wasn't all that surprising. That he involved himself in an organizational power struggle was.

As the Army band played "Hail to the Chief," a White House announcer addressed the audience of 4,000: "Ladies and gentlemen, the president of the United States—and Harlon Carter!" Reasserting his opposition to gun control, Reagan said, "We've both heard the charge that supporting gun owners' rights encourages a violent 'shoot-em-up society.' Don't they understand that most violent crimes are not committed by decent law-abiding citizens? They're committed by career criminals."[24] (The president, of course, wore a bulletproof vest while the Secret Service made sure that the entire law-abiding audience of NRA members was disarmed.) During the speech, Reagan pointedly praised Carter and Cassidy, noting his "great respect for your fine, effective leaders in Washington—Harlon Carter, Warren Cassidy—and your Institute for Legislative Action."[25]

Although Knox failed in his attempt to return to ILA, he was elected to the board of directors by the membership. Yet even this small victory was short-lived. By January 1984, he had the dubious distinction of being the first director to be voted off the NRA board. The action stemmed from Knox's having lobbied against that congressional session's version of McClure-Volkmer. While the NRA had endorsed the measure, Knox, lobbying as a private citizen, saw it as weak and flawed. At the board meeting, Senator McClure expressed hope that the warring factions could settle their dispute. In castigating Knox for his heresy, ILA head J. Warren Cassidy charged:

> In Knox's campaign to discredit ILA and to wreak vengeance upon the organization to which he once swore loyalty, he has spared no effort in contradicting, disputing, and disagreeing with every major move made by us since his firing, and while so doing, has sown dissension, confusion and distrust among friends and allies.[26]

Knox, said Cassidy, had chosen "once more to bite the hand that fed him for four long years."[27]

Endnotes

1. "Report of Proceedings," House of Representatives Subcommittee on Crime, (October 1, 1975) at 1221.
2. Tartaro, Joseph, *Revolt at Cincinnati,* Hawkeye Publishing, Buffalo (1981) at 7.
3. *Ibid.* at 6.
4. *Ibid.* at 5.
5. *Ibid.* at 8.
6. *Ibid.* at 19.
7. *Ibid.* at 21.
8. *Ibid.* at 22.
9. "Our Strength is In Unity," *American Rifleman,* (May 1977) at 20.
10. Tartaro, *supra,* at 34.
11. "Concerned NRA Members Redirect Their Association," *American Rifleman,* (July 1977) at 16.
12. "Gun Lobby's Aim is True Despite Infighting," *San Jose Mercury News,* (May 11, 1981).
13. Tartaro, *supra,* at 48.
14. "Hard-Line Opponent of Gun Laws Wins New Term at Helm of Rifle Association," *New York Times,* (May 4, 1981).
15. *Ibid.*
16. "Gun Lobby's Aim," *supra.*
17. Yeager, Chuck, *Yeager,* Bantam Books, New York (1985) at 5.
18. "Voters Overwhelmingly Reject Handgun Law," *Los Angeles Times,* (November 3, 1982).
19. "Issues in NRA Controversy," *Gun Week ,* (October 8, 1982).
20. *Ibid.*
21. Epstein, Fred, "Aiming to Please," *Rolling Stone,* (October 12, 1983) at 61.
22. "Rebels in Gun Lobby Say Leaders are Getting Soft on Controls," *Washington Post,* (May 5, 1983).
23. "What the Federation Bylaws Really Mean," *Federation Gazette,* (April 22, 1983).
24. "President Reagan Addresses NRA," NCBH Press Release, (May 6, 1983).
25. Epstein, *supra,* at 61.
26. *Minutes of the Meeting of the Board of Directors of the NRA,* (January 28-29, 1984) at 86.
27. *Ibid.* at 87.

Chapter Three

From One Great Warrior to the Next

By 1984 Harlon Carter was the NRA—a superhero who packed heat. Carter had redefined the role of the executive vice president. He was more than the chief executive of the organization, he was the leader of the "Cause," inspiring in NRA staff and members a radiant mix of devotion, humor, security and strength. According to former NRA lobbyist David Conover, the "family" at headquarters felt that they "were on a mission, fighting the good fight, battling big enemies." Although some staff and members never knew if they could have complete faith in the NRA, they believed in Carter.

The NRA adopted Carter's personality as its own—and it was a tremendous success. Under his eight-year reign, membership leaped from 930,000 to nearly three million. The organization was genuinely feared by elected officials across the country. And the NRA's presidential endorsements of Ronald Reagan—and its spending on his and other Republicans' behalf—assured it power and influence at the White House.

It was a gun lovers' Camelot, but a short-lived one, with Carter himself bringing about its end. In the spring of 1984, bowing to the wishes of his wife, Carter informed the board that he wished to retire once again from active service in the NRA and return to Arizona.

Carter's final mission was to find a new leader worthy of his legacy. The candidate profile called for "a recognized charismatic leader with a high sense of integrity, demonstrating inner toughness, courage, and mental stamina" and, in a nod to the NRA's past, a familiarity with the military.[1] Carter had predicted the search would take years. It ended eight months later.

At the January 1985 board meeting, in what appeared to be a well-scripted transfer of power, Carter announced to the "complete surprise" of board chair Howard Pollock that after "more than a year's solitary planning and thinking" he was quitting.[2] Under the bylaws, Executive Director of Operations Gary Anderson automatically became EVP upon Carter's resignation. Anderson would serve until the members elected a new EVP at the annual meeting to be held that April in Seattle. However, Carter explained, Anderson had "no desire to get entangled in the mercurial, unpredictable and fickle tides of NRA internal politics."[3] If Anderson declined the office, said Carter, the board could then elect a new EVP to serve until the April membership vote. As it spread through headquarters, the news of Carter's resignation was met with shock and tears.

Although his daily presence would be gone, Carter's influence within the organization would not diminish. "Let me remind you," he warned, "I have been elected to the Executive Council of NRA for life. . . . You are not, therefore, seeing me go. I am changing my relationship with the National Rifle Association. . . . I am not leaving."[4]

After Carter's announcement, the nominating committee announced its choice per the recommendation of an outside consulting firm hired for the search: former NRA board member G. Ray Arnett. Arnett's name was then placed in nomination with that of Institute for Legislative Action head J. Warren Cassidy. In a secret ballot Arnett was elected 54 to 15. At Cassidy's request the vote was made unanimous.

As advised by the consulting firm, Arnett's salary was set at $150,000 annually (compared with Carter's $87,500) plus "normal fringe benefits." These benefits, unmentioned in official announcements to NRA membership, included a Lincoln Town Car and driver. Carter would be kept on at his EVP salary until the 1985 annual meeting in Seattle. At Seattle he was retained as a consultant for a five-year term—$40,000 for the first year and $30,000 for each year thereafter.

At the January board meeting, Carter admitted that his one possible failure was his inability to end the "civil war" between the different NRA factions. Carter recognized the floor battle that could ensue between his and Knox's supporters at the 1985 annual meeting. Arnett's board-orchestrated ascension would allow the full force of the NRA's publishing and direct mail organs to be marshaled to assure his election by the membership when they voted that April. The choice of Arnett, a personal friend of Reagan's—and until the NRA vote assistant secretary for fish, wildlife and parks at the Department of the Interior, represented the consummation of the NRA's White House alliance.

A man's man, Life Member Arnett stood at six feet, five inches and weighed 260 pounds. He was the rare man who wouldn't look a fool in pith helmet and khaki hunter togs. Arnett's ticket had been punched in all the right places: World War II veteran with the Marine Corps Raider Battalion; recalled for active duty with Naval Intelligence during the Korean War; former board member and two-term president of the National Wildlife Federation; a former Bakersfield, California, police department commissioner; director of the California Department of Fish and Game under Governor Ronald Reagan; and first board chair for both the Wildlife Legislative Fund of America and Wildlife Conservation Fund of America. In February 1981 Reagan named him to the Interior post.

Arnett was prime NRA material on paper. His actions and reputation, however, ran counter to his résumé, as well as the stated goals and ethics of the NRA. Arnett was known in hunting circles as a "slob hunter," one who placed conservation and the standards of ethical hunting second to his own personal enjoyment. Such a label was not surprising judging from his activities at Interior, where he quickly became the James Watt of the animal kingdom.

The National Wildlife Federation's *Ranger Rick* magazine—whose namesake is a raccoon dressed in a forest ranger's uniform—was attacked by Arnett for attributing human characteristics to animals. The cartoon figure, he argued, could cause children to be "rabidly antagonistic toward hunters."[5] In proposing a federal tax on binoculars, bird seed, bird feeders and birdhouses, he argued that "it's time that Americans who do their hunting with binoculars instead of shotguns be given the opportunity to shoulder part of the responsibility for conserving fish and wildlife."[6]

As the primary Reagan official responsible for protecting endangered species, the "animal czar," Arnett did what came naturally: he deregulated them. U.S. big game hunters were allowed to bring back African leopards as trophies, and the importation of kangaroo hides for jogging shoes was approved. In 1982 while on an Interior Department travel junket to the Cayman Islands, Arnett was reportedly involved in shooting protected birds. Returning from a hunt, one of his party was overheard bragging that he had "winged a couple of parrots." The only parrot on the island was the protected Grand Cayman Amazon parrot. No charges were filed.

In spite of these events, a no-holds-barred effort was launched to ensure Arnett's election by the membership in Seattle. Arnett's appointment was presented in NRA publications as a *fait accompli*, the actual membership vote a mere formality. Writing in his "President's Column," Howard Pollock, praising his long-time friend Arnett, told the membership, "Never has our Association been as blessed with so smooth and peaceful an evolution in the succession of outstanding leadership. The torch has been passed from one great warrior to the next. The future for the NRA looks bright indeed."[7]

The April covers of *American Hunter* and *American Rifleman* featured an Oval Office shot of Reagan and Arnett. Superimposed over the photo was a congratulatory letter from the president, praising the NRA for "having the wisdom to seek a man of your outstanding qualifications, well-known all across America for your uncompromising stance in defense of our Second Amendment right to keep and bear arms."[8] A second congratulatory letter from Vice President Bush appeared inside the magazine. A primary reason for this show of power was the unchastened Knox. Carter's resignation had given the former ILA head a chance he hadn't expected until 1986; at the Seattle meeting Knox's name was certain to be one of those offered from the floor for the EVP spot. But if Knox failed to win the EVP post in Seattle he'd be locked out until 1990. The Reagan endorsement was the final effort that would push Knox out the door and lock it behind him. At the annual meeting a Knox-led faction was, as usual, crushed, and Arnett was voted in as the NRA's new head.

A week after the Seattle vote a confident Arnett reportedly told NRA members at the FBI training facility in Quantico, Virginia, how good it was to be free of all the bosses he had worked under at Interior. When a member asked about the NRA board of directors, Arnett reportedly replied, "I don't worry about them—I have them all in my pocket." Arnett may have won over the board, but his problems were only just beginning. Their names were Ted and Françoise Gianoutsos.

They're the NRA

The Gianoutsoses, dressed in blaze-orange hunting vests, cradling their shotguns and framed by their two black labradors, look like a living "I'm the NRA" ad. In 1983 the couple bequeathed their estate, consisting primarily of insurance policies taken out in their name, to the U.S. Fish and Wildlife Service to improve hunter ethics. Under the terms of the bequest, the Fish and Wildlife Service would be required to invest the money in long-term Treasury bonds. The

Gianoutsoses were soon told, however, that no mechanism existed within the government agency to accept multiyear gifts. The couple then conducted a two-person campaign to create an agency-linked foundation that could. For the next year they prowled the halls of Congress to win passage of a bill establishing a federal conservation foundation. Their membership in Democratic big-ticket contributor clubs gave them access to sell their idea. Finally, in March 1984 Congress established the National Fish and Wildlife Foundation. Noting his "serious reservations," President Reagan grudgingly signed the bill. A year later, however, Reagan claimed credit for having "pioneered" the foundation and "got the ball rolling."[9]

Things went quickly downhill after that for the Gianoutsoses. As Democrats, they were denied membership on the board of directors of the foundation they had founded. And a year earlier Ted Gianoutsos had been fired from his position as a senior management analyst at Interior for acting as a whistleblower and helping to expose fraud and mismanagement. Right before his termination, he met with a senior official who offered him a higher-level position in a different division if Gianoutsos "let go" of his charges of corruption. Gianoutsos walked out, calling the offer a bribe. The Interior official was G. Ray Arnett.

When Ted and Françoise Gianoutsos joined the NRA in 1982 they assumed they were joining an organization that shared their beliefs regarding hunting ethics and firearms safety. Their regard for the NRA was such that by 1984 both had become NRA life and benefactor members and contributed thousands of dollars to the organization.

Over time their idealized views soured. The NRA leadership, they felt, had lost touch with its membership and seemed more concerned with fund-raising and preserving the perquisites of power than in promoting safe and responsible gun ownership. At a 1985 finance committee meeting the couple witnessed an exchange they felt characterized the new NRA. ILA Executive Director J. Warren Cassidy expressed his concerns to Harlon Carter regarding member complaints stemming from incessant ILA fund-raising mailings. Carter turned to him with a smile, shaking his head. "Warren," he said, "as long as they've got a few coins in their pocket, if you don't get them, someone else will."

The appointment of Arnett confirmed the Gianoutsoses' worst fears. How could a man who represented the worst in hunting ethics head an association that supposedly taught the best?

If the leadership wanted Arnett, the Gianoutsoses were sure the membership would not—if they had the facts. Immediately after the 1985 Seattle annual meeting, they launched a recall petition against Arnett, charging:

> We ... have had direct dealings with G. Ray Arnett which cause us to have serious questions about his character, honesty and integrity. He ... offered high level jobs to Ted in exchange for his silence about wrongdoing, illegalities, fraud, and millions of dollars of waste. . . . In addition, Mr. Arnett gave his solemn word . . . to strongly support the creation of the National Fish and Wildlife Foundation. As fellow NRA members . . . we believed and trusted him. He testified in Congress several times against it in an attempt to kill it. The midnight transfer of power from Harlon Carter to G. Ray Arnett this past January precluded us from fully bringing these charges to the attention of all our fellow members. . . . [This petition process] offers the best and most open way to bring all of the information concerning Mr. Arnett's past conduct and fitness for office to the attention of all members of the NRA.

In collecting signatures for the petition the Gianoutsoses came into contact with thousands of NRA members. One thing became immediately clear: these people weren't happy. Some attacked the NRA for its hard-line stance against all firearms controls and its willingness to alienate the police, while others vilified it for going soft. They all felt used and ignored. The organization, they felt, catered to the needs of the select few at the top and had lost touch with its members.

The couple's efforts did not go unnoticed. In July 1985 Arnett released a four-page memorandum for NRA board and staff. The subject: Allegations by Theodore Gianoutsos. Damning him as a "Kennedy Liberal Democrat," Arnett, noting in the memo that "all of Gianoutsos' allegations, are lodged firmly . . . in his world of fantasy," wrote that his fellow NRA member had a

> history of abusive and discourteous behavior aimed at superiors and co-workers alike and . . . [maintained a] work record . . . littered with deliberate non-performance of assigned duties. . . . His accusations subsequent to his firing certainly point to one item on Gianoutsos' agenda: discrediting the Reagan administration.

Arnett described his offer of a promotion as a "lateral transfer" to shift his work environment and

> restore Gianoutsos to a useful, productive employee. . . . Gianoutsos' NRA membership applications seem to coincide with his employment problems at the Department of Interior. Was he attempting to enlist the aid of NRA in his personal vendetta against the Department of Interior and its officials? If indeed it was Gianoutsos' intention from the very beginning to garner NRA's support for his personal objectives, then certainly my election . . . could have angered him beyond reason and prompted his petition campaign against me.[10]

Arnett dismissed other aspects of the petition as figments of "Gianoutsos' warped and over fertile imagination."

In October 1985, however, Arnett himself handed the couple ammunition any NRA member could understand. That month Arnett and five others were in a boat hunting off Virginia's eastern shore. Arnett was being filmed for an "I'm the NRA" television commercial that would feature the EVP in his natural milieu. As he was hunting, federal and state game wardens observed Arnett fire at Clapper Rail game birds while his motorboat was under power—a violation of federal game laws.

Arnett's actions violated a litany of NRA sporting doctrine, including the *Hunter's Code of Ethics* and a 1970 resolution condemning the improper use of motorized air, water and land vehicles in hunting. Arnett paid the $125 fine, later likening the citation to a speeding ticket.

Although his violation was reported in the news media, no great NRA uproar followed. While most members were unaware of the incident, the board chose to ignore it. The month before the board had been less forgiving, expelling a Texas life member who had been sentenced to a year in jail and fined $10,000 for shooting deer from a helicopter.

The board had, however, shown leniency two years earlier when NRA President Pollock was cited for violating federal game laws while bird hunting in Delaware. Pollock, along with four others, was cited for hunting over an area that less than three weeks earlier had been baited with more than 200 pounds of cracked corn by one of his fellow hunters. When Pollock returned to his Arlington, Virginia, apartment that day in 1983, he could count on at least one sympathetic ear—then-roommate G. Ray Arnett, who at the time was still at Interior.

Pollock appealed his violation and won. Although the U.S. Attorney's office "recognize[d] the technical violation of the statute," it exercised its prosecutorial discretion in the "interest of justice."[11] This response was met with disbelief by the lead agent involved in the case, who wrote:

> Based upon my experience of having apprehended waterfowl hunters throughout the majority of the states on the East Coast of the United States I know of no judicial district in which these defendants would not be charged.[12]

The decision stood.

Prior to his citation, Pollock favored swift and sure punishment for game law violators and spoke against the type of
prosecutorial discretion he had benefited from. At an October 1978 board meeting Pollock offered a resolution stating:

> The National Rifle Association is on record in support of
> certainty of punishment for criminal offenses, and . . .
> recommends and supports legislation setting forth mini-
> mum penalties for game law violations to be uniformly
> applied in each state through the medium of a mandatory
> fine, or in some few instances, short jail terms more truly
> reflecting the seriousness of the offense, such fines and / or
> sentences not to be subject to suspension or waiver by any
> court.[13]

One year after his citation, in his May 1984 "President's
Column," Pollock brought a "long-standing problem of deep
concern" to the attention of NRA members:

> Each year there are dozens of cases of innocent, unknow-
> ing, law-abiding waterfowl hunters being invited to hunt
> in a water blind or a pit blind, who often have never been
> to the hunting site until perhaps a half hour before legal
> shooting begins, who are subsequently arrested or cited
> by federal or state officials for shooting over a baited
> blind. . . . [T]he innocence or prior knowledge of the
> hunter is immaterial.[14]

Pollock urged amending the federal baiting regulations
without mentioning his own violation. The NRA eventually
brought a court challenge, taking up the cases of two game
law violators in federal court. The constitutionality of the
regulations was affirmed and the convictions upheld.

Two months after Arnett's citation, the Gianoutsoses were
informed that their petition to recall the EVP lacked the
necessary number of valid signatures. They appealed, charging that the number of signatures had been purposefully
undercounted. The next month they went to the quarterly

board meeting to present their petition along with evidence supporting their charges. When the subject of their petition came up, the board went into executive session. The Gianoutsoses were sent out to the hallway to await the outcome. The board once again denied their petition. In a letter mailed to the board following the meeting, Ted Gianoutsos decried this action:

> Do you realize what message you have sent to our friends and enemies? What will they think when they see the shocking spectacle of the ENTIRE NRA LEADERSHIP, THE FULL BOARD , AND ALL THE OFFICERS so afraid of two NRA members, armed only with the truth, that they had to retreat with knees knocking and hands trembling behind closed doors to hold an executive session! Is this the mighty NRA in action? What have our enemies to fear from such an organization?

With their appeal denied, the Gianoutsoses planned their next attack: the 1986 annual meeting, to be held in April in New Orleans. On the floor, Ted Gianoutsos would present his evidence in an effort to have the membership vote Arnett out. Once again the leadership was pulling out the stops to ensure Arnett's election. In a March 1986 letter to Arnett, reprinted in the April 1986 *American Hunter* and *American Rifleman,* Vice President Bush gushed his enthusiasm over his and Barbara's invitation to attend the annual meeting, noting that the NRA's membership had "been a tremendous source of support for our Administration on a broad range of issues." Bush had accepted his life membership in a May 1985 Old Executive Office Building ceremony attended by Arnett and other NRA officials.

Ted Gianoutsos' hope was that the vice president, if informed of Arnett's violations, would withhold his support of the EVP. His April letter to Bush, informing him of Arnett's and Pollock's game law violations, opened with "Dear Mr. Vice President and fellow NRA member." The Gianoutsoses never heard from Bush. They did, however, hear from

Arnett's lawyers, who had evidently been sent a copy of the letter by the White House. They demanded a retraction of the "defamatory statements" contained in the letter and a written apology.

That month Ted Gianoutsos received a call that would supply him with information the board could not ignore. The voice on the other end of the phone belonged to a federal agent who told him of a letter Arnett had written for a convicted cocaine dealer prior to his sentencing. As reported in *Regardie's* by investigative journalist Dan Moldea, while at Interior Arnett had written a character reference for Duane Wendall Larson. Nicknamed "The Duke," Larson was a "major catch" for federal law enforcement authorities and was described by agents as "a major drug dealer from Tucson to Minneapolis for years." In 1984 Larson was convicted of possession with intent to distribute approximately three pounds of cocaine and was subsequently convicted of money laundering and income tax evasion.

Arnett had known Larson in the late 1970s through the World Beefalo Association, its namesake a high-protein, low-cholesterol bison and cattle hybrid. Arnett had been the association's executive vice president. In his April 1984 letter to Chicago attorney Raymond Smith (a former assistant U.S. attorney who, since leaving government, had represented Chicago organized crime figures, according to Illinois law enforcement officials cited by Moldea), Arnett mentioned his administration position while noting:

> During the years Mr. Larson was a WBA member . . . all of my dealings with him were cordial and honorable. His integrity and honesty were exemplary; he was a valued member and a person with whom it was always a pleasure to associate. Based upon the experience I had with Mr. Larson, I can vouch for his character and honesty without equivocation or mental reservation.

Larson got ten years in prison and was fined $25,000 on the cocaine charge.

Arnett's letter of recommendation in hand, the Gianout-soses began talking to select board members. They received no response until the April meeting. On the night of their arrival in New Orleans, they met with a former NRA director acting as the organization's intermediary. Acknowledging the Larson letter, he told them that Arnett would be removed following the elections in November. The Gianoutsoses held to their plans to call for his removal at the meeting. At a second meeting that night they were asked to wait only two or three weeks for Arnett's resignation. The couple again declined.

On the floor of the meeting of members the next day, Ted Gianoutsos confronted Arnett with his hunting violations and demanded his resignation. Gianoutsos refrained from mentioning the Larson letter, feeling that the Virginia incident should have been enough to enrage the membership. He was wrong. When a member asked to see evidence of Gianoutsos' charges, board member David Caplan interrupted on a parliamentary point, silencing him. Arnett then took the floor to defend himself. Following his speech, Carter led a standing ovation for Arnett, and a vote of confidence was offered. It was seconded and carried by acclamation. Ted Gianoutsos promised he'd be back, a second recall petition in hand. Soon after, the couple received telephone death threats. Not only against themselves, but against their hunting dogs. They began sleeping with a loaded shotgun by their bedside.

Though Gianoutsos had failed, the board knew that the Larson letter was a time bomb waiting to explode. Arnett had to go. He soon supplied the board with its excuse to oust him. One day after Congress finished action on the McClure-Volkmer firearms decontrol bill, Arnett fired the NRA's 15-member public education division staff. At 8:30 a.m. on May 7, staff were told to have their desks cleared out by noon. Their activities, it was explained, would be handled by the NRA's public relations firm. The purge was described by the NRA as purely a business decision.

Others suspected a different reason. NRA publicist and competitive sporting clay shooter Tracey Attlee was a not-infrequent Arnett travel companion. Both, however, denied rumors that their relationship was anything more than a friendship based on a common love of shooting. Attlee had been a publicist in the public education division. She was eventually promoted by Arnett to the eighth floor executive offices, where she was placed in charge of publicizing international shooting. Attlee's new salary was $38,500, even though the authorized salary for the position was $25,000. When public education head John Aquilino—a conscientious objector during the Vietnam War turned gun aficionado after the shooting had stopped—complained about the loss of Attlee, he soon found his whole department dismantled. As Aquilino told reporter Moldea:

> It was very bizarre. Arnett read this laudatory memo describing what I had done for the NRA over a decade and what the division had done. Then he said, "For economic reasons, we're disbanding you." Arnett's people called all of my people together and told them they had two hours to get the hell out of the building, because they were changing the locks. They treated us like we were the Lindbergh kidnappers. We were almost thrown out of the building.[15]

Not surprisingly, morale at NRA plummeted. The ousted and bitter Aquilino quickly channeled his resentment, founding *The Insider Gun News*, an NRA scandal sheet. In it he noted that Arnett had tried in desperation to establish "personal trademarks," such as "sunrise devotional" 7 a.m. staff meetings and a loathing of the word "which." Such actions, according to Aquilino, failed to win over his staff, which spent a great deal of time gossiping about the EVP's frequent travels and joking about his sex life.

Arnett acknowledged the perils of leadership and attempted to rise above them. In a 1985 letter written to an NRA member who had criticized some of the EVP's earthy aphorisms in a *Philadelphia Inquirer* interview ("Gun control is like a condom, it gives you a false sense of security," while "statistics are like a bikini bathing suit. They reveal what is interesting, but hide what is vital"), Arnett noted:

> Because of my exposure and high visibility, it is necessary for me to be always on guard and totally aware of the jackals who delight in ridicule and character assassination, and who will stop at nothing to denigrate the NRA. Long ago I learned the higher up the mountain of life one climbs, the bitter wind blows more strongly. The exposure can become almost unbearable at times, so to survive it helps to develop a hide like a rhinoceros.

On May 17, 1986, the rhinoceros was out of a job. At a special meeting that day the executive committee, unable to fire Arnett outright under the NRA's bylaws, voted to suspend him without pay. The vote was a foregone conclusion. The charges and resolutions had been drafted at a secret meeting the night before by a select group of board members.

"In view of the critical situation that has recently developed at NRA headquarters," the executive committee released a memo outlining its actions to the full board. In the wake of Arnett's suspension, ILA Executive Director J. Warren Cassidy was named acting executive vice president. The positions of Arnett's three top aides were abolished. The committee directed Cassidy to review the organization's PR activities, including the contract Arnett had signed with the public relations firm and restore any members of the public education division who he saw fit. Eight fired staffers were eventually rehired. Aquilino was not among them. Attlee was transferred back to her prior position in the now-defunct education division, her employment at NRA terminated. Carter was instructed to make himself available in Washington for the next month to help Cassidy, and Wayne LaPierre, director of federal affairs, was elevated to acting executive director of ILA.

The "causes for removal" included:

- Mr. Arnett's actions in conducting the affairs of the Association have contributed to a decrease in the morale and efficiency of the employees of the Association, of which he appears unaware;

- As the Executive Vice President, Mr. Arnett has acted contrary to Board policy of the National Rifle Association with regard to abolishing the Public Education Division and by the inconsiderate matter in which he did so;

- Mr. Arnett has neglected his duties as the Executive Vice President by frequent absence from Washington, D.C. on hunting and other personal trips and has used funds of the Association for his personal enjoyment in connection with these trips;

- Mr. Arnett has made personnel decisions on the basis of his personal interest rather than the interests of the Association;

- Mr. Arnett has demonstrated that he will use his authority without regard to the policies of the Board of Directors and has ignored and will ignore the power and duty of the Board of Directors to manage and have general charge of the affairs of the Association.

The committee also instructed the organization to begin proceedings in the New York state courts to remove Arnett. Arnett, arguing that the executive committee did not have the authority to suspend him, labeled himself the victim of a "kangaroo court." A lawsuit requiring "a major investment of NRA resources" would soon be filed, he threatened. The NRA's membership, he promised, would be "enraged. It's a travesty and I expect to see the action overturned."[16]

Arnett's threats were soon quieted when the NRA offered him a settlement package rumored to total more than $400,000. Under the terms of the agreement Arnett was to receive more than $150,000 in cash, payment of all attorneys' fees, use of the NRA-owned Lincoln Town Car and other benefits.

In NRA publications, Arnett was allowed a brief letter to the membership that made no mention of his battles with the board. His brief, yet cheery, farewell shared space with schedules for NRA firearms schools and an article on a fund-raiser involving commemorative belt buckles. Beneath a small, smiling photo of the former executive vice president was a three-sentence letter from NRA President James Reinke expressing the board's gratitude.

Among those who questioned the board's right to force out Arnett was Neal Knox, who argued that its actions had "usurped the members' rights by firing Arnett." Knox noted that "I helped write . . . [this amendment to the bylaws] to safeguard the Federation's candidate: Harlon B. Carter."[17]

Knox wasn't alone. In a July 30, 1986, letter with the heading "Private and Confidential—Not for Publication Nor Dissemination Except to Members of the NRA Board of Directors," Howard Pollock expressed his concern over Arnett's ouster, writing:

> The members of NRA must really be wondering what's going on. The Annual Meeting of Members was on Saturday, 26 April, and Ray was defended from attack by a tiny nucleus of dissidents, given an overwhelming vote of confidence, and a standing ovation for his performance by everyone, including all Board members. If his performance was sufficiently bad to warrant immediate removal, why were the members not given this information? As you very well know, Ray got an extraordinary settlement from NRA, about which the Board will certainly want to inquire. Why was Ray given such a large settlement, if he was the one in the wrong?

If the NRA had proof of Arnett using "funds of the Association for his personal enjoyment" (an amount rumored to total between $50,000 and $90,000), why did it settle? The answer was drugs, guns and the taint of organized crime. A perceived link between the NRA and those involved in the drug trade would never be tolerated by the NRA's membership. A court battle over Arnett's firing could have led to wider dissemination of this information through the news media while inviting increased scrutiny of the NRA and its leaders by the press. Involvement on the part of the NRA— however tangential—with drug dealers and organized crime would only give credence to the "guns & drugs" image bestowed upon the organization by many in the news media. Four hundred thousand dollars was a small price to pay for helping to keep this information a secret.

Endnotes

1. *Minutes of the Meeting of the Board of Directors of the the NRA,* (January 26-27, 1985) at 61.
2. *Ibid.* at 27.
3. *Ibid.* at 31.
4. *Ibid.* at 33.
5. Moldea, Dan, "Shootout on 16th Street," *Regardie's,* (April 1987) at 116.
6. *Ibid.*
7. "The President's Column," *American Hunter,* (April 1985) at 42.
8. *American Hunter,* (April 1985) at front cover.
9. "President Reagan Gives His Views on Wide-Ranging Conservation Issues," *National Wildlife,* (June-July 1985) at 19.
10. Memo from G. Ray Arnett to NRA, (July 26, 1985).
11. Letter from Joseph Farnan, Jr. to Hamilton Connor, (December 22, 1983).
12. Letter from Darcy Davenport to Hamilton Connor, (February 24, 1984).
13. *Minutes of the Meeting of the Board of Directors of the NRA,* (October 29, 1978) at 16.
14. "The President's Column," *American Hunter,* (May 1984) at 46.
15. Moldea, *supra,* at 122.
16. "Bloodletting at the Gun Lobby," *Washington Post,* (May 20, 1986).
17. *Bullet Trap,* Newsletter of the Arizona Gun Club, (July 1986).

Part II

Lovers & Friends

Chapter Four

To Serve and Protect

In the summer of 1986 the Bureau of Alcohol, Tobacco and Firearms denied an import application for the Striker-12—a foreign-made assault shotgun favored by South African security personnel. The gun, the agency ruled, was not suitable for "sporting purposes."

Soon after, ATF officials were visited by Institute for Legislative Action lobbyist James Jay Baker and NRA lawyer-on-call Stephen Halbrook. They had come to plead the importer's case.

Prior to the Striker, noted Baker, there had "never been a denial of importation of a 'long gun' based on lack of a sporting purpose. . . ." Therefore, he argued, "long guns by their nature have a sporting purpose."[1] Halbrook added that the shotgun, with a revolving cylinder capable of firing twelve rounds in three seconds, was ideally suited for hunters, who would have at their disposal a variety of ammunition—all at once. Meetings attended by the NRA, ATF and West Virginia Democratic Senator Robert Byrd were to no avail. ATF refused to allow the gun into the country.

The NRA's willingness to lobby on the gun's behalf was not surprising. It was business as usual. This is because the National Rifle Association has evolved into the unofficial trade association for the firearms industry. A common misperception is that the NRA assumes this role as the result of shadowy big-dollar industry payments. But there's nothing covert about it. In 1990 eight percent of the NRA's budget—more than $7.4 million—came from industry ads placed in NRA publications. During the 1960s, when membership and revenues were far lower, advertising at times accounted for more than a quarter of the NRA's budget.

However, the NRA is not in bed with the industry for money. It's definitely for love. The common goal of this long-standing union is expansion of the domestic firearms market. Guns equal dollars—increased sales for the industry and new members for the NRA. Though the NRA is quick to attack those who link it to gun manufacturers, the relationship is so close that the NRA supplies membership slips for manufacturers to include in their weapons' packaging. For both the industry and the NRA, gun control is literally bad for business.

As is often the case, love is blind. The NRA's success in stopping regulation of the gun industry protects all of its members—from mainstream manufacturers catering to sportsmen to small catalog houses fulfilling the desires of paramilitary survivalists. The result is a world of companies, products and publications few Americans ever see—until it bubbles up in the form of criminal activity, new technological threats or bona fide gun nuts. The firearms industry, like any other, can manufacture any product that isn't outlawed. Unlike virtually all other industries, however, there are practically no constraints placed upon it. And this is because of the NRA.

In its early years the organization was far more open about its industry ties. In the early part of the century, there existed a revolving door between the NRA and arms and ammunition manufacturers not unlike the Pentagon and the defense industry today. For five years the NRA was actually part of the firearms industry. In 1927 the NRA Service Company began selling shooting supplies, including rifles and ammunition, to members at discount prices. The company soon became a financial drain, helping to push the NRA into the red, and in 1935 the venture was abandoned.

In addition to being its protector, the NRA is also the industry's cheerleader. Firearms reviews in *American Rifleman* and *American Hunter* are almost always positive. The NRA is a ubiquitous presence at the SHOT (Shooting, Hunting, Outdoor Trade) show, the annual trade exhibit for the industry. (Pre-registration forms are available at the NRA's National Firearms Museum.) The most popular attraction at the NRA's annual meeting is the exhibitors' hall, which features weapons displays from virtually all the leading firearms manufacturers. In the blizzard of contests that seem to dominate NRA mailings, firearms are often the featured prizes. The "1990 Institute for Legislative Action World-O'-Guns Sweepstakes" promised participants

> a fantastic armchair trip across America and around-the-world for a look-see at all the incredible rifles, pistols, shotguns and revolvers you stand to win! For starters, we'll load up on prizes for you at Weatherby in California . . . then Freedom Arms in Wyoming . . . Browning in Utah . . . Springfield Armory in Illinois . . . and then we'll really stock up on gun prizes for you in New England—at Smith & Wesson, Ruger, Colt and Thompson Center. Then it's on to Europe where we'll pick up some dandy sweepstakes prizes for you at Glock in Austria . . . Heckler and Koch and SIG-Sauer in Germany . . . and Benelli in Italy.

(One note of reality does intrude on the NRA's world of guns. The contest rules note that the NRA and sponsors "shall not be liable for injury, loss or damage of any kind resulting from participation in this promotion nor from the acceptance or use of the prizes awarded.")

The 1991 NRA members' "Premium Pak" offers "60 money-saving coupons worth over $3,700" for various manufacturers. Mixed in with ads for ammo-belt quartz wall clocks and sweatshirts that "send a message to Mr. Hussein and dissident flag burners" are coupons for mail-order ammunition and firearms. Nine millimeter, .357 Magnum and

.45 auto handgun ammunition can be ordered at "NRA low prices."

Coupons for surplus weapons importer Century International Arms dominate the booklet. Members can order $280 Argentine Colt 45s, $130 South American .38 Specials and $90 Spanish .32 revolvers and have them shipped to their local firearms dealer. Other weapons, such as pre-1898 Argentine Mauser rifles, can be purchased directly through the mail. Because of their age the weapons—although functional—are viewed as antiques, not firearms. Bayonets are extra.

The NRA's greatest achievement on behalf of the industry has not, however, been in merchandising, but in shielding it from direct involvement in the political debate. On Capitol Hill, when the issue is gun control, manufacturers never testify, the NRA does. And because the NRA's arguments are framed in terms of Second Amendment freedoms, self-defense and crime, gun control has come to be viewed almost solely in a political context. The NRA has become the industry's fall guy. Handgun control advocates and editorial-page cartoonists excoriate the organization at the slightest provocation yet rarely bother to take a look at the industry that manufactures, distributes and sells the products they criticize the NRA for defending. Former presidential spokesman James Brady once referred to the NRA as the "evil empire" in congressional testimony. Yet the NRA is only the empire's messenger.

The NRA's ability to frame the gun-control debate on its own terms, coupled with the industry's ability to evade public scrutiny, means that firearms—most notably hand-guns—are rarely seen for what they are: inherently dangerous consumer products. Guns don't appear magically in gun stores. They are manufactured by corporations—with boards of directors, marketing plans, employees and a bottom line—just like companies that manufacture toasters.

The romantic myths attached to gun ownership and use stop many people from thinking of them as dangerous toasters. As a result, the standard risk analysis applied to other potentially dangerous products, such as pesticides, prescription drugs and toasters, has never been applied to firearms. Firearms are seen as a class in and of themselves. They're beyond mere consumer products—they're totems. For many they're nothing less than the physical embodiment of freedom.

The federal government shares this misplaced romanticism. Firearms and ammunition (along with alcohol and tobacco) are specifically exempted from the purview of the Consumer Product Safety Commission (CPSC), although the agency does have jurisdiction over non-powder firearms such as BB guns. The CPSC's mission is to protect the public from unreasonable risk of injury associated with consumer products. Firearms were originally included in the Senate version of the legislation creating the commission in 1972 but were removed before final passage. Instead, these products are regulated by the Bureau of Alcohol, Tobacco and Firearms, a division of the Treasury Department. Firearms were placed under the jurisdiction of Treasury in 1919 as the result of a revenue law that placed a federal excise tax on the sale of firearms and ammunition. ATF lacks the common regulatory powers, like standard-setting and recall, granted other government agencies such as CPSC, the Food and Drug Administration, or the Environmental Protection Agency.

ATF's powers are limited to issuing manufacturer and dealer licenses and monitoring compliance with the few skeletal federal firearm controls that do exist. Although the agency is granted limited control over imported firearms as the result of a "sporting purposes" test designed to weed out Saturday Night Special handguns and surplus military rifles and shotguns, it has virtually no control over domestic firearm design and production. Increased enforcement powers can come only from congressional legislation. During the few times that the agency has attempted to increase enforcement, it has come under rapid attack by the NRA and its friends on Capitol Hill.

The result is a rogue industry. Weapons flow from manufacturers through a vast, nearly unregulated distribution network consisting of wholesalers, stocking gun dealers operating storefront enterprises and free-lancing "kitchen table" dealers who typically operate out of their homes.

Few good industry statistics exist. ATF collects data on the number of firearms produced each year and breaks them down by manufacturer, caliber and firearm type (rifle, shotgun or handgun.) This information is available only under the Freedom of Information Act (FOIA). The number of firearms actually sold per year isn't known, and because most manufacturers are either privately held or divisions of larger corporations, little information is available on the industry's profits.

What is known is that ATF estimates that 67 million handguns, 62 million shotguns and 73 millions rifles have been available for sale in America since 1899. The ATF firearms population figures are generally regarded to be high. There is no measure, for instance, of the number of guns that have been destroyed, confiscated by police or rendered inoperative through abuse or neglect. In 1991 there were 1,035 firearms manufacturers in the United States and 912 firearms and ammunition importers. The spectrum of manufacturers ranges from old-line companies like Smith & Wesson, Colt and Remington to smaller "boutique" manufacturers offering "this week's assault weapon." Also included in this figure are small, independent customizing shops.

Based on the federal excise tax levied on firearms, the total wholesale value of firearms manufactured in fiscal year 1989 totaled more than $826 million. The value of handguns manufactured that year totaled $382 million, while the value of rifles and shotguns totaled $444 million.

To become a manufacturer, an individual must pay a $150 three-year licensing fee and undergo a background check to ensure that he or she is not in a proscribed category. ATF has no minimum standards concerning the number of weapons that must be manufactured annually. The license's low cost reflects the fact that the original intent of federal dealer and manufacturer licensing was not to restrict the number of licenses, but to keep track of those who had them. During the 1934 congressional hearings at which the initial standards were established, NRA President Karl Frederick urged that the price of a license be "fifteen cents or 10 cents, or anything which will not prevent compliance with it because of its burdensome nature."[2]

License to Kill

The NRA's goal of a non-burdensome federal regulatory system is best illustrated by the widespread availability of Federal Firearms Licenses (FFLs), the license required to sell guns in the United States. Broad privileges are granted by an FFL, including the ability to ship firearms in interstate commerce and to purchase unlimited quantities through the mail at wholesale prices. Currently there are more than 240,000 FFL holders in the country—nearly one for every 1,000 citizens. There are more gun dealers in America than gas stations.

FFLs are inexpensive and easy to obtain. Applicants, who cannot be convicted felons or under indictment for a felony, must merely mail in a two-page form to ATF with a $30 fee. No fingerprints, pictures or proof that the applicant has obtained any necessary local permits are required. "FFL kits" are available in numerous gun publications, including *American Rifleman,* which lists them under "Business Opportunities."

Not surprisingly, ATF estimates that only 20 percent of FFL holders actually operate storefront enterprises, such as gun stores or sporting goods dealers. The remainder are non-commercial dealers who obtain the license to enjoy the discounted prices and mailing privileges. These "kitchen table" dealers typically operate out of their homes, often unbeknownst to neighbors, police and zoning authorities, and are responsible for approximately 20 percent to 25 percent of all new and used firearms sales annually—an estimated 1.5 million to 1.9 million guns.

FFLs represent a convenient loophole for criminals wishing to evade state and local firearms laws. David Taylor, a resident of a South Bronx housing project, had a long criminal record. His rap sheet included an indictment for murder at the age of 16, a year in jail for drug possession and guilty pleas to assault, unlawful possession of a weapon and disorderly conduct. Under New York City law Taylor couldn't own or sell guns. However, because he had no felony convictions, he was eligible to obtain an FFL.

Taylor received his FFL in August 1986. In less than a year, he purchased more than 500 firearms from wholesalers in Ohio, Georgia and Wisconsin. They were delivered via United Parcel Service in shipments of up to 100 weapons at a time. According to police, drug dealers and other criminals were the final recipients of the guns.

ATF estimates that as much as 20 percent of the illegal firearms that enter New York City each year arrive in a similar manner. At the time of Taylor's arrest in 1987, ATF records showed that 882 individuals and companies in New York City had valid FFLs. New York police had no idea how many license holders had criminal records or if the licenses were being used for criminal purposes.

New York is far from unique. A 1980 study of New Haven, Connecticut, FFLs found that more than three-quarters of all licensees were in violation of at least one local, state or federal law. Nearly half were in violation of two or more firearms, tax or zoning requirements.

End of the Model T

The NRA's least publicly recognized gift to the industry has been its success in stopping federal control over firearms design. For the most part, the only limitations facing manufacturers are their own imagination and technological skill. Glock of Austria had both. And in 1986 the company had one word for the industry: plastics. It couldn't have come at a better time.

Since the turn of the century, little real innovation had been seen in the firearms industry. While Detroit unveiled a new model every year, gun manufacturers continued to churn out Model Ts—six-shot revolvers, low-capacity pistols, hunting rifles and shotguns. The inevitable result was a sales slump as soon as the primary market, white males, became saturated. This day came when handgun production plummeted from 2.6 million in 1982 to 1.9 million in 1983. Production continued its downward slide, bottoming out at 1.4 million in 1986.

To its entrepreneurial credit, the industry quickly recognized the opportunities presented by the introduction of powerful, high-capacity technically advanced weapons. Innovation became the new watchword. Many changes stemmed from the application to the civilian market of military and law enforcement advances. The days of the Model T were gone forever.

Of the many developments—assault weapons, new ammunition loads, the increasing popularity of semi-automatic handguns—plastics stood alone as truly revolutionary. In 1986, Glock unveiled the Glock 17, the first handgun to use significant amounts of plastic in its structural design. The handgun was 83 percent plastic by mass. Although plastic had practical applications in firearms technology—fewer moving parts, lighter weight, rust resistance and improved aesthetics—its primary benefit was its consumer appeal. Writing in the April 1985 issue of *American Firearms Industry* magazine, Andy Molchan, president of the National Association of Federally Licensed Firearms Dealers, enthused:

> The American plastic gun will shortly make its appearance. Plastic is the "common" word, but it's really liquid crystal polymer. Polymer is without question, going to be the material of the future . . . if a 100% plastic gun works, this would be great for sales. What this does is make everything that has been produced in this century obsolete. That is exactly what our industry desperately needs. This will give us a whole new, and real reason to resell every hunter and shooter in America.

Plastics quickly raised concerns among gun control advocates and members of Congress, who questioned whether the guns would be less detectable by airport security than standard handguns. In January 1986, columnist Jack Anderson reported that Libyan leader Muammar Khadafy was attempting to buy 100 Glock 17s. Anderson detailed how a Pentagon security expert smuggled a Glock past an airport checkpoint by stripping the weapon down and disguising its metal components—essentially the barrel, slide and spring—in carry-on luggage.

The Glock was merely the Sputnik of plastic handguns. A 1986 congressional Office of Technology Assessment study concluded that although all-plastic guns did not yet exist, technology was available to produce firearms in which the only metal parts would be a few small springs. Gun control advocates seized on the OTA report as further proof that legislation was needed to protect the public from plastic "Terrorist Special" handguns.

On November 10, 1988, Reagan signed a bill banning the production, importation and sale of new, non-detectable plastic firearms. Under the law, new firearms either had to trigger metal detection devices at the same level as a firearm containing 3.7 ounces of stainless steel, or they had to be readily discernible as a firearm by X-ray systems. (Although guns that can be detected by X-ray do not necessarily have to trigger metal detectors and vice versa, no weapon has yet been marketed that exploits this loophole.)

Another milestone was reached in the winter of 1990 when Ram Line of Colorado began marketing the injection-molded Syn-Tech Exactor—a virtually all-plastic handgun. The only metal parts of the futuristic-looking, 15-round, .22 Exactor are the plastic-shrouded barrel, springs, pins, receiver, bolt, disconnect and hammer. And unlike the Glock, a high-quality weapon that retails for $400 or more, the Exactor is marketed as an inexpensive (approximately $200) "plinker" to be used for shooting at tin cans. As the result of the 1988 law, the plastic contains an additive that makes it detectable by airport security.

Although the Exactor has been deemed detectable, its use of injection molding technology brings the industry one step closer to the day when all-plastic "stealth" handguns can be developed by foreign companies or governments.

Bigger is Better

Accompanying the plastics boom of the 1980s was a new trend toward powerful, high-capacity pistols—in both traditional and assault weapon configuration. In 1980, pistols accounted for only 32 percent of the 2.3 million handguns produced in America. The majority were revolvers. By 1989 this number had virtually reversed itself to the point where pistols accounted for 69 percent of the two million handguns produced that year.

The smaller 38 caliber load traditionally favored by police and home owners was quickly surpassed in popularity by the larger and more deadly 9mm—a chic version of the .45, the gun of choice of fictional tough guy Mike Hammer. Nine millimeter developed a cachet that made it *the* load of choice among drug dealers, gangs and television and movie script writers. Still flush with the success of the 9mm, the industry went one better with the new 10mm. Wrote *Gun World* columnist Tom Ferguson in May 1990: "The 10mm bandwagon is rolling now, with many manufacturers eager to jump aboard." Recognizing that the new caliber would aid in reselling the market, the NRA breathlessly cheered on the industry.

The first mass-marketed 10mm handgun, the Bren Ten, appeared in the early 1980s. Plagued by production problems and a lack of ammunition magazines, the gun did not take the market by storm. Even its role as the handgun of choice for detective Sonny Crockett on television's showcase of high-powered weaponry, *Miami Vice*, couldn't stave off its inevitable disappearance. But the 10mm returned in 1987 when Colt introduced the Delta Elite. Today the 10mm is ubiquitous—from derringers to assault rifles.

The renaissance of the 10mm was due primarily to the 1989 announcement by the FBI that it planned to adopt the cartridge for its agents' handguns and had ordered 12,000 pistols. FBI tests found that 10mm ammo was far more lethal than the .38 or 9mm and as deadly as a .45 with less kick. The FBI decision guaranteed popularity on two levels: other law enforcement agencies would follow its lead while the load would gain newfound prestige on the civilian market. As Robert Hunnicutt wrote in the March 1990 *American Rifleman*, describing the "emerging 10mm craze" at the 1990 SHOT show:

> The FBI's determination to adopt a 10mm autoloader seems to have opened the floodgates . . . and it was a rare pistol manufacturer or importer that hadn't come up with a way to swim with the tide.

The agency's plans to standardize all of its firearms to 10mm—including its assault rifles—has acted as a similar catalyst to the assault weapons industry.

Handgun ammunition can actually reach 50 caliber before falling under the strict licensing controls of the National Firearms Act of 1934. As a result, Magnum Research of Minneapolis offers the 50 caliber Desert Eagle handgun, which can "unleash eight rounds of the most powerful ammo available for a pistol." Not quite. In early 1991 Protection and Survival International announced the "first NEW production run in some 25 years . . . of GyroJet handguns, carbines and rocket ammo." The GyroJet, "The World's First and ONLY Interplanetary, Recoilless Rocket Gun," comes in 12mm (.495) and NFA-controlled 13mm (.51).

The federal government is reviewing new ammunition technology that, when perfected, will most likely be marketed to civilians. In 1982 the Army began research to replace its Colt M-16A2 assault rifle. Among the firearm prototypes currently being considered is one from Steyr of Austria that uses steel flechettes (darts) instead of bullets. Flechettes offer superior penetration with reduced recoil. (Flechette shotgun shells are already available to civilians.) Colt's entry fires a cartridge with two projectiles. The first travels to the point of aim while the second veers slightly to increase hit probability.

The largest technological leap, however, has been taken by Germany's Heckler & Koch, which has developed a rifle using "caseless" ammunition in which the propellent serves as the ammunition cartridge. One of the gun's "advantages" is that it leaves "no cartridge case [or] spent case signature." Although of benefit in wartime, this characteristic would devastate civilian police investigations, in which the matching of shell casings is a key research tool. As a District of Columbia firearms technician summed it up, "It would make our job impossible." The advance, as Heckler & Koch boasts, is "a quantum leap forward." And unless federal laws are passed to limit the availability of these new types of ammunition, anything that dates current firearms will find its way onto the civilian market.

Bottom Feeders of the Gun Industry

The NRA offers it umbrella of protection to all strata of the firearms industry. NRA board member Robert Brown, publisher of *Soldier of Fortune* magazine, is the organization's nod to the survivalist segment of America's gun culture. When SOF held its 15th annual convention/expo at Las Vegas' Sahara Hotel in September 1990, NRA field representative Fred Romero was there. Romero shared speaking honors with Iran Contra's Richard Secord and former CIA Cold War veteran Ray Cline.

In a commentary in the official program titled "Get Involved or Lose Your Guns," Brown urged all gun owners to join the NRA and

> VOTE the [pro-control] bastards out. Most politicians are whores whose only mission in life is to pig out at the public trough. And the only way they can continue their pigging is being reelected. Defeat them at the polls and the rest of the scumbags will get the message.

Brown's *Soldier of Fortune* contains a litany of ads for anti-personnel products and information. Trigger activators are manual devices that, when attached to semi-automatic weapons, give them full-auto firepower. The Tri-Burst "installs in seconds" and "allows three-round bursts from any semi-automatic weapon." The Ultimate allows the user to "fire single rounds, five, ten or even fifty round bursts without government red tape. The Ultimate is not regulated by BATF—it's 100% legal."

Laser sights—which cast a narrow beam of light undetectable to the target, except as a spot on their body—offer the user point-and-shoot assassination capability. At the special "SOF 15th Anniversary Sale" price of $199, the API Predator is "for those who must have the best!!"

A constant presence in SOF is the Brown-linked Paladin Press. Its glossy catalog includes sections on sniping, survival, weapons, explosives, guerilla warfare, silencers and terrorism. An essay in the 1988 catalog titled "New Age Survival" reassured readers that "we don't want to alarm you into heading for the hills today—but we will help you become prepared to do so tomorrow." Included in its more than 300 titles are:

> *The Anarchist Handbook.* All you need to know to construct . . . an expedient silencer; a pipe hand grenade; plastic explosive; and a rocket launcher. . . . [S]upplies a list of materials easily acquired from drug or hardware stores, hobby shops, supermarkets or even junk piles; simple diagrams and how-to-use instruction for certain weapons.

> *Improvised Explosives—How to Make Your Own.* Ten simple but powerful formulas for explosives and incendiaries ... to construct actual bombs, booby traps and mines.

> *How to Kill* (volumes one through six). Makes no moral judgments, but merely describes what has been known for years by the professionals who are part of the shadowy world of international espionage and intrigue.

As the author states in his preface, "My only premise is that there are times when one must attack with complete ruthlessness and fight with lethal fury. This fury and ruthlessness must be harnessed and directed to the gravest possible damage—to kill."

In addition to operating a 24-hour-a-day, toll-free order line and offering a "no questions asked" money-back guarantee, Paladin Press also offers gift certificates, which "make excellent gifts for you to send to friends and relatives."

Other magazines that cater to this segment of the gun culture include the biweekly, 200-page *Shotgun News*. Geared primarily to Federal Firearms Licensees, it is also the primary outlet for the "Neal Knox Report," the ex-ILA head's biweekly column devoted to analysis of the gun issue and what's wrong with the NRA. Each page of *Shotgun News* is filled with classified and display ads for assault weapons (both semi- and fully automatic), handguns, rifles, shotguns, stun guns, ammunition, military surplus and gun shows. Additional classified ads offer Asian brides, impotence cures ("helps most men, it helped me"), "Nazi, SS, Klan, Confederate & Pro-Gun" memorabilia, mannequins for "museums & uniform collectors" ("Don't hide your uniforms. Display them!"), "Dolf" Hitler and Eva Braun teddy bears and Hitler 100th anniversary beer steins.

Shotgun News gained attention in 1989 when a classified ad appeared offering for sale "The Whitman Collection." The ad stated:

On August 1, 1966, Charles Whitman climbed to the top of [the] Administration Building of the University of Texas in Austin, Texas and began what *Life* magazine called "The Most Savage One-Man Rampage in the History of American Crime." Ninety minutes later 12 people plus Whitman's Mother & Wife lay dead and 31 more people lay wounded. The firearms and misc. items are now For Sale as a single unit.

Firearms in the "collection" included a scoped Remington rifle, sawed-off shotgun and assorted handguns. The asking price was $7,500.

The monthly *American Survival Guide* is "the magazine for safer living." Its article headings include "Survival Weapons," "Survival Gear" and "Survival How To." Its "Survivalist Directory" is a post-apocalypse personals column offering a "confidential listing of survivalists who wish to become known to others of like mind," including:

> **Melbourne, Florida.** Teenage military organization that does U.F.O. research would like to recruit members. Also would like to set-up information exchange and meet others in this area for training. All races and sexes are welcome. Ages 12 and over only. No racists or religious fanatics need apply.

> **Northern Arkansas.** Young, conservative male seeks correspondence with other survivalists in area. Special interest is nuclear survival. No liberals, atheists, druggies or alcoholics. Females welcome. All ages reply.

> **Baltimore, Maryland.** Urban group which meets biweekly is looking for interested local survivalists wishing to exchange information. We are not Rambos, racists, or extremists, but family-oriented and interested in workable, realistic solutions to short and long term survival scenarios.[3]

Specialized weapons catalogs, often available through such publications, offer shop-at-home convenience for survivalists and other gun owners with "special" needs. In the fall 1990 *Rhino Replacement Parts* catalog "General Rhino" warns his "warriors":

> With all our troops sent by Bush to the Middle East, that leaves no military forces here at home to protect U.S. soil. And, at the same time congress is scheming to take away our guns. "Now is the time for all good men to come to the aid of their country!" Be sure you have plenty of spare

gun parts, ammo, water and food on hand. The enemy just might drop in while the wolf is away.

Rhino offers complete full-auto fire control component parts sets—useful for converting semi-auto weapons to full-auto machine guns—for UZIs, MACs and AK-47s, as well as deadly ammo. Its products are available to anyone with a phone, credit card and mailbox.

In a "notice-warning" General Rhino adds that it is

> a felony for any "individual" to convert a semi-automatic firearm to fire automatic. We . . . know and appreciate your unique needs for firearms accessories and parts, but NEVER ask us to do anything illegal! We respect your privacy—your names and purchases are kept in STRICT confidence.

Under federal law parts sets to convert semi-automatic firearms to full-auto are banned. However, if the conversion kits are renamed "replacement part kits," ATF allows their sale. In 1981 the NRA passed a resolution criticizing conversion kit manufacturers. The resolution expressed "deep concern" not over the availability of the kits, but the fact that some manufacturers did not adequately inform purchasers of the legal ramifications of performing an illegal conversion.

Also included in the *Rhino* catalog is specialized anti-personnel ammunition. Sabot Slug shotgun shells not only "go through a car door and out the other side" at 50 yards but also "penetrate a very high quality police vest in the process! WHAT A BLOWJOB!!" The "Bolo" shotgun shell—"It slices! It dices!"—is loaded with a five-inch piece of piano wire with a half-inch ball molded on each end. "When fired, the balls swirl like a BOLO. [A] devastating effect is created when your objective is struck, as the wire rips completely thru its target—ALONG WITH THE BALLS!" When "Blammo Ammo," available in a wide array of handgun and rifle calibers, strikes its target "it EXPLODES sending hundreds of pieces of the spent bullet throughout the deeply penetrated area. Naturally, life threatening trauma and shock occur immediately upon impact."

The Phoenix Systems, Inc. catalog is a compendium of anti-personnel equipment and information. At 30 feet the ballistic knife offers penetration "three times that of a manual stab." Noting that "Congress outlawed the springs—but you can still buy the knife!" it comes "in legal kit form" lacking only the spring. U.S. military practice grenades come "with ALL the mechanical parts IN THE FUSE ASSEMBLE!!!—NO EX-PLOSIVES." The catalog warns that "activation of these devices requires prior ATF approval."

The catalog's "Recommended Reading List" includes: *How to Make Disposable Silencers*; full-auto conversion manuals for UZIs, MAC-10s and AR-15s; *Improvised Munitions Handbook* ; and *Expedient Hand Grenades* .

And for the recreational hours, there are guns—and women. An ad in *Shotgun News* for "Rock n' Roll #3—Sexy Girls & Sexy Guns," promises:

> You've got to see this [video] tape to believe it. 14 out-rageous, sexy girls in string bikinis and high heels blast-ing away with the sexiest full auto machineguns ever produced.

The "Hotshots" video promises "eight topless beauties, captured on tape firing exotic weapons into the Sierra Nevada mountains. Experience the same thrills they do. . . . This is the tape that does it right, with Hot Guns and Hot Girls."

An ad for the "Your Survival Companion" poster set fea-tures four half-naked women holding hunting and military firearms: "The Hunter's Mate," "The Urban Soldier," "Lock and Load" and "The Most Wanted." The back pages of *Soldier of Fortune* offer "China Bitch, Beautiful Color Photos of Women BAREing Military Weapons." For $10 correspon-dents receive three photos "personally autographed with your name & message by one of the women of CHINA BITCH." And an ad in *Machine Gun News*—"the magazine for full-auto enthusiasts"—for the FULL-AUTO machine gun calendar promises each month "a stunning model, posed with an exotic machine gun." September's couple features a lingerie-clad woman in high heels posed on a school desk, a teacher's pointer in her hand. The tip of the pointer rests against an exploded diagram of a belt-fed machine gun, the weapon next to her. The caption reads, "The Extractor Stud Rides in the Cam Groove and Forces the Lever On."

Endnotes

1. "BATF Excludes Long Gun," *Monitor*, (October 15, 1986) at 7.
2. House Hearings on National Firearms Act, (April/May, 1934) at 57.
3. *American Survival Guide*, (August 1988) at 66.

Chapter Five

In Bed with Uncle Sam

Each summer, Camp Perry, perched on the banks of Lake Erie, hosts the Super Bowl of target shooting—the National Matches. In 1989 approximately 3,650 shooters from across the nation—the majority of them NRA members—participated in this federally subsidized shootfest. Total taxpayer cost: $1.4 million. Or nearly $400 per shooter, including subsidies for transportation, lodging and meals.

The National Matches are merely the most public example of the deep and long-standing relationship the National Rifle Association enjoys with the United States government. In its early years, the financial security of the NRA was virtually guaranteed by the establishment of government programs and benefits available only to NRA members. This relationship has only grown with time. Government lands are made available to the NRA for its use. NRA-drafted laws are passed that benefit firearms criminals at the expense of public safety. NRA employees attempt to reap financial gain from little-noticed changes slipped into federal law. And a government agency is nearly dismantled—at a projected cost of $22 million—simply because the NRA doesn't like it. The NRA is not an outsider to government, it is its partner.

Federal Fund-raisers

Following its temporary shutdown in the late 19th century as the result of New York state's perfidy, the NRA targeted a more appropriate funding source for its patriotic activities: the U.S. Treasury. The result was the Civilian Marksmanship Program (CMP). The program was established by Congress in 1903 with the formation of the National Board for the Promotion of Rifle Practice and the establishment of the National Rifle and Pistol Matches, which would be open to civilian and military shooters. "The immediate effect of this law," noted the NRA in *Americans and Their Guns,* "was to approve and lend the support of the federal government to the principles and program of the National Rifle Association of America." The program's supporters promised that it would increase interest in marksmanship among draft-age men, who would be better trained in time of war and could facilitate the training of unskilled inductees. By 1905 military rifles, ammunition and other equipment were being sold at cost to rifle clubs that met the specifications of the National Board. With minor changes in their bylaws, all NRA-affiliated clubs soon met the standards. With surplus weapons eventually available by law only to NRA members, *Americans and Their Guns* notes that the "semiofficial status" granted by this "important milestone"

> permitted a great broadening in the services of the National Rifle Association of America. Until given the support of federal recognition for its services and launched on an expanded, attractive program for all American shooters, it had operated under severe difficulties.

The NRA's government franchise was more conspiracy than coincidence. In 1909 the NRA revised its bylaws and enlarged its board to include three appointees chosen by the secretary of war as well as two from the secretary of the Navy. In addition, the National Guard heads of all states were added. The NRA's fondness for the military had some bizarre results. Members participating in early National Matches soon resembled drab Mounties, donning "the new khaki NRA official uniform—riding breeches, wrap-around puttees, and pleated shooting jacket topped by a wide-brimmed Anzac-style hat."[1]

The NRA's efforts bore fruit in 1916 with the passage of the National Defense Act, which created the Office of the Director of Civilian Marksmanship (DCM). The act was hailed by the NRA as another milestone, incorporating "into government policy many of the ideas that the NRA advocated for years." The impending world war supplied the rationale for Congress to expand civilian marksmanship. The act budgeted $300,000 for civilian marksmanship training, authorized the distribution of government guns and ammo to shooting clubs, supplied military instructors to assist civilian rifle clubs, allowed civilian shooters access to military ranges and subsidized the travel costs of civilian teams to the National Matches.

For the next 50 years the program remained the NRA's sacred cow. One of the few concerns raised during hearings on the 1938 NRA-drafted Federal Firearms Act came from the War Department, which feared that proposed regulations regarding the interstate sale and transport of firearms might affect DCM sales to NRA members. The department suggested that an amendment be added to the bill stating:

> That nothing herein contained shall be construed to prevent shipments of firearms and ammunition to members of the National Rifle Association and to the institutions, organizations, and persons to whom such firearms and ammunition may be lawfully delivered by the Secretary of War....[2]

NRA Executive Vice President Milton Reckord, a member of the executive committee of the National Board for the Promotion of Rifle Practice, while questioning the need for the amendment, lauded its sentiment. "Under the National Defense Act we [the NRA] have the privilege," correcting himself, he continued, "or the citizens of the United States as individuals, have certain privileges of purchasing rifles from the War Department. So I would be the last person in the world to object to that."[3] It was decided that the amendment was unnecessary.

Although the marksmanship program was an easy target for budget cuts during wartime, by 1966 nearly 167,000 handguns, 655,000 rifles, and 8,600 shotguns had been sold at deep discounts to NRA members. (These totals do not include weapons sold during the prime postwar years of 1945 to 1957.) The DCM today refuses to release figures on the total number of weapons that have been sold, labeling the information classified.

Beginning in the 1960s, however, the program came under repeated congressional attack. A new class of gun owner had become aware of the benefits of NRA membership—criminals and terrorists. A spot check in 1967 of 9,663 prospective NRA gun buyers resulted in the rejection of 75, primarily because of prior criminal records. Among the NRA's newest members were domestic terrorist groups such as the Minutemen and the Revolutionary Action Movement, which had established their own shooting clubs to receive government weapons via the NRA.

In a 1967 hearing, Senator Edward Kennedy questioned NRA Executive Vice President Franklin Orth regarding the NRA-linked Minutemen. Said Kennedy:

> The charge was conspiracy to commit arson in the third degree, conspiracy to use explosives, 16 counts in the indictment. At the time of the arrest, there were 26 handguns, three submachineguns, 111 rifles, shotguns, and carbines. Now, what is the position of the 16 men who were indicted as far as the NRA is concerned?[4]

An unhappy Orth explained that under the organization's interpretation of New York state's non-profit laws, the NRA could not just oust its members—even those attempting to overthrow the government with NRA-sanctioned DCM weapons. Said Orth, "As soon as there is an indictment or any serious trouble, we flag the membership card of those people to see that they do not get any further services. They get the magazine, but they cannot get any other service."[5]

As a result of the Minutemen case and other high-profile incidents, standards for obtaining DCM firearms were tightened in 1968 to include fingerprinting and a background check. Yet following the end of the Vietnam War, funding for the program once again increased.

In 1979 an attempt to break the NRA's stranglehold on the program came from a surprising source—the National Coalition to Ban Handguns (NCBH). An NCBH suit filed against the Department of Defense argued that the program had "compelled hundreds of thousands of American citizens to join an increasingly political, hard-line pro-gun organization in order to receive governmental benefits that should be available to all Americans."[6] Federal Judge Harold Greene agreed, striking down the membership requirement and opening the program to all qualified U.S. citizens. They would still, however, have to belong to DCM-affiliated gun clubs—most of which were also NRA-affiliated.

Throughout the 1980s, criticism of the federal gun-selling program continued, culminating in a May 1990 General Accounting Office study requested by the House Armed Services Committee. The report had been ordered after the committee found that annually only 200 Civilian Marksmanship Program "graduates" were enlisting in the military. The Armed Services Committee noted that with a 1990 budget of $4.7 million, the average cost per military recruit was $23,000, making the program "a very expensive recruiting aid."[7] These figures echoed a 1965 study by Arthur D. Little, Inc., which found that of a sampling of 12,880 Army trainers, only 3.1 percent were veterans of the Civilian Marksmanship Program prior to induction. And although affiliated clubs were required to have at least ten members between the ages of 13 and 20, 53 percent of the club members were of the undraftable age of 26 or older.

The GAO report noted that in 1989, 6,000 M1 rifles were sold by the Department of Defense at the discounted price of $165 (market value estimates of the guns started at $300). An additional 24,000 rifles, handguns and airguns were on loan or in storage at clubs. Nearly 1.8 million rounds of ammunition were sold to affiliated clubs at the discounted rate of two cents per round (the market value of the ammo ranged from eight to ten cents a round) while approximately 38 million rounds were given away. Nearly nine million rounds were donated to Boy Scout camps across America. One congressional office estimated that the money lost to the government for the benefit of NRA members totaled $3 million in 1989.

"Army mobilization and wartime training plans have changed," the GAO study found, "but the CMP's mobilization objectives have remained essentially as they were conceived during the early part of the century." The conclusion: "If usefulness is defined as a measurement of whether this program contributes to the military preparedness of the United States today, we believe that the CMP is of limited value." As a result of the GAO report, funding for the program was cut to $4 million and the program was required to become self-supporting by 1992.

In 1991, warning that the program "may be lost forever," the NRA, flush with Middle East war fever and showing a remarkable lack of prescience, charged:

> Last year when anti-DCM legislators rammed through a law to gut the program, they did not consider that our young people, many without proper firearms training, might be called into hand-to-hand combat in the Persian Gulf.

The NRA promised:

> When our youth are being asked to put their lives on the line in the Persian Gulf, it is reassuring to know that those who have participated in DCM programs will be better soldiers and marksmen and therefore better able to survive on the battlefield.

Despite its best patriotic appeals, the NRA's 88-year federal membership subsidy is scheduled to end in 1992.

Gentlemen's Agreement

The Department of Defense is not the NRA's only bureaucratic friend. In 1990 the NRA reached "memoranda of understanding" (MOUs) with both the Bureau of Land Management (BLM) and the National Forest Service (NFS). These public-private partnerships granted the NRA the right to construct target ranges on government property. NRA membership recruitment depends on introducing more Americans, especially youth, to shooting. The number of ranges in the country, however, is limited. Zoning laws hinder the construction of new ranges, and encroaching urbanization threatens those already established.

The government's vast land resources offer range-building opportunities without the cost of securing private land or the hazards of zoning complaints. In addition, aiding the government in the stewardship of federal lands adds to the NRA's prestige.

In May 1990, the BLM, an agency of the Department of the Interior responsible for the management of 271 million acres of public land primarily in eleven Western states and Alaska, signed an agreement with the NRA at the organization's headquarters to "provide a framework for cooperative efforts relating to the management of the public lands administered by the BLM."

In the December 1989 *American Hunter,* BLM director and NRA Life Member Cy Jamison was hailed as "a man who understands from firsthand experience the government's responsibility to provide access and recreational opportunities to public lands for the shooters, hunters and sportsmen of all states."[8] The measure was initially approved in January 1990 by the NRA's Hunting and Wildlife Conservation Committee, whose responsibilities include "encouraging hunters to affiliate with the NRA." (Initial drafts contained the decidedly non-sporting statement that "the NRA was formed to protect and defend the Constitutional right of the public to own and use firearms." It was removed by the time of the final draft.)

If the BLM and the NRA shared the common goal of expansion of public lands to hunters and shooters, their interpretation of the NRA's role differed wildly. In its public explanation of the agreement, the BLM portrayed the NRA as a cadre of grown-up Boy Scouts, "organizing litter clean-up details, building boat ramps, or improving outdoor facilities such as rest rooms, picnic tables and parking lots."[9] The NRA never shifted from its focus on shooting ranges.

Numerous hunting organizations are involved in conservation MOUs to benefit their members, while organizations such as Defenders of Wildlife and the Audubon Society have taken part in government partnerships regarding "watchable wildlife." The NRA's range-building privileges are, however, the first of their kind.

In October 1990, the National Forest Service—controlling 191 million acres in 43 states—in a second ceremony at NRA headquarters, joined the BLM in opening up public lands for NRA construction. The Forest Service hailed the agreement as a framework in which the government and the NRA would "work together to promote natural resource conservation and safe and ethical firearms use."[10] Among the "mutually beneficial work projects or activities" planned were the "development, maintenance, and operation of shooting ranges."[11] An internal Forest Service memorandum acknowledged that this new relationship was not without risk:

> The signing of the MOU may generate some negative reaction from some anti-hunting segments of the public. NRA's opposition to gun control legislation will contribute to that. The establishment of additional shooting ranges for public use on National Forests may also become an issue. Although currently allowed, shooting ranges are only permitted if compatible with other resource

uses, and if private facilities are unavailable in the area. The MOU will lead to more organized planning, development and maintenance of managed shooting ranges.[12]

By January 1991 both agencies were in the process of establishing contacts with local NRA affiliates to begin the development of projects. The possible public outcry mentioned by the Forest Service failed to materialize.

Felons' Relief Act

The NRA endorses swift and sure punishment of criminals who use firearms in the commission of a crime. And up until 1986, those convicted of gun crimes were forbidden from purchasing or possessing firearms. This changed with passage of the NRA-drafted McClure-Volkmer firearms decontrol bill. Under the law, individuals who had been convicted of felonies involving a gun, had involuntarily been committed to a mental institution or had violated provisions of the Gun Control Act of 1968 could now apply to the Bureau of Alcohol, Tobacco and Firearms to receive "relief" from the "disability" of not being able to own a firearm.

McClure-Volkmer, however, only *expanded* the ability of convicted felons to arm themselves. Prior to 1965, those convicted of a felony lost their gun-owning privileges. This changed with passage that year of a bill amending the Federal Firearms Act of 1938. As a result, convicted felons could now legally arm themselves if the crime of conviction had not involved a gun.

The law was a congressional favor to firearms manufacturer Winchester, a division of Olin-Mathieson Chemical Corporation. In 1962 Olin was indicted by a federal grand jury as the result of a kickback scheme involving Vietnamese and Cambodian pharmaceutical importers. Olin pleaded guilty to a reduced number of felony counts. As a result of the plea, Winchester could no longer ship firearms in interstate commerce. The law was enacted to allow Winchester to stay in business.

Under the law, relief can be granted if it is established

> that the circumstances regarding the conviction, and the applicant's record and reputation, are such that the applicant will not be likely to act in a manner dangerous to public safety and the granting of the relief would not be contrary to the public interest.

And although established to aid a specific corporation, the measure was so broadly worded that it quickly created a convicted felons' second-chance club.

One of the law's most notable beneficiaries is Alan Gottlieb, head of the pro-gun Citizens Committee for the Right to Keep and Bear Arms and founder of the Second Amendment Foundation. In 1984 Gottlieb pleaded guilty to income tax evasion. Two years later he applied for relief. In a pre-investigation interview Gottlieb explained to ATF agents that because of his involvement with the gun lobby and the fact that he was a director of the U.S. Ammunition Company, it was "awkward for him not being able to handle the ammunition product of the company . . . [and it was] also awkward for him not to handle firearms when he represents Citizens Committee to Keep and Bear Arms and the Second Amendment Foundation."

ATF conducts field investigations for all relief applicants. Gottlieb's, which was not unusual in its comprehensiveness, included interviews with regional law enforcement agencies, neighbors, business associates and Gottlieb's arresting officer and probation officer. In recommending relief, his probation officer described Gottlieb as a "very devoted gun person . . . into conservative Right Wing stuff." In the last decade, ATF has processed more than 22,000 applications for relief. ATF is required to print notice of the granting of relief in the *Federal Register*, including the reason for restoration. The latter is always a boilerplate explanation:

> It has been established to the Director's satisfaction that the circumstances regarding the applicants' disabilities

and each applicant's record and reputation are such that
the applicants will not be likely to act in a manner
dangerous to public safety, and that the granting of the
restoration will not be contrary to the public interest.

But ATF is not specifically required to print the crimes for
which the individuals were convicted. When the Firearms
Policy Project of the Violence Policy Center, a non-profit
educational foundation (of which I am executive director),
requested copies of the conviction records and ATF investigations under the Freedom of Information Act in October
1989, ATF conducted a year-long stonewall, citing privacy
laws and a court decision of dubious relevance in its defense.
In the spring of 1990 ATF finally agreed to release a sampling
of cases. Yet after reviewing them the agency abruptly
reversed its decision. The Firearms Policy Project then obtained the original court records of randomly chosen applicants. The reasons for ATF's anxiety over release of the
documents quickly became clear. Gottlieb was one of the best
of the bunch.

A random sample of 30 cases ("You will know no more
after looking at 10 files than you will after looking at 100,"
promised Robert Pritchett, chief of ATF's Disclosure Branch)
yielded drug dealing, sex crimes and terrorism.

Some examples: Robert Christopher Gunn pleaded guilty
in February 1980 to two counts of delivery of a controlled
substance, narcotics or cocaine. He was sentenced to three to
20 years for each charge to the Michigan House of Correc-
tions, to be served concurrently. In 1989, having been
released from prison, Gunn received his relief from disability. Another convicted felon who received relief from
disability that year was Jon Wayne Young. In 1976 the 19-
year-old Young pleaded guilty in Minnesota to aggravated
assault and aggravated robbery. Young had a history of
sex-related offenses dating back to the age of 13. According
to court documents, at Young's sentencing the judge stated:

You placed another person's life in jeopardy, in danger, and that person could have been killed by you.... As a matter of fact, you don't have enough control of your own actions to prevent that sort of thing. It is just lucky, fortunate that the girl wasn't killed, and the reason probably that she wasn't killed is that she submitted to you but had she fought you undoubtedly she might have been killed, probably would have been killed.

The judge noted that in analyzing Young, a doctor had written:

I was struck by the number of times therapy had been terminated with the feeling that he was unlikely to get into trouble again only to have him return once more. At this point I believe that the best predictor of Mr. Young's future behavior is his past behavior despite his protestations.

Yet both Gunn and Young pale in comparison to Jerome Sanford Brower, who pleaded guilty in U.S. District Court for the District of Columbia in February 1981 to conspiracy to transport explosives in foreign commerce with intent to use unlawfully, violating the Arms Export Control Act of 1976 and unlawfully transporting hazardous materials in foreign commerce. Brower had been part of an international terrorist plot masterminded by former CIA agents Edwin Wilson and Francis Terpil.

In 1976 Brower, a federally licensed explosives dealer, met with Wilson and Terpil and agreed to supply explosives for an unspecified "operation" in Libya. In June, after meetings with Libyan officials, Terpil drafted a "secret proposal" outlining a six-month terrorist training program to be conducted for the Libyans. Brower transported explosives to Libya and instructed the Libyans in defusing the explosive devices. He was eventually allowed to plead guilty and received a four-month prison sentence and a $5,000 fine. He received his relief four years later.

Brothers in Arms

Although the NRA paints its legislative battles in terms of constitutional rights and personal freedom, NRA employees have exploited for their own financial benefit legislation they have helped enact.

Rene Carl Vos, a partner in an Alexandria, Virginia, gun store, was a friend of NRA lobbyist Wayne LaPierre and a sometimes NRA consultant. In 1986 Vos served as a contract NRA lobbyist to aid in the passage of the McClure-Volkmer firearms decontrol bill. He raised a few eyebrows when he reportedly made the prescient move of increasing his gun store's stock of automatic weapons prior to the machine gun ban added to the bill as a last-minute amendment by gun control advocates. The measure was supposed to have been a complete surprise to the NRA. The ban increased the weapons' value dramatically and raised questions of full-auto "insider trading."

The previous year Vos and LaPierre had set up the firm of Blue Sky Productions, and by the summer of 1986 Vos and Blue Sky were involved in a $13 million arms transaction to import 200,000 M1 rifles that would make his machine gun deal look like peanuts. Each weapon—purchased at a price of between $51 to $76—had a resale value in the United States of $300. The gross from the sale of the guns would exceed $60 million.

Vos' M1 rifle deal wouldn't have been possible without the help of the NRA, LaPierre and Republican Senator Robert Dole. Prior to 1984, the importation of surplus military weapons—the most famous of which was the Italian Mann-licher-Carcano used to assassinate John F. Kennedy—was banned as the result of the Gun Control Act of 1968. This changed with an innocuous-sounding amendment attached by Dole that year to the conference report of the Trade and Tariff Act. The provision read:

> Amends section 925 of title 18, United States Code, to authorize the importation by a licensed importer, of all

rifles and shotguns listed as curios or relics pursuant to section 921(a)(13) and all handguns listed as curios or relics, provided that such handguns are generally recognized as particularly suitable for or readily adaptable to sporting purposes.

As *Guns and Ammo* cheerfully noted in 1991:

Most senators who voted to approve the amendment did not realize that all bolt-action and semi-automatic military rifles and most military handguns made prior to 1946, as well as many made after, were classified as curios and relics by the BATF. Even notoriously anti-gun Senator Edward Kennedy voted to approve the amendment!

The result was a new wave of surplus military rifles once again coming into the United States. A new twist was the ready availability of after-market parts, such as folding stocks and high-capacity ammunition magazines, that could make these "curios and relics" similar to modern assault rifles.

With an inexpensive and easily obtainable ATF collector's license (any citizen over 21 years of age who is allowed to buy firearms can obtain the license at a cost of $30 for three years), the guns (except for handguns) could be ordered through the mail—just like in the good old days.

LaPierre claimed to have severed ties with Blue Sky in the spring of 1986, before the M1 deal. The company had originally been formed, he claimed, to promote rock concerts. Yet four days after the company was incorporated, Blue Sky applied to ATF for a federal license to import and sell firearms. Under "specific activity applicant is engaged in" was written "importation of surplus weaponry, plus items of current manufacture." The application, signed by Vos, listed himself as president and LaPierre as secretary-treasurer. The firm's address was Vos' gun store, the Old Town Armory, a location that would have most likely offended the political sensibilities of most rock stars. Although involved in passing the 1984 amendment, LaPierre said that he had been unaware of the subsequent license application.

By the time the first shipment of 40,000 guns arrived in September 1986, Vos had sold Blue Sky, removing himself from the gun deal. Much to the consternation of Blue Sky's new owners, upon arrival in San Francisco and Seattle the guns were immediately seized by U.S. Customs. Because the weapons had originally been sold by the United States to South Korea, federal regulations forbid their reimportation. Still, in January 1987 Customs allowed the initial shipment into the country but refused to reissue a permit for the remaining 160,000 weapons.

That fall Vos was suddenly back in the picture—testifying with immunity before a grand jury investigating the relationship between the NRA, Blue Sky, Old Town Armory, and select members of Congress. Part of the investigation was to see whether federal law had been manipulated for private gain. Vos' involvement came to an abrupt end in November 1987 when he died during a flying lesson in a Cessna 152 aircraft. (His body was identified by a friend by his $7,500 Rolex watch, boot heels and belt buckle.) Two weeks prior to the crash Vos told a friend that he was becoming more involved with the grand jury investigation, but that he was trying to protect his friends at the same time.

Although the crash raised suspicions of sabotage and murder—the Cessna had been flying normally when it revved and plunged nose-first into the ground, bursting into flames—the National Transportation Safety Board concluded that Vos had committed suicide, taking his instructor with him.

That December Representative Bill Chappell, Democrat of Florida, introduced a second seemingly innocuous amendment, attached this time to the continuing budget resolution. The amendment in effect reinstated Blue Sky's import permit for the remaining 160,000 rifles. As the result of the grand jury investigation, the amendment contained an unusual provision that gave the government 20 days to rescind the Blue Sky deal. It didn't.

Jack-Booted Fascists

Secure in its favorite-son status, the NRA has not shied away from attacking federal agencies it feels have betrayed its ideals. The most notable victim of this has been the Bureau of Alcohol, Tobacco and Firearms. Although the gun control lobby is the NRA's most public villain, ATF is its oldest. ATF never got any respect. According to its first director, Rex Davis, in 1970 President Richard Nixon attempted to place Watergate conspirator G. Gordon Liddy and White House aide Jack Caulfield in high positions in the agency, allegedly to turn the bureau into a "secret police" for Nixon. When ATF was later elevated to bureau status in 1972, Davis was forced to take on Caulfield as an assistant director.

When in March 1978 ATF, with the support of the Carter administration, announced plans to computerize its files to aid in gun tracing, the NRA immediately cried "gun registration." An NRA membership mailing resulted in a flood of mail to Capitol Hill and Treasury attacking the "gun police." Mail at ATF ran 16 to one against the measure. As a result, not only was the $4.2 million program denied funding, but when ATF officials said that they could use money from other portions of their budget to finance it, Congress cut the agency's appropriation accordingly. NRA hostility to the ATF proposal was personal as well as political. Earlier in the month ATF had confiscated weapons from the NRA's firearms museum, including four automatic rifles and two large-caliber handguns, charging that the guns were actually National Firearms Act weapons that the NRA had failed to register with the federal government. The NRA sued, arguing that the weapons were inoperable and therefore exempt. In 1980 the court ruled in the NRA's favor and returned its guns.

In 1981, seizing on the window of opportunity offered by the election of Ronald Reagan, ILA head Neal Knox launched a full-scale assault on ATF. Because the agency had been established by presidential directive, it could be dismantled solely on presidential order. The NRA's main weapon was

an $80,000 in-house documentary titled *It Can't Happen Here.*
A pamphlet promoting the film hailed it as

> the most important film ever produced on the issue of
> Gun Control. It is important becaue [sic] it shows the
> inevitable results of gun laws—the abuse of the rights of
> ordinary citizens. These are but a few of the victims. The
> National Rifle Association has seen scores more. This film
> is a message which must be told to all Americans. For,
> unless the existing Federal gun law is changed, it *can*
> happen here.[13]

In the film, Representative John Dingell, Democrat of
Michigan and NRA board member, charged that "if I were
to select a jack-booted group of fascists who are perhaps as
large a danger to American society as I could pick today, I
would pick BATF. They are a shame and a disgrace to our
country."

The movie showcased the lives of common folk ground
under the boot heel of the federal government. Vietnam
veteran Richard Boulin—a federally licensed firearms dealer
and "avid gun collector"—had "asked BATF if he could
legally sell his private guns, without recording the sales in
his dealer records. He was told such sales were legal, then
was prosecuted and convicted for the private transactions."
Paul and Billie Hayes owned a "mercantile store and small
gun shop and were on the verge of retirement when they
were entrapped into a sham gun-law violation by undercover agents of the BATF. The Hayes have been forced to
battle the government for four years and the fight has robbed
them of their savings and their retirement."

The cases, however, were not as clearcut as the NRA
represented. Boulin had in fact been convicted of using his
FFL illegally to launder guns through his private collection.
One purchaser claimed to need the weapons for a band of
illegal mercenaries fighting for a white Rhodesia (a violation
of export laws as well as federal firearms laws). By acquiring
the guns as a licensed dealer, transferring them to his private

collection and then selling them as a private individual, Boulin evaded ATF reporting requirements as well as his state's seven-day waiting period. As Boulin himself told an undercover ATF agent, "It's hard to stay straight. It's hard 'cause you can't make a living."

Paul and Billie Hayes *were* acquitted of illegally selling guns to undercover ATF agents. Yet transcripts of their tape-recorded conversations with the agents—which were not allowed to be presented in the agency's case against the couple—revealed a different Paul Hayes than portrayed by the NRA. On the tape, Hayes advised an undercover ATF agent on how to evade the ban on out-of-state sales, offered to remove the serial number from a weapon to make it untraceable, boasted of an illegal miniature shotgun he owned and explained how to funnel unregistered firearms to illegal aliens.

As a result of the NRA's campaign, in November 1981 the Reagan administration announced that ATF would be abolished. The more than 700 positions overseeing alcohol and tobacco regulatory functions would be switched over to the Customs Service. Its 1,731 firearms, explosives and arson regulation and enforcement personnel would be shifted over to the Secret Service. The transfer date was April Fools' Day, 1982. Reasons cited for the transfer included improving "morale and productivity . . . based on job security plus better image."

The NRA's joy over the demise of its archnemesis was tempered with concern over how the Secret Service would handle its new firearms enforcement responsibilities. The final showdown over ATF occurred in early 1982 before a subcommittee of the U.S. Senate Appropriations Committee. The purpose of the hearings was to determine whether Congress should supply the approximately $22 million necessary to implement the reorganization of the agency.

At the hearing, Dingell reiterated his charge that ATF's agents were "jack-booted fascists" and noted that a mere shift of ATF responsibilities was a little like rearranging the deck chairs on the *Titanic*. You have a rogue agency which has abused the rights of the citizens consistently. Quite frankly, I carry no grief for BATF. I think they are evil. What is needed is not reorganization, but . . . just retribution. . . . There is a saying which aptly fits the dilemma faced by this committee. "Mix dirty water with clean water, and you get dirty water." I see no reason that agencies which have a long history of distinguished and respected public service should be contaminated by this kind of transfer.[14]

Characterizing ATF's agents as "knaves and rogues," Dingell added, "I would love to put them in jail. I would dearly love it. That is," he added, "after trial and proper procedures."[15] Echoing the Michigan Democrat, Knox—who throughout the hearing refused to say whether the NRA actually supported the shift—warned that "so long as the same agents are enforcing the same law it makes no difference whether they carry badges marked BATF or Secret Service."[16]

It soon became clear that the shift was a Pandora's box for the NRA. ATF, beaten down to the point where it feared any misstep that might bring the ire of the gun lobby, was a ready whipping boy for the NRA. The Secret Service—well known and respected—would be a more difficult, and most likely impossible, target for attack. And unlike ATF, which kept most of its firearms records on little slips of paper, the Secret Service already had a vast computer network.

The NRA's concerns were heightened when handgun control advocates refused to come to the aid of the agency. Michael Beard, executive director of the National Coalition to Ban Handguns, noted at the hearing that "the time has come to admit that BATF has outlived its usefulness and has, in effect, been destroyed by a massive, cynical campaign waged by the National Rifle Association." He characterized the agency's history as "one of failed objectives, unclear priorities, intimidation by the gun lobby, budget fights, and loss of morale among employees." In testimony, Knox noted that in addition to NCBH, both Handgun Control, Inc. and

Senator Edward Kennedy supported the change. Senator James Abdnor, Republican of South Dakota, mused to Knox, "I am wondering . . . if we are not jumping from the frying pan into the fire by going from the BATF to the Secret Service."[17]

By the end of the hearings, Knox was forced to undertake an embarrassing about-face for the NRA, telling the committee that the NRA opposed the transfer. He instead urged a purging of top ATF management, passage of McClure-Volkmer and the enactment of new policy guidelines restricting the agency's enforcement powers. To placate the NRA, Abdnor and Senator Dennis DeConcini, Democrat of Arizona, offered a substitute plan that would keep the firearms enforcement responsibilities of ATF intact but reduce the staff from 700 to 300. The remaining agents would be transferred to the Secret Service to augment their protective services and criminal investigations. ATF would be renamed the Treasury Compliance Agency. In granting NRA approval to the plan, Knox noted:

> There would be fewer agents. That is . . . desirable. They have had more agents than they needed . . . they have dreamed up things to do. In most cases they have been a party to the offense. . . . It's an exact equivalent to Abscam. One of our basic concerns with the Secret Service is that the Secret Service has too few agents in election years, but they have too little to do three years out of four. . . . I don't want to see those [laws] in the hand of people with too little to do.[18]

Republican Senator Paul Laxalt, speaking for the administration, argued in favor of the original plan, but to no avail. Although voted out of committee, the measure never came to a floor vote. ATF, crippled and toothless, survived.

Endnotes

1. Trefethen, James, *Americans and Their Guns*, Stackpole Books, Harrisburg, PA (1967) at 198.
2. House Hearings on Federal Firearms Act, (June 22, 1937) at 14.
3. *Ibid.*
4. Senate Hearings on Proposed Amendment to the Federal Firearms Act, (July 10, 1967) at 563.
5. *Ibid.*
6. "The NCBH vs. The NRA," *Handgun Control News*, (March/April 1979).
7. *HASC TASKS—A Periodic Newsletter from the House Armed Services Committee*, (July 1989).
8. "Here We Stand," *American Hunter*, (December 1989) at 7.
9. "BLM, NRA Join to Improve Wildlife Habitat . . . ," *Inside Track*, (July/August 1990).
10. USDA news release, (October 5, 1990).
11. Master Memorandum of Understanding Between National Rifle Association and USDA, Forest Service.
12. Briefing Memorandum for James McSeley, (October 2, 1990).
13. *It Can't Happen Here*, NRA, (February 1981).
14. Senate Hearings on Proposed Dissolution of ATF, (February/March 1982) at 249.
15. *Ibid.* at 256.
16. *Ibid.* at 314.
17. *Ibid.* at 317.
18. "Senate Panel, NRA Join to Defeat Plan to Abolish Treasury Firearms Agency," *Washington Post*, (March 26, 1982).

Chapter Six

Fellow Travelers

Like many Washington lobbyists, each December John Snyder celebrates the holiday season by sending a custom Christmas card to members of Congress. Eleven months after the January 1989 Stockton, California, schoolyard assault weapons massacre, Snyder's card featured a winged Michael the Archangel—handgun on his thigh—in a darkened alley firing a semi-automatic assault rifle "to break up purveyors of illegal narcotics."

Dollars, drugs and a hypodermic needle fly from the dealer's hands as the bullets splay him against an alley wall. A Christmas tree shines through an apartment window and a Star of Bethlehem twinkles overhead. The greeting noted that "though rendered artistically in previous eras armed ordinarily with edged weaponry, it seems appropriate in the current era to present this Patron of Law Enforcement Officers equipped with suitably modern personal arms."

Previous Snyder Christmas cards—with equal portions of cheer, guns, religion and bad taste—included Santa, handgun on his hip and the gift of a rifle in his hand, kneeling beside a baby Jesus with outstretched arms. The inside of the card read, "And the word was made flesh. . . ."

Snyder, a cheerful man with a weakness for plaid jackets, works for the Citizens Committee for the Right to Keep and Bear Arms. The Citizens Committee is one of the handful of national pro-gun organizations that labor in the NRA's shadow. And while the NRA attempts to hide its political activities behind the veil of its hunting, training and sporting activities, for its second-tier competitors the battle against gun control is the only focus. The Citizens Committee still calls for repeal of the Gun Control Act of 1968, while Snyder has mused about a utopian society in which every citizen would openly wear a handgun. Of all the members of America's gun lobby, the NRA is, in fact, the most reasonable and mainstream.

Indeed, many of the NRA's gun lobby brethren view the oldest, largest and most influential pro-gun organization in America as a weakened and sometimes floundering giant that is all too willing to compromise the movement's pro-gun ideals.

The NRA, for its part, consistently works to distance itself from its competitors. Their discomfort is not lost on pro-control legislators, who rarely allow the NRA to testify alone on Capitol Hill. The NRA's lobbyists almost always find themselves at the hearing table flanked by such hard-liners as Snyder, their testimony presented as one view of "the gun lobby." Pro-control legislators take great joy in tormenting the NRA, often asking its lobbyists if they agree with the less than delicate answers of their colleagues.

At a 1988 gun control hearing before the House crime subcommittee, ILA lobbyist James Jay Baker found himself, as usual, sitting at a table with John Snyder and former ILA head Neal Knox. The question put to the three men by one of the representatives was whether they truly felt everyone in the hearing room would be safer if each person was armed. As the representative worked his way down the panel, Snyder and Knox both gave their enthusiastic endorsement to the idea. An embarrassed and chagrined Baker hemmed and hawed before giving a noncommital answer. After the hearing, NRA lobbyist David Conover sighed to gun control advocate Kristen Rand, "Someday they'll give us our own panel and we won't have to sit with those nuts."

The Citizens Committee for the Right to Keep and Bear Arms is the most public component of the small empire of publishing, direct mail and non-profit organizations run out of Bellevue, Washington, by diminutive conservative activist Alan Merrill Gottlieb. Gottlieb founded the Citizens Committee in 1974 "to defend the Second Amendment of the United States Constitution and to provide aid and information to individuals throughout the Nation seeking to maintain the right to keep and bear arms." Its educational arm, the Second Amendment Foundation (SAF), was founded the same year.

Members of the Citizens Committee's National Advisory Council have included Vice President Dan Quayle, Secretary of Defense Dick Cheney, Secretary of Housing and Urban Development Jack Kemp and Interior Secretary Manuel Lujan Jr. Its list of more than 120 "Congressional Advisors" includes Senators Bob Dole, Jesse Helms and Orrin Hatch.

Like other Citizens Committee officers, Snyder's past is intertwined with the NRA. From 1966 to 1974 he worked on the editorial staff of *American Rifleman*, leaving to open the Citizens Committee's Washington office in 1975. Its political director is former NRA Institute for Legislative Action head Robert Kukla. And the head of the Second Amendment Foundation is Cincinnati Revolt co-conspirator and *Gun Week* editor Joseph Tartaro.

Subtlety is not a Citizens Committee trait. A 1986 ad featuring photos of Hitler, Castro, Khadafy and Stalin announced:

> The experts have always agreed that gun control is the single best way to take freedom away from the people. It worked in Nazi Germany, and gun control works today in Cuba, Libya and the Soviet Union. Today, a bunch of do-gooders, politicians and their friends in the media are trying to make gun control work in America. These people feel that if you aren't allowed to own a gun, our nation will be a "better" place. And they're very close to making it happen.

Periodicals owned by SAF include *Gun Week* and *Women & Guns*. Books and pamphlets available from SAF include such titles as *The Gun Grabbers, Armed & Alive, Armed & Female, The Good Side of Guns, Gun Control—White Man's Law* and *Why Handgun Bans Can't Work.* One pamphlet, the Gottlieb-penned *Rights of Those Using Firearms for Self Defense,* offers gun-owning tips in an easy question-and-answer format:

> **Question:** How about an individual who constantly threatens to "punch my lights out"; can I shoot him the next time he jeers at me?
>
> **Answer:** No. Courts dislike your shooting someone who is only verbally insulting you. Even when he raises a fist at you, the courts would rather you retreat than draw your gun, despite your humiliation of having to back down. Even after you have pulled your firearm, and the assailant attempts to flee, you cannot shoot him in his back. . . .
>
> **Question:** After I have watched the neighborhood kids or their pets trample across my front lawn for the umpteenth time after I have warned them not to do so, may I wave my gun at them to scare them off?
>
> **Answer:** No. The kid's parents will complain to the police department, which most certainly will charge you with any of the following offenses: reckless endangerment, assault, disturbing the peace, disorderly conduct; and should you fire a "warning shot" into the air, you will be charged for violating the city ordinance that prohibits discharging firearms within city limits.

Gottlieb's dedication to the Second Amendment, however, appears second only to his dedication to money. Gottlieb's empire has been marked by charges of financial irregularity—including a stint by Gottlieb in federal prison for income tax evasion—and internal power struggles. In the introduction to Gottlieb's self-published book *The Gun Grab-*

1. *Neal Knox. A leader of the 1977 Cincinnati Revolt, Neal Knox viewed himself as the conscience of the NRA. By 1982 his hard-line stance had offended too many on Capitol Hill and he was forced to resign from the Institute for Legislative Action and was later removed from the board of directors. In 1991 Knox was returned by the membership to the board to help guide the new, no-compromise NRA.*

2. *Harlon Carter. The prime beneficiary of the Cincinnati Revolt, Harlon Carter ruled the NRA as a Second Amendment Il Duce. A bigger-than-life figure to NRA true believers, as executive vice president, Carter increased the NRA's power and prestige. All subsequent leaders would pale in comparison.*

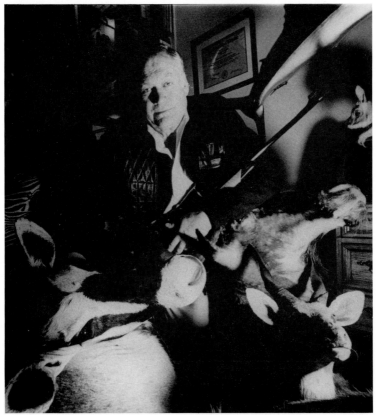

3. *G. Ray Arnett. Carter's handpicked successor soon found himself embroiled in a member recall petition. A game-law violator, it was revealed that as a Reagan administration official Arnett had written a letter of support for a convicted cocaine dealer. A year later he was stripped of power and resigned.*

4. *Howard Pollock. NRA President Pollack was one of the few to protest Arnett's ouster. In a secret letter to the board, he was concerned about member reaction to the $400,000 the NRA paid Arnett to avoid a legal battle over his dismissal.*

5. *Ted and Françoise Gianoutsos. NRA Life and Benefactor members Ted and Françoise Gianoutsos organized the recall petition against G. Ray Arnett. The Gianoutsoses joined the NRA hoping to participate in an organization that represented the best aspects of gun ownership. They quickly became disillusioned. The appointment of Arnett, they felt, symbolized the deep problems that had alienated the NRA from the public and many of its own members.*

6. *J. Warren Cassidy. Under Executive Vice President Cassidy the NRA went into a decline, losing members and political power. Although outside forces were mostly responsible for the change, Cassidy soon became the target of member and board wrath. After a sex-discrimination suit alleging misconduct by the NRA and Cassidy was settled for a sum in six figures, Cassidy resigned.*

7. Wayne LaPierre. Succeeding Cassidy as executive vice president in 1991, former Institute for Legislative Action head Wayne LaPierre promised members a reinvigorated, hard-line NRA that would never compromise. LaPierre counted among his supporters the ubiquitous Neal Knox.

A QUESTION OF SELF-DEFENSE.

"Tell them
what rape is.
Be graphic.
Be disgusting.
Be obscene.
Make them sick.
If they throw up,
then they have
the tiniest idea
of what it is!"
— Boston rape victim.

8. *In the wake of the handgun sales slump of the early 1980s, the NRA and the firearms industry targeted a new market: women. With rape as a sales pitch, handguns were offered as the only truly reliable means of self-defense.*

Photographs one to six are reprinted by permission of Brian Smale.

bers, Senator Steve Symms, Republican of Idaho, characterizes Gottlieb as "no stranger to controversy. During the years I've known him, he has overcome one adversity after another. I'm well aware of his classic battle with the Internal Revenue Service. I've seen him go through meat-grinder situations and come out stronger than ever."

Gottlieb's "classic battle" with the IRS came to an ignoble end in May 1984 when he pleaded guilty in federal court to income tax evasion. Gottlieb was charged with failing to report in 1977 and 1978 the gross receipts of Merril Associates, his direct-mail consulting firm. Gottlieb reported his 1977 taxable income as $13,335, with tax due of $142. In fact, the gross receipts of Merril Associates for the year were $138,000, Gottlieb's taxable income was $44,500 and the total tax owed by him was $11,000.

In 1978 Gottlieb reported taxable income of $17,329 with tax due of $3,354. For that year the gross receipts of Merril Associates were $260,000, Gottlieb's taxable income was $76,500 and his tax due was $32,750. Gottlieb plea bargained and was sentenced to a year and a day in jail and fined $5,000, despite pleas from his defense lawyer that "putting Alan in jail will not make him more sorry or more humiliated than he already is." After the sentencing Gottlieb hugged his crying wife and told reporters that the IRS had pressured the court to make an example of him. His indictment, he told them, was part of a Treasury Department campaign against pro-gun groups. Gottlieb served eight and a half months in prison and was released in March 1985.

While in prison, Gottlieb continued to control his holdings from his jail cell. Faced with complaints of questionable ethics from the Second Amendment Foundation staff, he quickly purged the organization. The ousted staff members then founded their own organization, SAVE-SAF. They charged that Gottlieb was using SAF for his own benefit and had betrayed its staff and supporters. Through a series of court and media battles the exiled staffers attempted to wrest the organization away from Gottlieb. Their counterattack failed, and Gottlieb retained control.

A Coopers & Lybrand review of the Citizens Committee's 1988 finances hints at the links between Gottlieb's non-profit organizations and other for-profit companies he owns. The Citizens Committee rents its office space for $4,083 a month from an "an officer and director," presumably Gottlieb. Other expenses that were paid in 1988 to "certain members of management of the Committee"—once again, presumably Gottlieb—who were "either principal owners or officers of various affiliated organizations which provide services to the [Citizens] Committee" included $200,000 to Service Bureau Cooperative, Inc. for data processing, accounting and telemarketing; and approximately $200,000 paid for mail, marketing and list rental to Merril Associates.

Gottlieb's money troubles have not been limited to his personal finances. In 1985 the Second Amendment Foundation agreed to stop using the name of New York subway gunman Bernhard Goetz in a solicitation for its "Citizens' Self-Defense Fund." Following Goetz's shooting of four black teens in December 1984, the foundation began making fund-raising telephone calls to its more than 400,000 members. Neither Goetz nor his lawyers had authorized the fund-raiser. They soon requested that SAF stop the solicitation "as the only honorable thing to do." At the time of the request SAF had raised more than $42,000.

The misappropriation of Goetz's name was nothing new. A 1977 Citizens Committee mailing done by New Right direct-mail marketing whiz Richard Viguerie featured a personalized letter that implied that the correspondence was endorsed by the recipient's member of Congress. Many hadn't been. Said Republican Representative Robert Walker of Pennsylvania, "I cannot believe there is anyone in the Congress more opposed to gun control legislation than I am. However, I cannot and will not condone this kind of irresponsible special interest appeal for money." When Walker called Gottlieb to complain about the "highly unethical and grossly ill-conceived" action, Gottlieb hung up on him. Gottlieb eventually agreed to return money obtained under the solicitation.

The Citizens Committee's hard-line competitor is Gun Owners of America. GOA was founded in 1975 by California Republican state Senator H.L. "Bill" Richardson, a former John Birch Society field representative. Founded to "preserve and defend the rights of gun owners," the group's members are "patriotic Americans working together to preserve the right to keep and bear arms, protecting and safeguarding our Constitutional freedoms for future generations."

In addition to its lobbying arm, GOA maintains an educational foundation, the Gun Owners Foundation; a political action committee, the Gun Owners of America Campaign Committee; and a statewide association in California.

In a 1991 column warning of possible Iraqi terrorist attacks, GOA Executive Director Larry Pratt—a former head of the American Conservative Union—warned that gun controls would deny citizens the ability to

> defend themselves and their families in the advent of terrorist strikes. Incredibly, politicians have already begun to use the threat of terrorism as an excuse for more gun control. [Virginia] Governor Douglas Wilder . . . claims the availability of guns will help terrorists perform their evil deeds. This is the rhetoric anti-gunners frequently use to argue for more gun control. But such reasoning is nonsense.

GOA is not above latching onto NRA issues for its own benefit. When the NRA launched its full-scale attack on ATF in the early 1980s, GOA joined in. A fund-raising letter at the time attacked the agency for its practice of giving visiting schoolchildren cards that made them honorary junior agents and urged them to be law-abiding. In the letter Pratt warned that ATF was

> encouraging them to spy on their parents and neighbors. Tomorrow while you're at work these kids could be sneaking around your property. You can expect them to be peeking in the windows of your house or car to find out more about your hunting rifle or gun collection. Then,

for the impressionable youngster, the most important part of all—sending a SECRET report to the government.

If both the Citizens Committee and GOA view the NRA as soft on guns, none can hold a candle to the American Pistol and Rifle Association (APRA), "the most dedicated, patriotic, uncompromising, freedom oriented gun organization in America." Located in Benton, Tennessee, APRA is headed by Dr. John Grady.

In its literature APRA dismisses other pro-gun groups as being too involved in the "entertaining and even wholesome" activities of hunting, competitive shooting and gun collecting. At APRA, says Grady:

> We support, defend and encourage responsible gun ownership by every mature man and woman in America—first, to prevent, resist and stop crime against person and property; secondly, to deter the abuse of power by elected officials, and prevent the establishment of totalitarian government, whether of foreign or domestic origin.

In a letter to prospective members, Grady adds that "unlike nearly every other national organization, APRA has no big salaries, slush funds, or wasteful expense accounts. Every dollar APRA spends goes into the fight to save our guns and our freedom." Preaching the gospel of post-nuclear survival, APRA proudly labels its members "survivalists":

> It is most regrettable indeed, that many people consider survivalists as a threat and regard them with suspicion and even hostility. Let's be honest and realistic: THE MOST DANGEROUS PEOPLE IN AMERICA TODAY ARE THE NONSURVIVALISTS. Every person who has not made provisions for surviving without food, water, fuel and other essential needs from the outside, is a mortal danger to his neighbor.

At the APRA Academy in Tennessee, men, women and children participate in Survival Schools, where they undertake firearms and survival training. APRA's schools have also served as survivalist networking parties for domestic terrorist organizations. In their book *The Silent Brotherhood*, authors Kevin Flynn and Gary Gerhardt relate how right-wing paramilitary extremist and APRA member Andrew Virgil Barnhill, while attending an APRA training workshop, met a group from the Identity camp of the Covenant, the Sword, and the Arm of the Lord. Barnhill later went to live at CSA's commune to train in military survival tactics.

Although APRA has talked of removing federal officials "by whatever means necessary," this hasn't scared away some politicians. A 1983 edition of *APRA News* features a photo of then-New Hampshire Governor John Sununu shooting at APRA's New Hampshire Birch Knoll Range. An accompanying article credits Sununu and other New Hampshire politicians, such as former Senator Gordon Humphrey (described as a member of APRA's National Advisory Board), with keeping New Hampshire a "bright spot of freedom in a world growing increasingly totalitarian."

Guns are not APRA's only concern. Busing, "perhaps the most obvious proof today that the American people suffer under the heel of totalitarian government," is decried as "federal kidnapping." South Africa is defended as a "European" nation in whose affairs "we have no legal or moral right to meddle in." Writes Grady:

> The betrayal and abandonment of South Africa constitutes national suicide for the United States. The only reasonable conclusion that can be drawn is that the top leaders of the United States, and those who manipulate them from behind the scenes, have for the past several decades plotted a course to undermine the United States and the freedom of her people, and ultimately destroy Western Civilization.

And in commenting on a Centers for Disease Control report on the link between inadequate health care and increases in syphilis and AIDS, a 1990 APRA newsletter asked, "Oh really? We didn't know that fornicators and homosexuals got syphilis and AIDS by not going to the doctor or to the free public health clinics which are readily available everywhere. We thought these diseases were caught and spread as a result of depraved behavior!"

The remaining pro-gun groups are small, personality-driven special-interest organizations. They represent machine gun owners, pro-gun Jews and Neal Knox fans.

Soon after the future production and sale of machine guns for civilian use was banned in 1986, the National Firearms Association (NFA) was founded. Sharing an acronym with the National Firearms Act of 1934, the all-volunteer NFA consists of machine gun manufacturers, dealers and owners. NFA head Linda Farmer paints licensed machine gun owners as a maligned segment of gun owners who have lost their rights as a result of the bad publicity associated with illegally converted machine guns and an unwillingness on the part of the NRA to defend their firearm of choice. Farmer is dedicated to convincing the public of the benefits of private machine gun ownership. "We had every reason to be proud of what we do," she says. "So we decided to drag it out of the closet." For Farmer, the battle is personal. Her husband, J.D. Farmer Jr., is a machine gun manufacturer. "What they're saying," says Farmer, "is that my husband's talents are not suitable. God gave him that talent, excuse me."

Full-auto enthusiasts, says Farmer, are "the crème de la crème" of gun owners. In support of this characterization, she cites not only the strict licensing process of the National Firearms Act, but also demographic studies showing that the majority of legal machine gun owners are college-educated with annual incomes of more than $50,000. Says Farmer, "If a real estate person said to me that every person in this neighborhood was a machine gun owner, I know they'd mow their grass, wouldn't beat their wives on the weekend and wouldn't get drunk and run over my mailbox. I'd buy a house in a second."

Like the NFA, Jews for the Preservation of Firearms Ownership (JPFO) was founded as the result of a perceived need. JPFO was established in 1989 by Vietnam veteran Aaron Zelman, a self-described firearms distributor and gun writer. Labeling itself "America's Aggressive Civil Rights Organization," JPFO's logo is a Star of David bracketed by two assault rifles.

In a 1989 *Gun Week* profile, Zelman explained the need for JPFO:

> One of the major problems we gun owners face is the heavy influence (some call it stranglehold) of left wing, liberal Jewish anti-gunners in the media and government. JPFO can . . . challenge those individuals without the fear of being labeled anti-Semitic. The other gun groups . . . must daily tiptoe around the truth for fear of the anti-Semitic label, which would be used by the liberal media in the blink of an eye and without mercy. . . . [C]an you imagine a representative of any pro-gun group saying what I have just said . . . even though it is the truth? It's not that they would not want to, it's just that they're afraid of being clobbered by the "anti-Semitic weapon"!

A swastika-headed ad for the organization warns:

> Stop Hitlerism in America! Gun haters who support gun banning, registration, and waiting period schemes are elitist Fascists who want *total* control of people's lives. Gun haters, knowingly or unknowingly, are advocating the Hitler doctrine of the 1990s. Gun control is a tragic mistake of the past. Millions of tortured and mutilated corpses testify to that fact. The Hitler Doctrine and those that favor it, must not be tolerated in America. Politicians, police officials, and media liberals who support the Hitler Doctrine of gun hate are un-American and have betrayed the public's trust. BE ANTI-NAZI!! Help eradicate gun hate in American [sic]. . . .

Membership, the ad notes, is open to "all Anti-Nazi gun owners. (NON-JEWISH GUN OWNERS WELCOME)." Readers are urged to make copies of the ad "and send it to gun haters today!"

"A minority within a minority," Zelman hopes to also "combat the growing anti-Semitism in America, partly caused by anti-gun Jews. We may even possibly educate some Jewish anti-gunners and 'convert' them to the pro-freedom, pro-American pro-gun viewpoint." According to Zelman, Jewish involvement in the gun control movement stems from two factors. The first is the willingness of Jews to "blame outside influences for their misfortunes." The second is that gun control can act as a stepping stone to fulfill their "insatiable desire to be accepted into social circles that previously excluded Jews," such as the pro-gun control Kennedy family.

Following his ouster from the NRA's Institute for Legislative Action in 1982, Neal Knox formed the Firearms Coalition. Originally named the Neal Knox Hard Corps, the Coalition is operated by Knox's consulting firm, Neal Knox Associates, and is the primary vehicle by which Knox maintains his hand in the gun debate. Since July 4, 1984, he has been a registered lobbyist for the Coalition. Callers to the Coalition are welcomed by a tape-recorded computer greeting allowing them to hear Knox's latest legislative report and views on the gun issue. His most public face, however, is the "Neal Knox Report," which appears in *Shotgun News* and other pro-gun publications. Although the NRA has at times dismissed Knox as a one-man show, his appeal among no-compromise gun advocates, who view him as the last true voice remaining in the pro-gun debate, is strong. Contributions to the Firearms Coalition total nearly $100,000 a year.

Part III

Fear & Intimidation

Chapter Seven

Selling Fear

Fear sells guns. Fear of crime, of government, of people who aren't like you. Since the 1960s, the NRA has offered private firearm—primarily handgun—ownership as the only truly dependable means of self-defense. In 1967 the NRA warned of government inability to guard "the doors of American homes from senseless savagery and pillaging" and endorsed the establishment of civilian "posse comitatus" groups. These statements, coupled with a notation that even sledge hammers and ax handles made useful self-defense tools, led to accusations that the organization was promoting vigilantism.

Since the early 1980s, the NRA has used fear to sell itself. Hunters and target shooters represent a limited membership pool, most of whom know of the NRA. And increasing urbanization, equipment costs and competition for leisure time can only decrease sportsmen's numbers. Self-defense offers access to the general population. So in 1983 the NRA instituted its Personal Protection Program, a twelve-hour training course for those buying handguns for self-defense. Since then, more than 500,000 Americans have participated in it.

The fear peddled by the NRA can be general or specific. In 1987 it placed in national newspapers six full-page ads "as chillingly real as the NRA's advertising agency . . . could create." Designed to "strike an emotional chord within all law-abiding citizens who feared or were infuriated by rampant crime," the ads featured bold *New York Post*-style headlines and photos presented in grainy black and white crime verité. Readers opened their papers to a variety of crime scenes. A store clerk behind a counter throws up both his hands to cover his face from attack. The ad asks:

> What Does a Convenience Store Clerk Think Just Before He is Attacked? He has no time to think. Instead, his instinct to survive takes over as he attempts to defend himself. He deserves a fighting chance in the face of vicious criminal assault. That's why our constitution guarantees his right to own a firearm.

A nattily dressed yuppie is beaten to the ground by a baseball bat-wielding young tough. The headline reads:

> Why Can't a Policeman Be There When You Need Him? He's somewhere else, responding to crimes already committed. If police can't protect you, who will? You alone. You bear ultimate responsibility for your own protection.

And as a white-haired granny is pushed to the ground by a muscle-shirted man in running shoes, her groceries spilling across the sidewalk, the question arises:

> If You're Attacked On Your Porch, Do You Want Your Neighbors To Be Opposed To Gun Ownership Or Members of The NRA? Crime strikes without regard for your personal beliefs about firearms ownership. Faced with the cruel reality of criminal assault, your philosophy no longer counts. Your survival does.[1]

Handguns do kill some criminals and stop some crimes. The proof is provided each month in an *American Rifleman* and *Hunter* column, "The Armed Citizen." Originally titled "Guns vs. Bandits," each month the column features news clips citing the self-defense use of firearms. Todd Gray, "wearing only a smile," nabs a thief breaking into his roommate's car and holds him at bay with his .45 handgun. Louie Fonduk grabs the pistol from his nightstand to catch a crowbar-armed intruder in his living room.

The NRA promises that each year gun-wielding citizens kill 1,500 to 2,800 criminals and stop nearly a million crimes. In reality, handguns are rarely used by citizens to kill criminals or stop crimes. For every time a handgun is used by a citizen in a justifiable homicide against someone unknown to them, 118 innocent lives are ended in handgun murders, suicides and accidents. From 1981 to 1983, nearly 69,000 Americans lost their lives in these three categories. During that same period, only 583 homicides were reported to the FBI in which a citizen used a handgun to kill a stranger justifiably (assuming that Americans aren't arming themselves for protection against those known to them, such as friends and family). More Americans are hit by lightning each year than justifiably kill strangers with handguns.

How many times are handguns used to stop crimes without killing criminals? According to the federal Bureau of Justice Statistics, in 1987, the most recent year for which figures are available, in only one-half of one percent of all intended or actual incidences of violent crime was a firearm even available to the potential or actual victim—both gun owning and non-gun owning. Of these approximately 28,000 instances, it's not known whether the gun was even successfully used to stop the crime.

Criminals are not the only element to be feared in the NRA's world. Whenever civil strife or invasion strikes a foreign land, the NRA is there to warn that there but for a heavily armed civilian population... Following the imposition of martial law in Poland in 1981, full-page newspaper ads displayed "An Open Letter to all Polish Americans" from Institute for Legislative Action head Neal Knox. Wrote Knox:

> Poland has precisely the firearms laws that the NRA has been opposing in the United States.... [T]he courageous Polish people are willing to ... fight against ... a tyran-

nical government . . . but "the authorities have all the guns." Fortunately for us, the Founding Fathers had great foresight. And so long as the Second Amendment is not infringed, what is happening in Poland can never happen in these United States. Thank you, Mr. Jefferson.[2]

Responding to Knox's revolutionary fervor, firearms researcher Franklin Zimring, then at the University of Chicago, noted in a *Chicago Tribune* op-ed that in an age of heavy artillery and standing armies

> revolvers are no better against tanks in Chicago than in Warsaw. Under these circumstances, a constitutional right to bazookas and heat-seeking missiles would seem more promising than rabbit guns as a counterforce to tyranny. But there are problems. Would this give power to the majority of the people or to the people with the majority of the artillery? What happens when two heavily armed groups disagree? Are these "scenarios" the lessons of Solidarity? Or is a democratic spirit, unarmed but fabulously powerful, our real insurance policy against darkness?[3]

When tanks rolled into Tiananmen Square in June 1989, the NRA was there—in spirit. Beneath the picture of a battered Chinese student surrounded by helmeted troops, the text of an NRA newspaper ad read:

> The students of Beijing did not have a Second Amendment right to defend themselves when the soldiers came. America's founding fathers understood that an armed people are a free people. Free to defend themselves against crime and violence. Free to rise up against tyranny. That's why the individual armed citizen remains one of democracy's strongest symbols. The National Rifle Association's defense of firearms isn't just about hunting, or competitive shooting, or even personal protection. The right to own a firearm is a statement about freedom.[4]

And when Iraqi tanks rolled across the Kuwaiti border, *NRAction* attacked "Gun Control: Iraq's Ally." The article featured a Kuwaiti refugee couple who, "now safely in America, reflect on the devastating effects that gun control had on Kuwait."[5] Dr. Jagan Sharma "saw . . . the effects of a total gun ban when tyranny is unleashed: massive lootings and the rape and murder of defenseless people." Added Sharma, "Private firearms ownership is a must. The tyranny unleashed in Kuwait can happen to any country."[6]

This same theme was heard in 1968 following the Kennedy and King assassinations, when the NRA told of U. S. troops in Vietnam, who "believe devoutly in the right of American civilians to keep and bear arms," writing home "distressed, about the ease with which the Communists capture disarmed Vietnam villages."[7]

That nations such as Great Britain and Japan have banned handguns yet managed to remain democracies has little effect on the NRA mindset. The NRA was also noticeably silent when the disarmed "captive nations" of Eastern Europe peacefully gained their freedom in 1989.

In addition to its broad themes of self-defense and government oppression, the NRA has also focused on specific society segments. They are children, women and blacks.

In a 1985 address to the board, NRA President Alonzo Garcelon outlined the need for the NRA to expand its appeal in order to increase its political power. He said:

> The youth of America are our future. . . . [W]ithout their interest and involvement, there will be no gun ownership or hunting. Another segment of our population which needs more emphasis is women of all ages and avocations. We can easily double or triple our ranks by enlisting millions of women. . . . This so-called minority, as well as the *real* minorities in our society, represent great potential for increasing our ranks and strategies. . . . [T]hese areas I've discussed and given new priority to will provide the needed additional strength, numbers and resources for the [gun control] battles which lie ahead.[8]

Children's Crusade

Throughout its history the NRA has beckoned to America's youth. A 1907 NRA advertisement headed "Boys!! Become a 'Junior Marksman' " encouraged children to organize NRA rifle clubs in their schools to "instill the principle of manhood and loyal citizenship in the youth of the land." One advocate of this "gun in every schoolroom" approach was President Theodore Roosevelt, who in a 1908 address to Congress called for publicly funded rifle ranges in all military schools and large public schools.

In January 1985 the NRA board reaffirmed a 1980 resolution that stated:

> WHEREAS, The future of the shooting sports in America rests with the youth of the nation . . . [i]t is the official policy of the National Rifle Association to introduce as many of our nation's youth as possible to the legitimate use of the [sic] firearms, and to provide specific assistance to involve them via other organizations in firearms related activities.[9]

The result of this resolution is a children's crusade that reaches from safety in the home to hunting in the field. One of the first "I'm the NRA" ads featured eight-year-old Bryan Hardin, "second grade student and a member of the National Rifle Association." Holding an air rifle, Hardin admits, "I like to play football best. But I like my dog and I like my new BB gun. My Dad's a member of the NRA and so am I because he says they need kids like me to grow up and keep shooting a safe sport." A March 1982 *Rifleman* article titled "Kids Rifle" extolled the Chipmunk, a scaled-down .22 children's rifle. The caption beneath the photo of a child being helped to aim the rifle notes that "Lisa Howard at seven years' age and a height of 4 ft. 3 inches, seems to be a potential customer."[10]

The NRA portrays kids and guns as an inevitable fact of life. In the instructional guidelines to the grade-school oriented *My Gun Safety Book,* the NRA notes:

> There are close to 200 million guns in the United States. Whether or not the students' families own guns, there is a great chance that children will come in contact with a gun at some time during their young lives.

The six-page coloring book opens with "Dick and Jane found the gun." Upon seeing the revolver, left on a living room coffee table, an alarmed Dick tells a quizzical Jane, "Stop, Jane. Don't touch the gun." Apron-clad Mom is then told of their find. A sheepish Mom hugs the tykes, telling them, "I am proud of you for telling me so I could put it away."

David's First Hunt is a 31-page coloring book featuring a freckle-faced protagonist. In the story, David jumps out of bed to load up the family pickup truck so he, Dad and the family labrador, Ace, can begin their journey to visit a local farm to hunt pheasant. After gaining permission from the farmer, the two "courteous hunters" tramp into the woods in search of game. David shoots a pheasant, flushed by Ace, in midflight. Moments later Ace proudly returns with David's bird. David holds up the "beautiful" pheasant, a look of Christmas-morning awe on his face, and gasps, "Wow, look at all these pretty colors." With a tail feather from the bird in his hat, David expresses hopes that his father too will find a bird that day. His dad reminds him that "true hunters love being outdoors and seeing the beauty of mother nature. The killing of an animal should never be the most important part of the hunt." On the ride home in Dad's pickup truck, David, tired from the day's activities, dreams of Mom serving up the steaming bird.

The NRA's "Father Shoots Best" safety programs are almost quaint in their separation from the reality of youth and firearms violence. By focusing on accidental shootings—both in the home and in the field—the NRA ignores the vast majority of youth firearms violence. A 1989 National Center for Health Statistics study found that in 1987 more than 10 percent of the deaths of children over a year of age were linked to firearms. For that year, the study found that 3,392 youth aged one to 19 were killed in gun-related incidents. Forty-eight percent died as the result of firearms murders, 42 percent from firearms suicides, and the remainder, 10 percent, died in firearms accidents.

The reality of youth violence wouldn't make a good coloring book. And unlike Dick and Jane, the victims are disproportionately black males. In 1986, the teenage homicide rate for black males was 51.5 per 100,000, compared with 8.6 per 100,000 for white males. As a result, for black teenage males murder, usually involving a firearm, is the leading cause of death. The scenarios bear little resemblance to the NRA's world of absent-minded Moms and friendly farmers.

Fifteen-year-old Jermaine Daniel counted among his friends Washington, D. C., Police Chief Maurice Turner, who had become the chubby teen's mentor. When Daniel got into an argument with his 14-year-old best friend—whose girlfriend Daniel had threatened to slap—the friend allegedly pulled out a pistol and pumped three shots into Daniel's chest.

When 14-year-old Shamel Knight yelled at another Queens teen to get off his moped, the youth dismounted and returned brandishing a pistol. Knight told him, "If you want to pull a gun, you have to use that gun." Pointing the handgun at Knight's face, the other teen replied, "You think I'm joking here?" He then squeezed the trigger. The gun clicked but didn't fire. A second squeeze of the trigger sent a bullet through Knight's mouth and into his brain.[11]

In New York City, ten-month-old Rayvon Jamison—a pudgy baby nicknamed Mike Tyson by his family—was toddling in his blue walker over to the refrigerator while his family watched Donahue. "All of a sudden it was like a nightmare," said the boy's grandmother. "I heard these gunshots. . . . BOW! BOW! BOW! . . . The shots came repeatedly. They were coming through the door, ripping the door up." Jamison died from bullets intended for an uncle, who had drawn an unflattering sketch of the hairstyle of one of the suspected gunmen.[12]

NRA Junior Membership, which promises to "make your shooting experiences fun and rewarding," denies the existence of kids like Jermaine Daniel and Shamel Knight. Instead, through its publications and shooting activities, it focuses on "tomorrow's leaders" who "want to help protect our right to keep and bear arms." Each month NRA junior members receive the "NRA News for Young Shooters," *InSights* magazine. The thin, glossy publication focuses on hunting, shooting and the joys of NRA membership. Established in 1981, by 1990 circulation, reflecting current NRA junior membership, stood at 32,000. In an April 1985 article, 50,000th Junior Member Jared Goegeline promised, "I plan to tell all my friends about how much fun shooting is and that if they love to shoot a lot, they will want to join the NRA."[13]

A profile later that year of 17-year-old member Jeff Brantley noted that since the age of 13 he

> has been conducting his own one-man crusade to preserve the right to possess firearms and lawfully use them. He's spent countless hours writing his congressmen and senators, researching local, state and federal firearms laws, signing up members for the NRA, writing the editors of national news magazines, submitting articles to major outdoor publications, reading newspapers and magazines for firearms news, monitoring anti-gun bias on television programs, making speeches and writing class papers on safe use of firearms and talking with his friends and classmates about the positive aspects of gun ownership.[14]

Like its older brothers, *American Rifleman* and *American Hunter*, *InSights* acts as a sales vehicle for manufacturers. Springfield Armory offers M1A rifles and 1911A Colt 45 handguns. The Winchester .22 rimfire rifle commemorating the Boy Scouts of America promises "This Gun is a Tribute to More Than 70 Million Great Americans." While the receiver is engraved with Scout symbols and lore—including the Boy Scout oath—the gun's finger lever is engraved with scouting knots. An April 1991 article, "Youth Guns for '91," notes that "quite a few firearm manufacturers are offering guns specially designed and built for junior hunters and shooters this year." Rifles and shotguns from Marlin, Remington, Mossberg and Navy Arms are featured in the article. The magazine also notes that "there is no reason a junior can't learn to handle a pistol safely and competently."

As part of its promotional efforts, the NRA also works with youth organizations such as 4-H and the Boy Scouts of America, supplying necessary materials and instructor training. The 4-H shooting program began in 1976 in Texas when ammunition manufacturer Federal Cartridge Company called the NRA with an idea to link 4-H to the company's youth shooting programs. Soon after, other 4-H state chapters expressed interest in the Texas program. The result was "a major financial grant" from the NRA to establish a national 4-H shooting program. According to 4-H spokesperson Michael Ambrose, the association's shooting program has increased dramatically in the past decade, getting a "lot of kids involved in 4-H that wouldn't be." Manufacturers that have supported the 4-H program, says Ambrose, include Winchester, Sturm, Ruger & Co., Smith & Wesson and Browning. The program, they tell him, has helped the industry.

The NRA has enjoyed a longer relationship with the Boy Scouts of America. Among the marksmanship merit badge requirements listed in the 1911 Boy Scout handbook was qualification as an NRA junior marksman. (The requirement has since been dropped.)

According to Daniel Ruth, associate national director for council services for the Boy Scouts, the organization's connection with the NRA today is limited and clearly defined, with no direct affiliation or ties. The Boy Scouts utilize the NRA's educational materials in their shooting activities, and all Boy Scout camps must have NRA-certified instructors. There are currently four Scout shooting merit badges. But even the Boy Scouts have doubts about the NRA's agenda. Says Ruth, "Some of these things they stand for are ridiculous. And some people [at NRA headquarters] don't agree with some of the things they're doing, although they won't go on the record."

The New Equality

Women are the new target for handgun sales. Although the NRA had tried to involve women before (most notably in its WINRA, Women in NRA, program), the handgun sales slump of the early 1980s—which stemmed from saturation of the primary market of white males—resulted in the most broad-based effort ever conducted to bring women into the gun culture. Niche marketing had worked for cigarettes and alcohol, why not guns? Writing in the September 1984 *American Firearms Industry* magazine, National Association of Federally Licensed Firearms Dealers head Andy Molchan cheered the efforts of Neal Knox to place a shooting program on cable television. Said Molchan, "The left-wing socialists who control ABC, CBS and NBC have frozen firearms people out, but *cable* is our key to the door. Cable is also the key to the women's market."

In addition, women gave the NRA a human side. "Our opponents would like to depict us as chauvinistic, redneck clods who dream only of machine guns in every pickup truck," complained NRA Personal Protection Program Director Tracey Martin in a 1988 *NRAction* article.[15] And the NRA's female members are not just beer-guzzling rednecks in drag. "Millions of intelligent, self-reliant women have chosen to defend themselves," say Martin. (According to one woman profiled: "I have two college degrees, 15 years of professional work experience and an IQ that has been measured high by anyone's standards.")

The NRA's women's gallery is a showcase of feel-good psycho-babble. "Wife, mother, businesswoman, national woman pistol champion" Ruby Fox reveals in the article that "competitive shooting has taught me to believe in myself." Norma McCollough, "wife, mother and high power shooting champion," finds shooting "very relaxing and personally satisfying." And the blond-tressed Jo Anne Hall, former Dallas Cowboys cheerleader and ladies' national pistol champion, explains that "women should know there's wholesome recreation connected with guns. It's something you can have fun with, besides having a means of self-protection." With handguns offered as another male bastion falling to women's equality, arguments against their ownership are often portrayed by the NRA as patriarchal attempts to deny women their freedom.

The NRA's primary marketing tactic to women, however, is not personal growth through gun ownership. It's fear. The pitch to women is simple. You're a woman. Someone's going to rape you. You'd better buy a handgun. People buy handguns out of fear, and rape is perceived as what women fear most.

In NRA pamphlets and advertisements the point is drilled home. The cover of the pamphlet *A Question of Self-Defense* offers a chilling quote against a black, blood-spattered background. " 'Tell them what rape is. Be graphic. Be disgusting. Be obscene. Make them sick. If they throw up, then they have the tiniest idea of what it is!'—Boston Rape Victim." *It Can Happen to You* opens to a drawing of an unsuspecting, elderly woman. Written from the female perspective, the pamphlet warns:

> In nature, the predator preys on the weak, the sick, the aged. It stalks. It waits patiently for the precise moment when the victim appears defenseless. Then, it strikes. . . . [T]here is no way of telling a criminal predator by the way he looks. He might be a potential suitor.

In its clumsy attempts to paint handgun ownership as a "choice issue," the NRA has appropriated the language of abortion rights advocates. In the first "I'm the NRA" ad to feature a woman touting a handgun for self-defense, Detective Jeanne Bray states, "A gun is a choice women need to know more about and be free to make. And the NRA is working to ensure the freedom of that choice always exists."

One ad in its 1987 self-defense series featured a stocking-masked man-of-all-races under the headline, "Should You Shoot a Rapist Before He Cuts Your Throat?" The text read:

> American women are realizing they must take responsibilty for their own self-defense. One choice is a firearm, a deeply personal decision that requires deliberation, knowledge and maturity. It's a choice guaranteed by our constitution, a right that can be as precious as life itself. Don't own a firearm if you choose not to. But never let anyone deny or delay your constitutional freedom to make that choice.[16]

And in a 1990 television commercial, Susan Howard of *Dallas* offers the image of the NRA as the good boyfriend, soothingly stating, "Owning a firearm is a deeply personal decision, but you don't have to do it alone."

The NRA has been joined by other pro-gun organizations in its women's pitch. A 1985 Second Amendment Foundation ad featured a beaten woman, eye blackened and lip swelling, wrapped in a bathrobe. "Last night I was raped. . . . Where were the police?" she asks. The text reads:

> The days when you thought you'd never be the victim of a rape—that it "can't happen to me"—are over. We all know of friends or family who have been raped, beaten, robbed or burglarized by thugs who don't think twice about hurting someone. You might be the next victim.

By 1989 SAF had purchased the nascent *Women & Guns* magazine, the self-described "leader in the women gunowners movement." The magazine presented a new-found firearms feminism, noting:

> Women have been conditioned to think they are not smart enough or strong enough to handle a firearm effectively. Let me tell you women out there: If you are smart enough to use a sewing machine or a word processor, you are smart enough to handle a firearm. And if you are strong

enough to carry a man's groceries and a man's baby, you
are strong enough to carry a man's gun.

Soon after the magazine's purchase, its founder, Sonny
Jones, became SAF's director of women's affairs. Upon as-
sumption of the post, she stated in *Gun Week* (which had been
purchased previously by SAF):

> More and more women are not only buying guns—for
> self-protection, recreational shooting and hunting—but
> they are also playing a bigger role in the firearms industry
> itself.

Jones urged that "the whole firearms community take up
the challenge" of a resolution passed at the 1988 Gun Rights
Policy Conference (the annual hobnob of pro-gun groups)
urging participants to "endeavor to actively recruit more
women in America to join as active partners in the defense
of our right to keep and bear arms."

With the political organizations supplying the fear, the
manufacturers offered the solution. In 1989 handgun
manufacturer Smith & Wesson announced its LadySmith
Program—"just possibly, an ideal answer to a very contem-
porary need." The catalog cover featured a 38 caliber handgun—one of "four revolvers that manage to be elegant
without sacrificing any of their practicality"—lying on a
table. Behind it rested a fur coat and a single yellow rose. The
text for the catalog read, "Independence. In the last few
decades, American women, regardless of their marital,
economic or employment status, have been striving for it—
and achieving it. And gaining independence means assuming the responsibilities that go with it. "

New Detonics offers the Ladies Escort Series of chopped
45 caliber handguns. Customers can choose between the
Royal Escort, purple with a gold-plated trigger and hammer,
or the all-black Midnight Escort. Lorcin Engineering Co., Inc.
warns, "Ladies, don't become an easy target. "Their answer

is the Lady Lorcin, "a gun designed with you in mind" available in "designer Pearl Pink & Chrome finish."

Yet for all its claims of equality, the firearms business remains male dominated. As a result, in addition to the relatively subtle sexism of exploiting women's fears of rape, there's often an even more awkward, explicit component. In gun trade publications, the fleshy Elizabeth Saunders, vice president of American Derringer Corporation, dresses in black lingerie and stockings, a high-heel shoe kicked rakishly aside, to announce that "Lady Derringer is Back."The handgun, "designed to appeal to your feminine customers," comes packaged in a jewelry box or walnut case.

In a *Gun World* review of the Royal Escort, author Tom Ferguson cheerfully notes that "since this is a ladies' gun I thought it fair to get a lady's opinion of it and handed it over to my wife, Tina, for evaluation. Purple is her favorite color and she liked the little .45 immediately." A photograph accompanying the article notes that "Tina Ferguson is fond of purple and insisted upon selecting an outfit to complement the colors of the pistol." And in much the same way that cigarette manufacturer R. J. Reynolds hoped to appeal to "virile women" through its Dakota cigarette, FIE Corporation developed the Titan Tigress, a gold-plated 25 caliber handgun with gold lamé carrying purse, its fake ivory handle inscribed with a red rose.

The NRA and industry pitch to women has not fallen on deaf ears. An April 1988 Gallup poll indicated that between 1983 and 1986 gun ownership among women had jumped 53 percent, to more than twelve million. The number of women considering buying a firearm quadrupled during the same period to nearly two million.

Not only would an expanded women's market result in years of growth, but as Franklin Zimring noted in his 1987 book *The Citizen's Guide to Gun Control:*

> The American woman of the late 1980s and 1990s . . . [is the] leading indicator of the social status of self-defense handguns in the more distant future. If female ownership

of self-defense handguns increases dramatically, the climate of opinion for drastic restriction of handguns will not come about.[17]

Gun Control As Race Control

The NRA's overture to American blacks is based less on their gun-owning potential than their gun-control views. Black Americans, disproportionately urban residents, are one of the most strongly anti-gun segments of the U.S. population. In general, city dwellers—of all races—favor gun control at rates far higher than the general population. The NRA hopes that increased black support will aid it in stopping gun control in American cities and help it in defeating urban pro-control legislators.

Toward this end, black Americans are warned by the NRA that gun control is a white plot to disarm a feared minority population. This conspiracy allegedly stems from a surprising alliance of racists and ivory tower liberals. The spring 1991 *D. C. Defender*, the newsletter of the District of Columbia NRA affiliate, warns of gun control advocates "who have been unable to neutralize their racist impulses when thinking in terms of an armed urban population." The premiere example offered in support of this charge is the 1976 Washington, D. C., handgun ban. The *D. C. Defender* charges that "students of race relations in this area quickly realized that a predominantly black population had been disarmed by the legal system and was surrounded by predominantly white populations that owned and had ready access to all types of firearms."

"The Second Amendment," according to the NRA, "is a sort of constitutional safety net for the poor, the underprivileged, and those in the minority."[18] At least once a year the NRA runs articles in its publications fulminating on the theory of gun control as race or class control. "Minority Gun Ownership . . . A Dunkirk for Today's Left?" asks, "If a gun ban is imposed, how is it enforced . . . whose neighborhoods are most likely to be scoured for guns? Rich . . . or poor?

Black ... or white? History has an answer." The article "The Second Amendment and Second Class Citizens" warns:

> Those in favor of restrictive gun laws—white, upper-middle to upper income Americans—are the ones least affected by them. .... [T]he common thread that binds together hundreds of years of repression [through gun control] becomes very clear. In almost every instance a powerful ruling class deliberately seeks to prevent the arming of a distinct lower class which they both despise and fear.[19]

This is nothing new. In 1968, *American Rifleman* featured an article on "Why Anti-Gun Laws 'Hit Hardest at the Negro.' " The article, written by a black NRA member, stated:

> Anti-gun measures would have the effect of disarming the American citizen in general and the Negro in particular. That is why I, as an American citizen and as a Negro, oppose them. Because I am a Negro, I conceive that I would have little or no chance of obtaining a firearms permit in most of the 50 states. Anti-gun bills could in fact disenfranchise the Negro of his right to bear arms and to protect himself and his property. To me as an American, they are un-American. To me as a Negro, they are anti-Negro. I take no pleasure in saying so, but feel it is my duty and right to express my views.[20]

Such a stance is ironic at best. None of the NRA's leadership is black, and its board is almost uniformly white. In looking at its annual report the number of black faces can be counted on one hand; often they appear to be clerical employees. (Like the NRA, the leadership—and most likely the membership—of the gun control movement is also white. The involvement of black America in the gun control debate for the most part has been relegated to the unenviable role of victim.)

Lacking natural support in the black community, the NRA puts its money and influence behind virtually any black leader willing to share its vision. Their best investment has been Roy Innis of the Congress of Racial Equality (CORE). Under Innis' guidance over the past two decades, CORE has become every conservative's favorite "civil rights" organization. In 1985 Ronald Reagan—defending his statement that mainstream black civil rights leaders worked to keep their constituencies aggrieved in order to protect their own positions—noted that "there are leaders of quite prominent black groups, like Roy Innis of CORE, who . . . agrees completely with what I said." In comparing Innis to Martin Luther King, Reagan stated, "Roy Innis is a worthy successor to the Nobel Peace Prize winner."

Innis has wholeheartedly devoted himself to the NRA. In the wake of the 1984 Bernhard Goetz shooting—described at an NRA board meeting as "what may eventually turn out to be the most significant window of opportunity ever offered"—Innis and the NRA announced a campaign to liberalize New York state's handgun carrying laws.[21] Said Innis—two of whose sons were murdered with firearms— "Never before have I seen white people and black people so together on one issue, and that issue is crime. We've got to find some way to bring some kind of fear into a criminal. We have to make the streets unsafe for criminals."

By May 1986 the NRA announced that it would join CORE in the development of the National Crime Fighters' Crusade. In a ceremony at CORE's Flatbush offices the NRA presented CORE with a $5,000 check. "What we hope to do," said the NRA's Richard Feldman, "particularly in the black community, is let decent citizens know how to lawfully obtain firearms." At the opening, members of the Federation of New York State Rifle and Pistol Clubs demonstrated gun safety techniques and handed out handgun permit applications. The club's president told attendees that "there's nothing wrong with self-defense and survival in a community that calls for it."

In 1986 the NRA spent more than $4,500 in direct contributions and independent expenditures to help finance an Innis run for the U.S. House of Representatives against New York

City Democrat Major Owens. "Roy Innis," said Owens, "is coming from Harlem with the backing [of people who believe] they can take money and really do what they want with an electorate."[22] Whether or not the NRA believed Innis could win—he didn't—it was able to inject its pro-handgun message into an urban environment. The NRA's willingness to support black politicians with little hope of success in order to air anti-control arguments was repeated in 1990 when it helped finance the Republican mayoral campaign of former Washington, D. C., Police Chief Maurice Turner. In a city 75 percent Democratic, Turner, even in the wake of former Mayor Marion Barry's drug and sex scandal, didn't stand a chance against his Democratic opponent, Sharon Pratt Dixon. Two thousand dollars in NRA contributions guaranteed that a pro-gun message would be a key tenet of his campaign platform.

Although the NRA failed in its effort to bring Innis to Capitol Hill, by 1989 it had the black face it was looking for— Representative Mike Espy, Democrat of Mississippi. Elected in 1986, Espy was the first black congressman to serve from Mississippi since Reconstruction. Espy received the NRA's endorsement in his 1988 campaign—and $12,400 of its money—and returned the favor the next year by becoming the first member of Congress to appear in an "I'm the NRA" ad. In the ad, Espy, holding a shotgun, states:

> I understand that interest in firearms is a regional issue. But I also understand that freedom to own a firearm—for recreation or self-protection—is a constitutional issue. And when government tries to infringe upon a constitutional right, we must be extremely wary and cautious. So the next time you hear about the NRA "gun lobby," remember: that "lobby" is simply millions of Americans saying they don't want government interfering with the rights of honest citizens. I hear them, agree with them and believe in them. I'd be a hypocrite to do anything else.[23]

Espy's pointed use of the word hypocrite seemed designed to contrast his views with another well-known black man who had recently gained fame with a firearm—syndicated columnist Carl Rowan. In June 1988 Rowan, who advocated a national handgun ban, shot Ben Smith, a Maryland teen, with an unregistered revolver his son, Carl Jr. , had left with him "for protection against the telephone nuts."

In his 1990 autobiography *Breaking Barriers,* Rowan wrote that he felt confident following the shooting that "no one would fault me for protecting my home and my wife." He was wrong. Mocked as "Rambo Rowan" and made the butt of jokes, he soon found himself labeled a hypocrite. Rowan blamed the attacks on an NRA disinformation campaign, writing in his autobiography, "The National Rifle Association, which considered me one of its most worrisome foes, would sucker the media into swallowing the . . . argument that I was a hypocrite to write in favor of gun control when a gun was on my property."

Yet the NRA was only taking advantage of the perfect set of circumstances Rowan had given them. If saying one thing and doing another could be defined as hypocrisy, Rowan was, without doubt, a hypocrite. Rowan favored banning handguns, yet owned one. He lived in city where handguns were banned, yet claimed that he enjoyed a special exemption because the gun belonged to his son, a former FBI agent. Rowan was the perfect ivory tower liberal. And while Rowan protested that Smith and his female companion weren't the well-scrubbed suburban teens portrayed by the news media, this had little effect on the fact that a handgun banner had used a handgun in "self-defense. "

While the shooting took a big bite out of Carl Sr.'s credibility, it gave Carl Jr. a new career. By 1989 Rowan Jr. had registered with the District of Columbia government as a $200-an-hour NRA lobbyist.

Endnotes

1. "Self-Defense Ad Campaign Rivets National Attention on Combating Crime," *NRAction*, (October 1987).
2. "An Open Letter to All Polish Americans," *Los Angeles Times*, (January 13, 1982).
3. Zimring, Franklin, "Poland's 'Real' Problem," *Chicago Tribune*, (January 13, 1982).
4. "Letters to Editors," *NRAction*, (July 15, 1989).
5. "Gun Control: Iraq's Ally," *NRAction*, (November 1990).
6. *Ibid.*
7. "Can Three Assassins Kill a Civil Right?" *American Rifleman*, (July 1968) at 16.
8. *Minutes of the Meeting of the Board of Directors of the NRA*, (April 22-23, 1985) at 90.
9. *Minutes of the Meeting of the Board of Directors of the NRA*, (January 26-27, 1985) at 123.
10. "NRA Comes to Town, With Eye On Image," *Philadelphia Inquirer*, (April 1, 1982).
11. "Queens Youth Reported Slain in Moped Dispute," *New York Times*, (August 3, 1990).
12. "Children Caught in 'Nightmare' of N.Y. Gunfire," *Washington Post*, (October 5, 1990).
13. "NRA's 50,000th Junior Member Follows a Family Tradition," *InSights*, (April 1985) at 11.
14. "Jeff Brantley: Battling Bias With Time, Energy and a Typewriter," *InSights*, (June 1985) at 10.
15. "Women Declare Firearms Ownership No Longer Just a Man's World," *NRAction*, (August 15, 1988).
16. "Self-Defense Ad Campaign," *supra.*
17. Zimring, Franklin, *The Citizen's Guide to Gun Control*, Macmillan Publishing Co., New York (1987) at 186.
18. "The Second Amendment and Second Class Citizens," *NRAction*, (January 1988).
19. *Ibid.*
20. "Why Anti-Gun Laws 'Hit Hardest at the Negro,' " *American Rifleman*, (March 1968) at 21.
21. *Minutes*, (January 1985), *supra*, at 94.
22. "Owens Endorses Gumbs," *Daily Challenge*, (June 3, 1986).
23. "Rep. Espy Touts NRA in Magazine Ads," *NRAction*, (February 15, 1989).

Chapter Eight

The Carrot and the Stick

A simple strategy has always guided the NRA's political activity: reward your friends and punish your enemies. The rewards are big-dollar campaign spending and purported legions of voters in orange caps who obey the wishes of NRA headquarters. Punishment is also meted out by members and money—focused to destroy a candidate.

The political power of the NRA, however, resides primarily in the threat of injecting the issue of gun control into a campaign. The volatile issue can quickly dominate a campaign and derail any politician's packaged message; most candidates hasten to avoid it.

Also, as a political issue, gun control tends to cut only one way. While the orange-capped hoard, with its myopic pro-gun vision, will never forgive an "anti-gun" politician, gun control supporters tend to view the issue as only one of many by which they judge a candidate.

This is not to say that NRA money doesn't talk. When in 1990 an amendment to the U.S. House crime bill was offered that would gut its assault weapon restrictions, the proposal came from a surprising source—Representative Jolene Unsoeld, Democrat of Washington. Unsoeld was a little-known, liberal, freshman member who had never before been involved in the gun control debate. In 1988 her margin of victory had been a mere 618 votes, her Republican opponent arguing that she was too liberal for Washington voters. On October 4, 1990, the U.S. House approved 257 to 172 the Unsoeld amendment. The next day she received a $4,950 contribution from the NRA along with newfound conservative credibility.

The growth of the NRA's lobbying arm, the Institute for Legislative Action, has mirrored the NRA's ever-increasing obsession with gun control. Since its founding in 1975, ILA has come to be the dominant division of the NRA in terms of money, publicity and organizational focus. Because ILA spending consistently outpaces its own fund-raising, its growth has been at the expense of the NRA's recreational program activities and has at times pushed the NRA's general operating budget into the red—e.g., $6 million in 1988.

In 1989 ILA expenses totaled $19.7 million and consumed more than 22 percent of the NRA's nearly $88 million budget. In 1988 and 1989, after member contributions, ILA's deficits totaled $11.5 million and $5.6 million respectively—a gap filled with money from other NRA program areas.

ILA is the primary vehicle through which the NRA works to motivate its membership politically. In the first seven months of 1990, ILA mailed 3.5 million legislative alerts to NRA members warning of gun control initiatives and 14.3 million fund-raising letters. (During the same period, 19.5 million NRA membership promotions were mailed.) In ILA's world the sky is always falling—and only money can shore it up. A 1979 ILA fund-raising letter issued in the wake of a bill introduced by Representative Abner Mikva, Democrat of Illinois, to ban handguns warned:

> Although . . . [they] claim they are only after our handguns, make no mistake. . . . THEY ARE AFTER ALL GUNS! *The only differences between a long gun and a handgun is a 75-cent hacksaw blade.* The past decade has taught us one fundamental truth: *Evil men with evil intent can inflict all manner of abuse under the color of an evil law.* Ten years ago, the 1968 Gun Control Act was "sold" to the Congress

and the public as a "compromise." Now those who devised GCA '68 are again saying we must "compromise" by giving up handguns, or risk losing our rifles and shotguns. Nuts! That kind of "compromise" means losing! It means voluntarily giving up more than the anti-gun forces are big enough to take.

Two years later, when Morton Grove, Illinois, became the first municipality in America to ban the private sale and possession of handguns, an ILA legislative alert warned:

> Morton Grove . . . has passed the unthinkable—a ban on the private possession of all handguns for all law-abiding citizens. . . . Having failed in their attempt to ban handguns statewide [in Illinois], the anti-gun groups are now going to the local government and, as with any disease, these fanatics must be stopped—NOW!

The NRA has not shied away from linking itself with the popular cause of the moment. In its battle against a national seven-day waiting period, a spring 1991 fund-raising letter recalled "a very special" letter received at NRA headquarters postmarked from Saudi Arabia and signed by 22 Marines "as they waited for the command to cross the Kuwaiti border." In the letter:

> These men asked that while they protect freedom abroad, the NRA and its members continue the fight to protect our Second Amendment freedoms right here at home. If our Marines could write this letter before they put their lives on the line, certainly you can take the time to write or call your Congressman. . . .

Under a handgun waiting period, warned ILA:

> You will no longer be able to buy the firearm of your choice when you need it to protect your family from violent criminals. You will be forced to wait—and wait— and probably wait some more—while the bureaucrats decide if you can own this firearm. Can you imagine a

federal law that will force these Marines when they come home to have to go through that?

With ILA as the engine that drives the NRA membership, the NRA's political action committee, the Political Victory Fund, motivates the candidates themselves. Founded in 1976, PVF judges candidates solely on the gun issue. As a result, although it leans more heavily toward Republicans, its contribution roster includes many Democrats. Historically, lawmakers' views on gun control are defined more on a regional basis and by rural versus urban constituencies than by party affiliation.

According to Federal Election Commission (FEC) documents, PVF's budget for the 1977-78 election cycle totaled more than $605,000, ranking it tenth among trade/membership/health PACs. Most of its political money was spent in direct contributions to candidates—more than $366,000. One hundred and fifty-six Republican candidates received a total of $272,035, while 122 Democrats split up $93,626. Independent expenditures—campaign spending conducted without the knowledge or approval of a candidate on his behalf or against his opponent—totaled a mere $58,330, of which $40,031 was negative campaign spending.

By the end of the 1985-86 election cycle, the peak PVF budget year as the result of Republican efforts to maintain control of the Senate, the NRA's PAC spent $4.8 million while raising only $4.6 million. That year the PVF ranked seventh in an FEC listing of the top 50 money raisers and third among trade/membership/health PACs, coming in right behind such heavyweights as the Realtors' and the American Medical Association's PAC.

Of the $898,564 contributed to candidates by the NRA during the 1985-86 cycle, $643,740 was contributed to 139 Republican candidates, while $254,824 was contributed to 68 Democratic candidates. Independent expenditures on behalf of Republican candidates totaled $693,030, with $60,790 spent on behalf of Democrats. Nearly $73,000 was spent on negative campaigning against candidates, 29 out of 33 of whom were Democrats.

According to FEC reports, PVF has contributed to the majority of congressmen who hold leadership positions on both sides of the aisle. Speaker of the House Thomas Foley, Democrat of Washington, leads the pack. Since 1977, Foley has received more than $33,500 in NRA contributions and independent expenditures. Majority Leader Richard Gephardt, Democrat of Missouri—a lawmaker of limited NRA sympathies—has accepted $850, the most recent contribution coming during the 1983-84 election cycle. Since 1977 Minority Leader Robert Michel, Republican of Illinois, has accepted $21,600, the largest contribution, $7,950, coming during the 1989-90 election cycle. Minority Whip Newt Gingrich, Republican of Georgia, accepted $6,757 during the same cycle, bringing his NRA total since 1977 to more than $12,000.

Senate President Pro Tem Robert Byrd, Democrat of West Virginia, has accepted more than $24,000 in NRA contributions and expenditures. Majority Whip Wendell Ford, Democrat of Kentucky, accepted $1,000 during the 1985-86 cycle. Minority Leader Robert Dole of Kansas has accepted more than $20,000, $17,400 of it for his 1986 re-election campaign. Assistant Minority Leader Alan Simpson of Wyoming has received only $2,050, the small amount reflecting the security of his seat and his steadfast NRA loyalty. Vice President Dan Quayle received $7,750 as a House member and Indiana senator.

Not surprisingly, with fewer members and greater influence held by pro-gun states, the U.S. Senate is a far better value. Current senators who have benefited from high-dollar contributions and independent expenditures by the NRA, totaling more than $50,000 in a single campaign, include: Texas Republican Phil Gramm, $337,752; Pennsylvania Republican Arlen Specter, $111,757; North Carolina Republican Jesse Helms, $96,827; and Idaho Republican Steve Symms, $58,503.

This is not to say that money always buys the NRA political happiness. There have been some expensive failures. In the 1986 battle for control of the Senate, wasted NRA expenditures included $128,466 to Kenneth Kramer in a race against Senator Timothy Wirth, Democrat of Colorado; $88,619 to James Broyhill to challenge Senator Terry Sanford, Democrat of North Carolina; and $59,144 to Mark Andrews to defeat Senator Kent Conrad, Democrat of North Dakota. Another notable loser is former White House Chief of Staff John Sununu, to whom the NRA contributed $4,950 in a failed 1984 attempt at a New Hampshire Senate seat.

The PVF's history with the Federal Election Commission has not been a cordial one. Since PVF's founding, the FEC has brought suits against the NRA five times. In December 1990, the FEC sued the NRA for more than $830,000 for allegedly using corporate funds illegally in the 1988 elections. The suit charged that the Institute for Legislative Action illegally transferred $415,000 in corporate funds to the PVF two weeks prior to the presidential election. The NRA claimed that its violation had merely been "technical."

Although the NRA contributes to pro-gun Democrats, since 1980 it has aligned itself primarily with Republicans. The reason for this was Ronald Reagan. In 1980, Reagan—whose vision of America mirrored the NRA's own—became the first presidential candidate to receive the NRA's official endorsement.

Following Reagan's 1980 election, the NRA quickly benefited from the rise of the political New Right that accompanied the "Reagan Revolution." Gun control, like opposition to the death penalty or support for abortion rights, was just another red flag to identify card-carrying liberals. The equation of gun control with liberal ideology had become so complete that by 1988 liberal Representative Barney Frank, Democrat of Massachusetts, was publicly calling for his party to abandon the issue.

The NRA and its supporters offered the Republicans an easy voter pool to tap into. In 1984, Joe Rodgers, finance chairman of the Reagan-Bush '84 Committee and a former

Republican National Committee finance chairman, announced plans to finance a national "non-partisan" voter registration drive using such conservative organizations as fundamentalist Christians, anti-abortion groups and gun control opponents. His plan called for the establishment of a private corporation named Leadership '84 to aid in the voter registration effort. Without irony, Rodgers announced that any profits from Leadership '84 would be contributed to the James S. Brady Presidential Foundation, a private foundation established in the wake of the 1981 shooting to benefit the victims of future presidential assassination attempts.[1]

Although the NRA had no doubts regarding Reagan's pro-gun credentials, others did. Following his election, word came from California via members of the Libertarian Party that Reagan was no true friend of gun owners. As governor, Reagan had participated in Project Cable Splicer, a secret, domestic war-games exercise. Other members of Reagan's California Cabinet who participated included Special Assistant Attorney General Edwin Meese and State National Guard Commander Louis Giuffrida. Cable Splicer would establish an effective state of martial law "in the event that forces of radical black nationalism joined forces, inside the State of California, with the anti-Vietnam forces to challenge the established authority of the State."[2]

Project Cable Splicer was part of a larger program, Project Garden Plot, a nationwide war-games scenario prepared for President Richard Nixon and Attorney General John Mitchell. The purpose of Garden Plot was to allow Nixon to declare martial law nationwide if he felt it was necessary to combat his "political enemies."[3] To NRA members, the willingness of a politician to endorse a plan of martial law—for whatever reason—smacked of the very evils they were arming against.

At the Reagan White House, Garden Plot soon resurfaced as REX 84 BRAVO. This time the political enemies were no longer black radicals and Vietnam protesters, but possible opponents of a U.S. invasion of Central America. The secret nationwide "readiness exercise" tested the ability of the

Federal Emergency Management Agency to institute a "State of Domestic National Emergency" that would involve suspension of the Constitution and the establishment of martial law concurrent with the launching of military operations in Central America.

Any qualms the NRA might have had about supporting Vice President George Bush for president in 1988 were quickly brushed aside when the Democrats chose Massachusetts Governor Michael Dukakis as their nominee. Dukakis was the personification of all that the NRA loathed and feared—a liberal, gun-hating technocrat. Writing in the October 1988 *American Rifleman*, NRA President Joe Foss warned:

> A nation under Michael Dukakis promises to be one based upon creeping socialism and unfettered federal power. I fear that a Dukakis presidency will bring about a reign of bureaucratic arrogance. Dukakis themes contain a contempt for individualism reminiscent of the aristocracy our forefathers fled and that we all still fear today.

In a special fund-raising letter, ILA head Wayne LaPierre told members:

> You and I cannot allow Michael Dukakis to become President of the United States and use the Justice Department, the Department of the Treasury, the Courts, and the anti-gun press to ban guns in America. I never thought that we would have a candidate for President worse than Ted Kennedy—but Michael Dukakis is worse. I need your help—or a President committed to taking away the firearms of every American hunter and sportsman may be elected.

Labeling Dukakis a man who "does not believe in the same things you and I do," the NRA letter envisioned a scenario where "Dukakis could easily pick anti-gun lawyers like Senator Howard Metzenbaum, Congressman Ed Feighan, Congressman Peter Rodino, and Congressman Bill Hughes to fill those Supreme Court vacancies." The NRA quickly backed up its words of doom with more than $1.5 million in independent expenditures against the Massachusetts Democrat.

A Dukakis administration, the NRA warned, would herald the death knell of gun ownership in America. This point was driven home in the October 1988 *Rifleman*. The all-black cover featured a quote attributed to Dukakis stating, "I do not believe in people owning guns, only police and military. I am going to do everything I can to disarm this state." The inside of the cover featured a full-page ad for a scope-fit Ruger rifle—"the perfect mid-size game rifle." Following a letter from Vice President Bush, the next page warned that "Dukakis Wants to Ban Guns in America." Facing it was a second full-page gun ad, this time for a Mossberg shotgun. Some NRA members feared that the organization's inflammatory language, coupled with the proximity of the Ruger and Mossberg ads, sent a deadly message. One Democratic NRA member wrote to candidate Bush, urging him to denounce the NRA campaign, warning that "we have already heard loose talk on ranges about killing Dukakis because he is seen as such a threat to gun owners."

A Very Big Stick

Although the NRA's reputation for political might had grown throughout the 1960s, it was not until the 1970 upset defeat of Senator Joseph Tydings that support of gun control was viewed as a form of political suicide. Although the 42-year-old Maryland Democrat's defeat stemmed from a variety of factors, and the NRA's role in the campaign was limited, the public and political perception was that the legislator had been martyred on the cross of gun control.

Tydings, a primary proponent of a federal registration bill, was seeking re-election to his second term. An anti-Tydings, pro-gun committee, Citizens Against Tydings, was formed to oust the popular senator. In the campaign CAT spent more than $50,000, mailed more than 350,000 brochures and distributed another 150,000 pamphlets in a door-to-door campaign.

After having won the Democratic nomination in a surprisingly close race, Tydings was eventually defeated in November by Representative J. Glenn Beall Jr. (whose father Tydings had defeated in 1964). The NRA was quick to credit the gun issue with taking down Tydings.

After the defeat, Tydings press secretary Ernest Lotito estimated that the pro-gun attacks had cost his candidate "at least 30,000" votes. Tydings had lost by a little less than that amount. Lotito promised that "nobody in his right mind is going to take on that issue again." In conceding defeat, Tydings worried that "one of the worst things about this is that it will be interpreted as a victory for the gun lobby." CAT head Michael Parker noted, "That was the point of the whole thing."[4]

Although the NRA was quick to paint Tydings as a victim of gun control, other factors had contributed to his defeat. In August of that year *Life* magazine had accused him of attempting to use his influence to aid an investment firm in which he was a stockholder. (He was later cleared of any wrongdoing.) And liberals were offended by Tydings' support for a Nixon-backed crime proposal for the District of Columbia that included preventive detention and a "no-knock" policy for police entries.

That gun control was only one more aggravating factor that led to Tydings' defeat didn't matter. The perception was that it had been the only factor. The Tydings defeat taught the NRA the political value of public executions.

It was this realization (coupled with Neal Knox's vow never to forget the NRA's enemies) that led the NRA to wage war on the 1979 nomination of Representative Abner Mikva, Democrat of Illinois, to fill a seat on the U.S. Court of Appeals for the District of Columbia. Not only was Mikva a handgun banner, but over the years he had taunted the NRA as "the National Rip-off Association" and the "street crime" lobby. Since federal judges serve for life, the Senate Judiciary Committee confirmation hearings and subsequent floor vote stood as the NRA's last chance to exact retribution.

Testifying before the committee, Knox cited Mikva's criticisms of Supreme Court nominees whose views had been "peculiarly hostile to the civil rights of Negroes." Said Knox:

> Congressman Mikva, while in public life, has been peculiarly hostile to the civil rights of gun owners. I submit to you that there is no qualitative difference between a judge who is prejudiced against blacks and one who is prejudiced against gun owners. The very nature of prejudice is the same. . . . He is an extremist. He is a radical. In his attitude toward firearms owners, Mr. Mikva is a bigot.[5]

(Knox's vision of gun owners as an embattled minority group was reduced to its essence in 1982 when NRA public education head John Aquilino told *The Washington Post* that "gun owners are the new niggers of society.") More than $700,000 was reportedly spent in the campaign against Mikva. In spite of this, in September 1979 his nomination was approved by the Senate 58 to 31. The vote wasn't a surprise. Senate confirmation of Mikva, well liked and respected by his colleagues, had been expected to be little more than a formality. The NRA's ability to turn the confirmation process into a full-scale battle was a measure of its influence and power. The NRA had lost, but its efforts would go a long way toward winning the war of intimidation.

This two-fisted—and at times personal—retribution, although muted, did not end with Knox's exit in 1982. In 1984 NRA President Howard Pollock—in the midst of Representative Howard Wolpe's re-election campaign—said of the Michigan Democrat, "I don't know whether he is a communist or not; his record would certainly indicate he's a sympathizer."[6] Wolpe, at the time chair of the House Foreign Affairs Subcommittee on Africa, had earned Pollock's ire for his attacks on South Africa, actions the NRA president characterized as "harassment" that benefited the "the Soviets and their stooges."

In 1990, Representative Peter Smith found himself on the receiving end of the NRA's ire. After signing a petition in 1988 promising that he would not support gun control, the Vermont Republican later endorsed a federal assault weapons ban. Citing Smith's betrayal, the NRA moved to make an example of him. In 1990 Smith lost to self-proclaimed socialist Bernard Sanders, who in both 1988 and 1990 had supported an assault weapons ban. The NRA attacked Smith's credibility, noting that even if they disagreed with Sanders, they could believe him. The NRA spent $18,000 to defeat Smith, distributing bumper stickers that advised Vermont voters to "Dump Peter Smith." Another bumper sticker distributed by Smith opponents said "Smith & Wesson (yes)/Peter Smith (no)." The bottom of the strip warned of "Vermont's big lie." As the result of the NRA's campaign, said Smith, "My mother was almost driven off the road. People were shooting my lawn signs at night. That is the level of emotion the NRA was able to stir up."[7] Presented with these incidents, ILA's James Jay Baker replied, "We certainly wouldn't condone any violence. We represent law-abiding citizens."[8]

Yet physical intimidation and threats do often characterize the response of the NRA membership to the organization's fear-laden mail. State and local legislators bear the brunt of such action. And the NRA is aware of this. A common component of NRA legislative mailings is an admonishment that members should not be abusive when calling their legislators. Many ignore this advice. In 1965 two members of the Maryland General Assembly described death threats and abusive telephone calls they had received as the result of their support for local gun controls. State legislator Angelo Palmisano told of receiving telephone calls and mail threatening his life and questioning his patriotism, parenthood and religion.

When in 1988 the Maryland House of Delegates was preparing to vote on a bill banning the sale of Saturday Night

Specials in the state, bill co-sponsor Gill Genn came face to face with the anger and fear the NRA could generate. The lobbying was so intense, says Genn,

> that [NRA] members would push and literally grab you by the lapels and say, "I can't believe you're taking away my constitutional right to bear arms."

The intimidation grew, with Genn receiving threats on his home answering machine. The callers would merely remind him that "we're gonna getcha."

On the day of the vote, the statehouse grounds, according to Genn, looked like an "armed encampment." It was merely the NRA's members. "Some delegates were concerned whether the National Guard had been called out to keep order, but as it turned out these guys were actually NRA members lobbying against the bill. They were in boots and fatigues. They were in war gear," says Genn. In the days surrounding the vote Genn and other legislators were given police protection as a result of the threat posed by NRA members.

In the final debate on the bill, NRA members were allowed into the gallery of the legislative chamber, and Genn came face to face with his phone messenger. Says Genn:

> I was on the floor, and this fellow leaned over and pointed down—and he's only about ten feet away and 15 feet up. I look up and there's a guy in fatigues, says right at me, "We're gonna getcha. You're dead. We're gonna getcha." Now whether I took that as a literal threat on my life—I have to be candid, I didn't—but you never know.

Another NRA member told Genn that their disputes stemmed from the fact that Genn didn't understand what guns meant to NRA members, how much "fun" they could be. He insisted that Genn go hunting with him. Genn, who considered himself open-minded, said that he'd consider the

offer, but would like to bring along a few of his fellow
delegates. At that point, says Genn,

> he said, "No. We're just going to go some place way out
> in the woods. Just you and me. We'll go hunting." And
> all of a sudden I started to think . . .

Although such incidents are often dismissed by the NRA,
its staff at times orchestrates such intimidation. When the
New Jersey Assembly held committee hearings on a
proposed assault weapons ban in 1990, Chairperson Marlene
Lynch Ford described the two-week period surrounding the
bill as "just incredible." At the public hearing held the day
before the vote, NRA members packed the room while an
NRA field representative—outfitted with a mike and head-
phones to eavesdrop on committee members and communi-
cate with supporters—orchestrated demonstrations. At one
point, according to Ford, a police chief sitting next to the
NRA staffer heard him say into his headpiece, "Okay, let her
have it." Immediately a "spontaneous" protest erupted both
in the committee room and outside, bringing the hearing to
a halt until Ford threatened to clear the room.

The night before the vote, the glass front door of Ford's
office was shattered. Arriving at the Assembly that day,
pro-gunners told Ford that the office had been firebombed.
During the day hundreds of NRA members roamed the
statehouse, following legislators down the halls, threatening
political and physical retribution. As Ford walked through
the Capitol hallways, accompanied by aides to protect her,
NRA members repeatedly yelled: "You're dead."

During floor debate on the bill, opponents sitting in the
gallery stamped their feet, sending vibrations through the
chamber and drowning out the voices of legislators. Outside,
protesters banged an American flag on a staff against the
two-story windows of the building. A window eventually
broke and the flag was pushed through it. The bill passed.

Political Boomerang?

In a March 1991 op-ed published in *The Washington Post*, Representative Les AuCoin, Democrat of Oregon, a former NRA "100 percenter," announced his abandonment of the NRA's "ideological straitjacket" and his willingness to vote for a seven-day waiting period and a ban on assault weapons. Wrote AuCoin:

> The conventional wisdom still is: If you cross the gun lobby, they'll have a silver bullet waiting for you at the next election. I'm betting those days are over. . . . [T]he conventional wisdom about the NRA's clout is hopelessly out of touch—and . . . the leaders of the NRA are out of touch too.

AuCoin's editorial was only one of the most public examples of the growing willingness of some public officials to use the NRA's reputation against it. As firearms violence has increased, so has public support for limited gun control measures. With this has come a newfound willingness on the part of some politicians to buck the NRA and attack it for its unwillingness to compromise.

When in 1988 Representative Jim Sensenbrenner, Republican of Wisconsin, voted in the House Judiciary Committee for a national seven-day waiting period, the NRA sent an emergency mailing into his district. The letters attacked Sensenbrenner, alleging that the bill would "put New York City style gun laws on the backs of all Americans." Wrote the NRA:

> If the . . . bill passes, you will have to wait to buy a firearm, and you will be forced to ask a government bureaucrat's permission. You will have to submit to a government investigation, and if you are turned down, there is nothing you can do. This bill . . . will spend millions and billions of your tax dollars investigating you and other honest citizens while criminals roam free untouched.

Alleging that the bill constituted "backdoor registration on American firearms owners," the NRA letter noted that Sensenbrenner had proclaimed "his fight for gun owners' rights against Metzenbaum and the Kennedys. HA! With support like that you might as well have Ted Kennedy representing you!" Instead of trying to placate the NRA, Sensenbrenner attacked it, defending his support of the waiting period.

According to Maryland state legislator Peter Franchot, a Democrat from suburban Montgomery County, "The NRA endorsement in many areas of the country is a kiss of death." As a result, says Franchot, many of their political tactics are eleventh hour. In the final weekend of Franchot's 1990 campaign, the NRA distributed a letter attacking him. Franchot immediately copied the letter and mailed it out to his supporters, voicing his determination not to be intimidated by the NRA and urging voters to do the same. Says Franchot:

> The smart politicians will take whatever the NRA does and disseminate it widely, because they don't have credibility with the public [but with] that small group of NRA members, paramilitary types and gun owners. . . . Their actions are often covert [because] if some sunshine reflects on it, it often turns out to have a boomerang effect. The political wisdom [now] is "make my day NRA" and come out and endorse my opponent.

"But," he adds, "they still have potency."

Endnotes

1. "GOP Fund-Raiser Plans 'Nonpartisan' Vote Drive," *Washington Post,* (June 6, 1984).
2. Affidavit of Daniel P. Sheehan, National Security Archive.
3. *Ibid.*
4. "Gun Lobby Hails Tydings's Defeat," *New York Times,* (November 8, 1970).
5. Senate Testimony of Neal Knox on Nomination of Abner Mikva, (July 12, 1979).
6. "NRA's Gunslingers Sling Mud Instead," *Detroit Free Press,* (September 23, 1984).
7. "Letter-Writing and Campaigns," *Congressional Quarterly,* (March 9, 1991) at 605.
8. *Ibid.*

Chapter Nine

Shot in the Back

During the 1980s America's police found themselves facing increased criminal firepower and an explosion of drug-related violence. Also during this decade, according to Philadelphia Police Commissioner Willie Williams, the police view of the National Rifle Association shifted "about 180 degrees."

Says Williams:

> At one time law enforcement . . . was probably very close in agreement . . . with the NRA. But as the violence in America changed, and the violence against the community and against police changed, the professionals in law enforcement's views began to change. The NRA changed, but they changed in the opposite direction.

For more than 60 years the NRA had taken its warm relationship with police for granted. In much the same way it had embarked on a crusade to train the citizen-soldier, beginning in the 1920s the NRA charted a similar course in law enforcement. Police across the country were soon happily under the NRA's tutelage, with many joining the organization as the result of its firearms training. Sharing a common firearms bond and a lock-'em-up approach to crime, the relationship continued on a smooth course—even through the gun control debates of the 1930s and the 1960s.

It was, however, a marriage of convenience. The NRA's true love was its own ideology. The result was an inevitable split when the NRA failed to acknowledge the changing realities of the street. The NRA's argument of the illegitimacy of placing a value judgment on an inanimate object meant little to officers whose views weren't based on abstract concepts but the public's—and their own—safety. The new threats to police resulted in a willingness on their part to call for legislation limiting firearms availability. And while police differed on the severity of additional gun controls required, there was a consensus that current federal laws should not be relaxed.

According to Aurora, Illinois, Police Chief Robert Wadman, the NRA looks at the issue "not through reasonable decision-making but through emotionalism. They're of the mindset that you're completely with them 100 percent of the time, or you're against them. [Once they reach that decision] they treat you like some liberal, commie bedwetter opposed to all firearms."

Two simultaneous legislative battles of the early 1980s would act as the catalyst to separate police from the NRA. The first was over armor-piercing ammunition capable of penetrating the bulletproof vests worn by police. The second was over Neal Knox's McClure-Volkmer firearms decontrol bill.

The Bond Breaks

In the early 1970s three men named Kopsch, Turcus and Ward developed a Teflon-coated, hard-metal handgun bullet with armor-piercing capabilities that enabled police to shoot through cars at criminals. Taking the first letter of each man's surname they named it the KTW. Police soon found the ammunition to be impractical, as the bullets had a tendency to pass not only through the car, but through the criminal, the other side of the car, and possibly through innocent passersby as well. Outside of special assault situations, armor-piercing ammunition had little practical police use. But the bullets, available on the civilian market, were ideally suited for a far less noble purpose—penetrating the bulletproof vests worn by more than half of America's police. Or as Arthur Kassel, chairman of the California Addict Evaluation Authority, warned, "Anybody that's using this bullet is out to kill a cop and that's just about what it's used for. Nothing else. Nothing else is it good for."[1]

Public awareness of the KTW began in 1982 following an NBC news segment. One of those concerned about the bullets was Chief Wadman, who at the time headed the Omaha, Nebraska, police department. He was struck by the fact that a bill had recently been passed in the state legislature that limited the use of lead shot by duck hunters. Its purpose was to protect bald eagles that, traveling along the flyway, were dying after ingesting lead-filled ducks. Wadman was disturbed that an ammunition bill could be passed almost immediately to protect the bald eagle, yet police remained in jeopardy as armor-piercing bullet legislation became mired in controversy. Wadman wrote to the NRA expressing his concerns. "What I received back," he says, "was the most brain-damaged swill I had ever received in my entire life."

In responding to their queries, the NRA promised Wadman and other police officers that "no police officer wearing a vest has ever has been killed or wounded by one of the [armor-piercing] rounds" and that "no police officer has ever been shot with a KTW."[2] The NRA was wrong on both counts. In 1974 Protective Service Officer John Rixham Jr. was patrolling the Social Security Building in Woodlawn, Maryland, when he came upon a drunken man and woman in a parked car. The man grabbed Rixham's service revolver and shot him at point-blank range. Rixham's bulletproof vest stopped the slug. Seconds later another shot was fired by the woman from her own handgun. The bullet, a 9mm armor-piercing round, penetrated Rixham's vest, passed through his stomach, and exited out the other side of the vest. Rixham was permanently disabled. In 1976, State Highway Patrolman Phillip Black and visiting Canadian policeman Donald Irwin were shot and killed with 9mm KTW ammunition in

Broward County, Florida. Their killers were arrested later with more of the bullets in their possession.

The NRA's stand on the ammunition shocked police. To the NRA, cop-killer bullets were merely the gun grabbers' most recent foot in the door. The NRA warned that "these attacks are much more a philosophy of opposition to firearms ownership in general."[3] The NRA stood its ground on principle—cop-killer bullets don't pierce bulletproof vests, criminals do. Testifying before Congress in 1984, Institute for Legislative Action head J. Warren Cassidy reaffirmed the NRA's doubts that

> legislation which attempts to control criminal behavior through the control of firearms and/or ammunition will ever be effective. Rather, we believe that stiff, sure, fair, mandatory penalties for misuse of firearms and/or ammunition are the only effective deterrents to criminal behavior. It is already against the law to shoot police officers.[4]

Cassidy's predecessor, Neal Knox, had noted in 1982, "There's no such thing as a good bullet or a bad bullet."[5] The NRA seemed surprised when the cops took it personally.

Unlike the NRA, the police didn't perceive a ban on armor-piercing bullets as coming under the rubric of gun control. Gun control to police was pointy-headed liberals whining about banning handguns and "victims of society." This was about their lives. This perception gave the gun control movement unprecedented access to the police. Handgun Control, Inc.—stalled on its primary agenda of handguns—moved quickly to push cop-killer bullets to the front of its political program. A relationship previously thought impossible could now be built. HCI's message wasn't subtle: the NRA was literally willing to sacrifice cops for the sake of ideological purity. To put it more bluntly—the NRA killed cops.

Representative Mario Biaggi, a 23-year veteran of the New York City Police Department who was wounded ten times in the line of duty (a fact consistently noted by his press releases and often met with questions as to how he managed to get shot that often), quickly became the most visible proponent of an armor-piercing bullet ban. A companion bill was introduced in the Senate by New York Democrat Patrick Moynihan. Initial versions of the bills proposed banning ammunition capable of penetrating more than 18 layers of Kevlar—the key material in bulletproof vests—when fired from a handgun with a five-inch barrel. The NRA argued that using penetration as the defining criteria would ban vast amounts of rifle as well as handgun ammunition.

By 1986 momentum was building for passage of a bill. The NRA soon let it be known that it would accept a compromise. As a result, the defining characteristic of the ammunition was switched from penetration to content. In August Congress completed action on legislation banning bullets composed solely of specific hard metals—tungsten alloys, steel, brass, bronze, iron, beryllium, copper or depleted uranium—that could be used in a handgun. Critics were quick to point out that hundreds of armor-piercing bullets would remain on the market, and that the measure did not even cover one of the eight bullets named by the FBI as armor-piercing. In addition, because the law required that the bullets be composed solely of the specified metals, it could be circumvented by merely adding a lead core to the ammunition. The NRA offered no objection to the bill, and it was signed into law by President Reagan the same month.

(Not long after passage, the NRA was allowed its moment to gloat. Representative Biaggi was convicted in August 1988 as part of the Wedtech scandal. The court found that Biaggi had extorted $1.8 million in stock from the company for lobbying on its behalf. He resigned from the House and was sentenced to federal prison.)

At the same time that it was opposing armor-piercing bullet legislation, the NRA was battling for passage of the McClure-Volkmer firearms decontrol bill. Sponsored by Senator Jim McClure, Republican of Idaho, and Representative Harold Volkmer, Democrat of Missouri, the bill would:

- Resume the interstate sale of all firearms (earliest versions allowed the "mail-order" sale of handguns);

- Restrict ATF enforcement, including the inspection of dealer records;

- Impose a higher standard of proof (violations would need to be "knowing" or "willing") while lessening penalties for dealer violations; and

- Allow gun owners to transport their firearms interstate regardless of local law.

In arguing for the legislation, the NRA portrayed it not only as a necessary remedy for undue restrictions placed on law-abiding gun owners, but also as a measure police supported.

McClure-Volkmer made limited progress in the House and Senate throughout the early 1980s. The Senate Judiciary Committee approved versions of the bill in 1982 and 1984, but it was kept from a floor vote. This ended in July 1985, when the Senate passed a version of the bill by an overwhelming 79 to 15 margin. The measure was the first firearms legislation to be considered by the Senate since the 1972 Saturday Night Special ban. The vote was rightly hailed as an NRA victory that reaffirmed its lobbying strength on Capitol Hill, with one Senate aide grumbling that "this place is marching in lock step with the NRA."[6] It was also the event that forced police from the sidelines.

Police had never viewed themselves as outsiders to government. The quick political lesson they had just received opened their eyes. As was the case with armor-piercing bullets, they were shocked that when the public safety aspects of firearms and ammunition were being debated in Congress, they were treated as just another special interest group.

According to Baltimore County Chief of Police Cornelius Behan:

The NRA has greater access to the people at the top of this government than law enforcement. More than once, legislators have said on the merits of the case you fellas are right, but I can't afford to go against the NRA. They'll hurt me. Instead of sitting down with us and saying how can we work together, [the NRA is] trying to find a way to defeat us and neutralize law enforcement in this country.

Recognizing the need for an organized lobbying effort to win the House vote on McClure-Volkmer, in November 1985 the Law Enforcement Steering Committee was formed. Initial committee members were the International Association of Chiefs of Police, Police Executive Research Forum, National Fraternal Order of Police, National Organization of Black Law Enforcement Executives, and the National Troopers Coalition. Organizations that later joined were the Federal Law Enforcement Officers Association, International Brotherhood of Police Officers, Major Cities Police Chiefs, National Association of Police Organizations, National Sheriffs Association, the Police Foundation, and the Police Management Association. Combined membership totaled more than half a million.

Following Senate passage, McClure-Volkmer remained stalled in the House. House Judiciary Committee Chair Peter Rodino of New Jersey had labeled it "dead on arrival" and refused to budge. As a result, Volkmer began a drive for a little-used congressional tool known as a "discharge petition" to force the measure to the floor. Under the process, if a majority of House members signed the petition, the bill would bypass the committee and move immediately to the floor, allowing Volkmer virtually to dictate the rules regarding the vote. As Volkmer neared the 218 signatures needed, the police became a conspicuous presence on the Hill, buttonholing congressmen and staff to argue against the bill. To forestall Volkmer, a compromise measure was eventually voted out by the House Judiciary Committee and brought to the floor in April 1986.

During the vote, representatives arriving on the floor were met by rows of police in dress uniform silently standing at rest at the doors of the chamber. The police could not stop the NRA's momentum, but they did slow it. Although Volkmer's bill was easily substituted for the Judiciary Committee compromise, an amendment retaining the interstate ban on handgun sales was approved 233 to 184. And in the final seconds of the debate the House approved in a voice vote a ban on the future production of machine guns for civilian sale.

"The police misunderstood the force of lobbying," said then-Louisiana Democratic Representative Buddy Roemer. "Lobbying is not standing in long lines at the door. Lobbying is good information early; it is a presence when minds are being made up. Minds were already made up."[7]

In May 1986 the Senate substituted by voice vote the House version of McClure-Volkmer for the version it had passed in July 1985. It then passed a police-backed "clarifying" bill that:

- Specified that firearms being transported interstate must be unloaded and locked away in some place other than the passenger compartment;

- Eased gun tracing strictures for terrorist crimes; and

- Required that dealers selling guns from their personal collections keep limited records of the transactions.

On May 19, 1986, President Reagan signed the McClure-Volkmer bill into law. In addition to its core components, the final version of the bill also:

- Allowed for the resumption of the mail-order sale of ammunition;

- Removed record keeping requirements for ammunition dealers;

- Expressly prohibited ATF from centralizing dealer records or establishing any system of firearms registration; and

- Banned the importation of barrels for Saturday Night Specials.

Following passage of the bill, the police view of the NRA, says former International Association of Chiefs of Police Executive Director Jerald Vaughn, "deteriorated rather quickly. . . . Many in law enforcement began to question not only the motives and tactics, but the basic integrity of the NRA." The NRA may have hoped that with the legislative battles over armor-piercing bullets and McClure-Volkmer finally completed they could begin winning back the police, but the split only widened that same year when Congress began to consider legislation to ban the production of all-plastic handguns capable of evading X-ray and metal detectors. The NRA attacked the measure—which required each handgun to contain a specific amount of metal—as a clever subterfuge to ban Saturday Night Specials.

In his Senate testimony, NRA lobbyist James Jay Baker labeled plastic handgun legislation "a Trojan horse to attack the ownership of all guns owned by honest, law-abiding Americans. . . ."[8] Added Baker:

> "Plastic" gun or "Terrorist Special" have become very elastic epithets, much like the "Saturday Night Special," used by politicians who are antagonistic to the private ownership of firearms to describe a firearm they don't like, meaning all handguns, or at least every handgun they think they have a chance to outlaw. If any article possessed by the public should be banned just because a terrorist may also possess it, that misguided argument will very shortly be made against rifles and shotguns too.[9]

In October 1988, Congress finished action on legislation to ban non-detectable plastic firearms. Because plastic handguns could be framed as a terrorist issue and not a gun control issue, support for the measure was widespread. When the NRA found that no guns currently on the market would be banned, it dropped its opposition. The legislation required that all guns trigger metal detectors at the same level as a firearm containing 3.7 ounces of stainless steel or be detectable by cabinet X-ray systems. It was signed into law the next month.

Political Pit Bulls

The NRA's unyielding stance resulted in a growing number of police officials who were willing to criticize it publicly. Although most were used to the vicious elements of politics, few were prepared for the NRA's reaction. The NRA didn't want merely to counter their arguments. It wanted to destroy them. The easiest way to guarantee the NRA's enmity was to appear in a Handgun Control, Inc. ad. Those who participated soon found that wherever they went, the NRA was never far behind.

Jerald Vaughn, a 20-year police veteran and executive director of the International Association of Chiefs of Police from 1985 to 1988, was one of the first police leaders to work with Handgun Control, Inc. He was also one of the first to bear the brunt of the NRA's ire. Says Vaughn:

> I was identified by the NRA for a period of time as public enemy number one. Along with that came a certain amount of hate mail and controversy. The tactics, the vindictiveness, the resources mustered against anyone who dares speak against them . . . no other group [can] even compare to the NRA.

Like Vaughn, Baltimore County's Behan had agreed to appear in an HCI advertisement. Says Behan:

> When I got into this I was rather naïve. It never occurred to me that when looking at the 20,000 deaths per year— that anyone would sustain an argument for more handguns. As a result, I didn't know they were the enemy.

Pretty soon I found out. When McClure-Volkmer heated up they began calling the elected officials around here asking for my removal. Here I'm exercising my First Amendment rights and they're trying to kill me for doing that. They're still after my head, trying to influence politicians to get rid of me.

Although the NRA failed in ousting Behan, other efforts have been more successful. Minneapolis Police Chief Anthony Bouza had inspired the wrath of the NRA, having appeared in an HCI newspaper ad and having worked with the now defunct National Alliance Against Violence. When Bouza was being considered to head the Suffolk County, Long Island, police department, the NRA urged its 20,000 Suffolk County members to block his appointment in what the organization described as "a massive telephone and letter writing campaign." The job went to another candidate.

Contrary to what the NRA wanted its members to believe, many of those it targeted weren't "liberal bedwetters." Former Memphis Police Chief and IACP head Joe Casey says very matter of factly that he doesn't support gun control. Yet he did support a seven-day waiting period as a reasonable measure. The NRA didn't agree, and tried to have him fired. The NRA, says Casey,

> started a letter campaign, wrote to the mayor and asked them to terminate me. They go after you hook, line and sinker. The leadership is out of touch. They've lost sight of what they claim they are—to teach people gun safety and to help sportsmen. That's not what they're about anymore. It's all right to disagree with somebody, but when you get to the point where you're trying to get their job, destroy them and ruin their position, that's going too far.

The NRA has reserved its most shrill attacks, however, for former San Jose Police Chief Joseph McNamara. McNamara, Harvard-educated, yet with a history as a Harlem-based street cop, was smart, articulate and willing not only to endorse strict handgun controls, including banning the private possession of handguns, but to attack the NRA directly as an industry shill. In a 1987 HCI ad he asked: "Has the NRA gone off the deep end?" In the ad McNamara, citing a litany of extreme NRA positions, states:

> In recent years, the NRA's leadership has repeatedly ignored the objections of professional law enforcement. Their actions make our jobs more difficult—and more dangerous. And they've poured millions of dollars into local elections, seeking to intimidate public officials who dare to speak out. The NRA has become one of the most powerful special interests in Washington. Like a loaded gun, that power must be handled with care. And should never be pointed in the wrong direction.

Following release of the ad, the NRA announced that it was considering suing McNamara if he continued his "untrue and unsupported" statements. It settled instead for attacking him for allegedly stating that he favored legalizing drugs. He hadn't.

Will the Real Police . . .

Initially, the NRA dismissed claims that it had lost the cops as a hoax perpetrated by the news media and gun control advocates. The reality has finally sunk in. This has resulted in two tactics. The first has been to develop ties with pro-gun police and police organizations. This is based on the public relations belief that to the general public a uniform is a uniform. The second has been to attempt to woo back police with small favors and a newfound attentiveness.

Gerald Arenberg, according to many police executives, is the Jim Bakker of law enforcement. From his base of operations in North Miami, Florida, Arenberg—whose 40-year law enforcement history includes stints as a small-town police chief, OSI special agent and park ranger—oversees a network of non-profit and for-profit organizations. More than 30 organizations have been registered with the state of Florida by Arenberg or his associates. Most have to do with law enforcement. A 1987 analysis of Arenberg's organizations by the International Association of Chiefs of Police found that he did not draw a salary from any of his organizations. Each organization, however, paid "management fees" to American Fraternal Programs, a for-profit corporation of which Arenberg was co-owner. Arenberg today says that American Fraternal Programs is now owned by the non-profits it serves and that his annual salary is little more than $51,000 per year.

Most of Arenberg's non-profit organizations bear a striking resemblance to their better-known counterparts. His 14,000-member National Association of Chiefs of Police (NACP) mirrors the International Association of Chiefs of Police (IACP). The NACP's *Chief of Police* magazine is similar in design and appearance to IACP's *Police Chief* magazine. Other police groups Arenberg is associated with include the American Federation of Police, American Law Enforcement Officers Association, Inc. and the Venerable Order of the Knights of Michael the Archangel, Inc. The combined budgets of Arenberg's organizations come to more than $3 million per year.

Arenberg's critics, most notably the IACP, label him a police carpetbagger. They charge that he plays off of the confusion his organizations engender. As proof of his illegitimacy, they point to the fact that membership in his organizations is not limited to police, and to investigations of his activities by the U.S. Postal Service and the Internal Revenue Service.

Arenberg dismisses criticism from other police organizations as carping by competitors. In 1984 he told an interviewer that "police are multimillion-dollar businesses, most of them, and we're in competition. It's as simple as that. You want to create problems for your competition."[10] The bottom line on the animosity between himself and other police organizations says Arenberg is "competition, greed and avarice."

Whether or not Arenberg is the mercenary huckster portrayed by the IACP and others, his organizations do offer the NRA the police cover it so desperately needs. Unlike the mainstream groups, Arenberg's are uniformly pro-gun. The religious Venerable Order of the Knights of Michael the Archangel (the patron saint of police officers) counts among its officers John Snyder of the Citizens Committee for the Right to Keep and Bear Arms. Others who have joined the group in the past, says Arenberg, include former FBI Director Clarence Kelly and Don Johnson from *Miami Vice*. Arenberg's groups may be held in contempt by many mainstream police organizations, but to most citizens, and most likely many lawmakers, the debate over who represents "real" cops is meaningless. They all look the same on television. As a result, Arenberg's organizations have begun to gain a higher profile on Capitol Hill, testifying before Congress and promising to represent the view of the "cop on the beat."

When the NRA needs a police voice, one of Arenberg's associations is there. During the cop-killer bullet debate, Arenberg's National Association of Chiefs of Police was notable for attacking not the NRA, but Handgun Control, Inc. An NACP press release warned:

> The posters and advertising sponsored by Handgun Control, Inc. had made persons who had no idea that there was a type of ammunition that would penetrate soft bullet-resistant jackets . . . fully aware of the way to overcome the little protection our officers have.

Repeating the NRA line that no officer had ever been killed with armor-piercing ammunition, the NACP warned that "if this comes to pass, as we fear it will, then Handgun Control will have to share the responsibility of helping to kill police."[11] In 1984 Arenberg's American Federation of Police filed a friend of the court brief with the Illinois Supreme Court to aid in the NRA's efforts to overturn the Morton Grove handgun ban. The brief noted that police have historically opposed gun control laws and warned that "overbroad and unreasonable gun control measures of the type enacted by Morton Grove cannot be effective, will only disrupt legislation that would work, and will serve only to breed contempt and disrespect for the law."[12]

And in 1986 NRA publications argued that "contrary to the impression fostered on the nightly news, a number of professional law enforcement groups fought with NRA to pass . . . McClure-Volkmer."[13] Among those cited were Arenberg's American Federation of Police and the NACP. In return, the NRA gives Arenberg's organizations the respect he seeks in its publications, political campaigns and events.

As an insurance policy, the NRA has formed its own police organization. In 1989, the NRA was "instrumental" in establishing Law Enforcement for the Preservation of the Second Amendment. LEPSA is headed by NRA board member and former San Jose police officer Leroy Pyle. In 1990, reportedly having received more than $100,000 from the NRA, the organization changed its name to the Law Enforcement Alliance of America, Inc. and moved its offices from New Jersey to northern Virginia. In a full-page May 1991 *American Rifleman* ad, LEAA champions itself as "a group willing to fight the bureaucrats who have abandoned the death penalty and other important crime-fighting measures while trying to pass useless gun control laws."

The NRA has, however, continued its attempts to recapture mainstream police organizations. In a pamphlet titled *Is The NRA Pro-Police—Here's Proof,* the NRA warns:

> Recent media trumpeting and hype have called our traditional ties [to police] into question. Unfortunately some [police] believed it. We'd like to set the record straight. Because the future of many American freedoms depends upon maintaining this bond of mutual support and strength. The NRA is pro-police. Always has been. Always will be.

As part of this effort, in 1989 the NRA established its department of Law Enforcement Relations. The department's newsletter, *The Badge*, was unveiled soon after. In the fall 1990 edition, NRA Law Enforcement Relations Director Sam Cross writes that "considering the near-warfare we're now facing from America's new breed of criminals," the NRA was instituting "a program which should erase some of the shadows clouding the long-term security of your wives and children"—death benefits. Effective August 1990, NRA police members would receive $10,000 in death benefits when "feloniously killed in the line of duty." That the NRA was defending the very weapons that were likely to be used to kill police didn't strike it as particularly ironic.

Although the NRA has finally recognized that a split exists, whether they will be able to win or buy their way back into the hearts of police is questionable. As former Chief Casey wrote in *The Washington Post* in 1988, "The NRA keeps taking positions in opposition to law enforcement while paying for expensive advertising that says, 'Next to his partner, the NRA is the police officer's best friend.' With friends like those, who needs enemies?"

Endnotes

1. Senate Testimony of Michael Beard on Armor-Piercing Bullets, (1983).
2. *Ibid.*
3. Letter from J. Warren Cassidy to members of Congress, (January 30, 1985).
4. Senate Hearings on Armor-Piercing Bullets, (March 7, 1984) at 99.
5. Beard, *supra.*
6. "Federal Gun Law," *Congressional Quarterly Almanac,* (1985) at 229.
7. "Congress Relaxes Federal Gun Control Laws," *Congressional Quarterly Almanac,* (1986) at 85.
8. Senate Hearings on Plastic Firearms, (July 28, 1987) at 51.
9. *Ibid.* at 51, 52.
10. "Spotlight-Gerald Arenberg," *The National Centurion,* (February 1984) at 24.
11. "Police Group Blasts HCI on KTW Issue," *American Rifleman,* (March 1984) at 52.
12. "More Police Oppose Morton Grove," *American Rifleman,* (March 1984) at 53.
13. "Law Enforcement Groups Back America's Gun Owners," *American Rifleman,* (August 1986) at 51.

Chapter Ten

Hunting for Humans

If the congressional battles over armor-piercing bullets, McClure-Volkmer and plastic handguns had driven the relationship between the NRA and police to the brink, assault weapons sent it right over. The extra push was added by a 24-year-old drifter named Patrick Purdy.

Purdy's criminal history was replete with sex, drugs and guns. In 1980 he was arrested for soliciting sex from an undercover police officer. Two years later he was taken into custody for drug possession. In 1983 Beverly Hills police picked him up on a dangerous weapons charge. The next year he was arrested in Woodland, California, for attempted robbery and criminal conspiracy. In 1987 Purdy was arrested in El Dorado National Forest for discharging a pistol and resisting arrest. While in custody he twice tried to commit suicide. The probation report described him as a danger to himself and others.

On January 17, 1989, dressed in camouflage fatigues and a flak vest with the words "Evil, Evil, Evil, Evil" written across it in felt-tip pen, Purdy walked onto the grounds of Stockton's Cleveland Elementary School. Purdy was armed with a Chinese-made AK-47 semi-automatic assault rifle, purchased in Oregon, and a 9mm Taurus pistol obtained from a Stockton, California, gun shop. Under California law, Purdy had waited 15 days for the handgun while a background check was conducted. Because Purdy had never been convicted of a felony (his sentencings were characterized by plea bargains, brief jail stints and probation), he came through with flying colors.

At 11:39 a.m. Patrick Purdy opened fire on the nearly 400 students, most of them the children of Cambodian and Vietnamese refugees, who were out on the school grounds at recess. In the next few minutes he emptied a 100-round and a 35-round ammunition clip. By the time he finished—ending his own life with the Taurus handgun—five children were dead and 29 others, including one teacher, were wounded.

As reports of the shooting came over the wire, the NRA followed its standard procedure: membership rolls were scoured to see if the shooter had ever been a member. Purdy hadn't been. Armed with his rap sheet, the NRA quickly pointed the finger of blame at the criminal justice system.

The Stockton massacre came nearly six years after James Huberty, armed with an UZI carbine, a handgun and a shotgun, had walked into a San Ysidro, California, McDonald's restaurant. Huberty had told his wife that he was "going hunting for humans." He was successful, killing 21 and injuring 19. Most of those massacred were children. It was the largest single mass shooting in American history. Yet outside of California, memories of the Huberty massacre quickly faded.

Stockton, however, pierced the public consciousness once and for all with a fact police had known already: a new breed of firearm—assault weapons—was rocketing in popularity. Semi-automatic (firing one bullet per trigger pull), high-capacity, military-style, anti-personnel handguns, rifles and shotguns— assault weapons appealed to the worst instincts in gun owners. And all too often the worst gun owners.

In the month following the Stockton shooting, restrictions on assault weapons were passed in Los Angeles, Stockton, Compton, San Diego and Santa Clara County. The NRA immediately challenged the local ordinances in court on the grounds that they violated California's statewide firearms preemption that forbid local communities from enacting gun laws stricter than statewide standards.

Stockton was horrifying—but it wasn't surprising. The phenomenon of assault weapons and the resultant carnage was, in fact, almost inevitable. Following the handgun sales slump that began in 1983, firepower, capacity and technology had become the new industry sales points. Assault weapons were everything handguns were on the visceral level, only more so. Yet the industry didn't force these guns on the public. We wanted them.

The infatuation may have begun with the 1981 assassination attempt of Ronald Reagan. While most Americans were transfixed by the image of a dazed Reagan being shoved into the back of his limousine, others were fascinated by the UZI pulled out from under the coat of the Secret Service agent standing over a prone Hinckley. The UZI was already admired by gun aficionados for its Israeli pedigree. The revelation that it was carried by the Secret Service only added to its aura. And although full-auto versions came under the strict licensing provisions of the 1934 National Firearms Act, semi-automatic models could be purchased just as easily as a hunting rifle.

Fattened on a television and movie diet of increasingly tantalizing firearms, Americans had become bored with six-shot revolvers and Colt 45 pistols. The .44 magnum revolver that Clint Eastwood wowed movie audiences with in the 1970s was a relic by the '80s. The firepower and looks of assault weapons were needed on the big screen to keep our gaze from wandering. In movie series like *Rambo, Lethal Weapon, RoboCop* and *Die Hard,* guns played key supporting, if not starring, roles.

The A-Team, Miami Vice and other cop-and-robber shoot-'em-ups acted as home video showrooms for firearms. "The MAC-10," a criminal purred in the opening of a *Miami Vice* episode, "it slices, it dices." The boxy assault pistol was then turned on three silver, naked female mannequins, cutting them in two. When the futuristic Steyr AUG assault rifle was featured on one episode, gun stores across the country received inquiring calls. The MTV mentality of *Miami Vice*—short takes, rock music and a flimsy plot line wrapped in fleshy thighs—did as much for assault weapons as it did for razor stubble. Guns were sexy. An Armani suit and a half day's growth of beard couldn't rescue a sagging waistline or an unattractive face. The image of the assault weapon, however, was intrinsic. It didn't matter whose hand it was in.

Firearms industry advertising reduced the barely subliminal *Miami Vice* message to a simpler point: real men carry real mean guns. As Action Arms advised, "When the going gets tough . . . the tough get an UZI." Often the industry's tough-guy role models were survivalists and criminals.

"Survival means different things to different people," observed Colt in an ad for its AR-15. "For a rugged individual in the wilderness, it means being prepared for any eventuality." "When you're determined to survive," warned Heckler & Koch,

> you leave nothing to chance. In a survival situation, you want the most uncompromising weapons that money can buy. The HK91 Semi-Automatic Assault Rifle. . . . In a world of compromise, some men don't.

(In a fit of political correctness, this line later changed to, "In a world of compromise, some don't.")

Other manufacturers seemed to revel in their weapons' suitability for criminal misuse. FIE urged gun owners to "Take the 'LAW' Into Your Own Hands" with its Franchi LAW-12 shotgun. Advertisements for the SWD 9mm MAC-11 showcased a '30s gangster holding the gun's presumed antecedent, the Thompson machine gun. The MAC—as "American As God, Mom And Apple Pie"—was "The Gun That Made The '80s Roar." In ads for the Street Sweeper—a revolving cylinder riot shotgun—SWD warned, "It's a Jungle Out There! Make you [sic] streets safe and clean with the help of *The Street Sweeper!*" Dealer literature for Intratec, Inc. pushed "high-spirited, high-profit" weapons "as tough as your toughest customers." For anyone who had doubts about who the "toughest" customers were, a 1989 study by Cox newspaper reporters Jim Stewart and Andrew Alexander had the answer. The TEC-9, because of its low price and concealability, was the criminal assault handgun of choice.

Such advertising was ready-made for Mitty-esque gun owners whose firearm fantasies included a "wicked" looking gun that could make Swiss cheese out of anything in its path. The weapons, however, were best suited to a far less innocent set of fans. Assault weapons quickly became the prestige firearm for paramilitary groups, teenage gang members, drug dealers and bona fide gun nuts. In a world where weapons were primarily used to intimidate, firepower and looks were everything. When used to kill, capacity removed any doubts posed by inexperience. In addition, many assault weapons could be converted to full-auto machine guns relatively easily.

Assault weapons changed the gun control debate in America. Previously, the gun control movement focused only on handguns. Its arguments against the weapons were based primarily on a benefit/detriment ratio: Did the harm inflicted by handguns outweigh any possible benefit? With assault weapons, the standard changed from benefit/detriment to one of utility—for what purpose was the weapon designed? Handguns were designed to kill people. Assault weapons, with their military pedigree, were designed to kill a lot of people. The new debate required a level of technical expertise and knowledge the gun control movement lacked—and that few in it were willing to acquire. Firearms knowledge, they seemed to feel, implied a tacit endorsement of the weapons themselves.

NRA Betrayed

In March 1989, Director of the Office of Drug Policy William Bennett, reacting to the growing media outcry, announced that ATF would ban the import of five types of assault weapons, including the UZI carbine and AK-47.

"There are a lot of policemen and chiefs out there who are saying . . . the main purpose of these weapons is carnage and mayhem," Bennett said.[1] Although ATF lacks control over domestically manufactured weapons, all imported rifles and shotguns are subjected to a "sporting purposes" test. By stating that the guns no longer met the subjective criteria, ATF could ban their import.

The day after the announcement, Colt Industries, to honor "the spirit of the law," pulled its AR-15 assault rifle off the market. Bennett praised the Colt move as "an act of civic responsibility." (Colt's civics lesson came to an abrupt end a year later when under new ownership—which included the state of Connecticut, with 47 percent of the company's stock—the AR-15, with some slight cosmetic changes, was returned to the marketplace.) NRA officials portrayed the five-weapon ban as a sop toward calming "media hysteria" and warned that the time was "long overdue for a cool-headed look at the facts regarding the legitimate, sporting purposes of certain semi-autos."[2] Two days later, ILA head Wayne LaPierre met with White House Chief of Staff John Sununu to discuss the ban.

Unwilling to attack Life Member George Bush, the NRA turned its ire on Bennett. In a letter released to the press, the NRA painted the drug czar, who had attended graduate school during the Vietnam War, as a draft dodger. "While you may not be familiar with the life of a serviceman," wrote Assistant Counsel James Warner,

> for many of these men the chance to bring home firearms while posted overseas is small recompense for the isolation, the boredom and the risk of overseas duty. Perhaps you can remember, when you were in graduate school, looking forward with great anticipation to some small pleasure to relieve the tedium of your scholarly pursuits.

When asked if he was accusing Bennett of being a draft dodger, Warner replied, "Let people's records speak for themselves."

Although five models of assault weapons were banned from import, numerous other foreign models could still be imported. Noting that the number of unaffected weapons scheduled to be brought into the country totaled more than 200,000, ATF Director Stephen Higgins recommended expanding the ban. Higgins warned in an ATF memo that "absent action on our part, [unaffected] importers will try to bring in the maximum [number of unbanned assault weapons] possible. Considering the premium price that assault weapons currently command in the U.S., we must assume that a loophole in coverage will be rapidly exploited." ATF also faced the possibility of court action by the banned importers, who were charging discrimination. As a result, in April the White House announced a temporary ban on an additional 24 types of assault weapons.

A "disappointed" NRA bemoaned "the emotion of the moment taking the Administration's attention away from the pledges George Bush made to us. . . ." Warning that "his Administration is starting down the path George Bush warned us Michael Dukakis would take," the NRA called upon the president to "stick to his guns."[3] That a spurned NRA would cast aspersions on the administration and not George Bush was understandable. Only four months earlier the president had been named its 1988 "Person of the Year" and lauded as the "one candidate [who] would stand up for the rights of millions of American gun owners."[4] (Disgruntled Alaskan NRA members expressed their anger more directly. Rallying as "The No Compromise Majority" they began a petition drive to expel Bush from the organization.)

In a May 1989 speech Bush contradicted the NRA's argument of the assault weapons "hoax," acknowledging the "increasingly sophisticated guns in the hands of a new class of criminals," and labeling semi-automatic and "so-called assault weapons" the criminal's "gun of choice."[5] Bush announced a crime package that included doubling mandatory minimum penalties for the use of a semi-automatic firearm in a crime involving violence or drugs; permanent enactment of the federal import ban following ATF review; and banning the future production and sale of ammunition magazines with a capacity greater than 15 rounds.

The proposal was quickly criticized by both sides. "Does the Bush administration seriously think that criminals who smuggle tons of cocaine and marijuana into our country won't also smuggle in as many firearms and high-capacity magazines as they want?" asked the NRA's LaPierre. Democratic Ohio Senator Howard Metzenbaum noted that even with the import ban, "some 75 percent of all assault weapons on our streets are made here in America."[6]

That same month, California became the first state to ban assault firearms. Passage of the law rendered the NRA's court challenge to the municipal bans moot. The California law banned the sale of 55 makes of assault rifles, shotguns and pistols and required current owners to register their weapons. New assault weapon models could be added to the list through court determination. An NRA suit challenging the statewide law was soon filed but was eventually dismissed. (A year after the law's passage, compliance was virtually nonexistent. Only 7,000 of the estimated 300,000 assault weapons in the state had been registered.)

In July 1989 ATF formally banned 43 types of imported assault rifles. Criteria for banning included the ability to accept a detachable ammunition magazine and bayonet; and the presence of a folding or telescoping stock, pistol grip, flash suppressor, bipod mount, grenade launcher or night sight. Other factors included whether the weapon was a semi-automatic version of a military machine gun and the type of ammunition it used.

Seven guns were given a reprieve. Six were .22-rimfire models of already banned assault weapons, including the AK-47, Galil and M-16. Traditionally, .22 rimfire is viewed as sporting ammunition. As a result, ATF decreed that even though the guns had characteristics similar to the banned rifles, they were, by definition, sporting weapons. This romantic notion of good versus bad ammo ignored the realities of the assault weapons market. Many assault weapons, marketed as high-capacity "plinkers," use .22 ammunition. One of the most popular domestic assault pistols is the TEC-22 Scorpion. Although less deadly per shot than 9mm or .45 ammunition, the overall effect of 30 rounds of .22 ammo is no less lethal.

The seventh exempted rifle, the larger-caliber Valmet Hunter, lacked a pistol grip, bayonet or flash suppressor. It still, however, accepted detachable ammunition magazines—flying in the face of ATF's own criteria. ATF had warned of the industry's ability to exploit loopholes. By focusing on the cosmetic aspects of assault weapons and allowing the importation of a gun that accepted a detachable ammunition magazine, it gave the industry just the opening it needed.

German Ingenuity

Germany's Heckler & Koch soon became the industry leader in evading the ban. H&K's first move was to unveil a handgun version of its banned HK-94 assault rifle, the P-94. Unlike long guns, ATF import standards for handguns are based on an objective set of criteria with point values assigned for specific design characteristics, such as barrel length, caliber, safety devices and quality of manufacture. Pistols or revolvers must accumulate enough points based on positive design characteristics to surpass the import threshold. The factoring criteria were established following passage of the 1968 federal gun control laws to weed out Saturday Night Special handguns—not assault pistols. (In fact, throughout the debate, Action Arms had continued to import its UZI pistol.)

The P-94 was a squat 9mm that packed a 30-round magazine and retailed for $1,100. Ideal for "small game hunting—varmints, squirrels, rabbits," explained Heckler & Koch's Marvin Wagner. He added, "I guess you could go after a deer with it."[7] The weapon, stated H&K, had been designed prior to the ban, the timing of its introduction merely fortuitous. The P-94 was easily approved for import.

H&K's next move was to resume importation of its banned HK-91 assault rifle. In February 1990 H&K gained ATF approval for a "sporterized" version of the gun, renamed the SR-9 Orion. Taking a lesson from the Valmet Hunter, the modified rifle lacked the bells and whistles of the HK-91. The flash suppressor had been removed and a full stock had been added. Yet the gun's "thumbhole stock" acted as a pistol grip, and the rifle accepted detachable ammunition magazines. As a result, it could still be fired from the hip and reloaded quickly and easily. According to ATF, any banned assault rifle could be reclassified as a sporting weapon if it did "not have the characteristics common to military assault rifles" and was "more in the configuration of a traditional sporting rifle." It also had to have a new name.

Approval of the SR-9, promised one ATF staffer in an honest assessment of the agency's decision, was "going to open the floodgates" as other manufacturers followed suit. He was right. By June 1991 ATF had granted import approval to an additional eight "sporterized" versions of banned assault rifles, including the AK-47 and Galil. The number of guns scheduled for import totaled more than 100,000.

"Sporterization" represented a triumph of style over substance. The guns looked less threatening, but were no less deadly. And with little effort they could be retrofitted to full assault weapon configuration. A catalog description of a sporterized HK-91 clone offered by Springfield Armory described it as having

> all the features that have made the original HK-91 one of the world's most enduring semiautomatic sporting rifles as well as such a reliable performer. With its standard thumbhole sporter stock, the SAR-8 functions exactly like the original HK-91; with its optional accurizing package of a black pistol grip, stock, handguard and flash suppressor, it still looks like it, too.

ATF warned Springfield Armory that the "accurizing package" was "a clear attempt to circumvent the prohibition against the importation of assault-type rifles."[8] The company dropped plans to offer the kit and ATF approved the gun. Springfield Armory told inquiring gun owners that the package would soon be available from another company.

By February 1991, some companies were openly mocking ATF's policing of "accurizing" packages containing the necessary parts to return the guns to their original assault weapon configuration. A full-page Cobray ad for the Egyptian-made MAADi A.R.M. assault rifle offered kits of original military stock, pistol grip and compensators for $35 a set. "Customs and ATF have approved the importation of these previously banned rifles simply by installing a thumbhole stock classifying them as sporting rifles!" the ad bragged, adding, "original military stocks available... check other sources."

Homegrown Failure

ATF's definitional inconsistencies guaranteed the failure of the import ban. But even if the ban had worked, it would have had no effect, of course, on domestic manufacturers, who supplied the bulk of the guns. For this congressional action was needed.

On Capitol Hill assault weapons injected new energy into the gun control movement and loomed as a potential PR disaster for the NRA. Assault weapons—just like armor-piercing bullets and plastic handguns—were a new issue in an old debate. And unlike the handgun battle, it was one the movement felt it had a far greater chance of winning.

The weapons' menacing looks, coupled with the general confusion over fully automatic machine guns versus semi-automatic assault weapons, increased the chance for public support for restrictions. Because of the guns' TV image, few could imagine a sporting use for them. While many Americans believed that standard handguns were effective weapons for home self-defense and that the Second Amendment offered protections to gun owners, assault weapons were believed to be a different story.

Assault weapons also brought the gun control movement's lack of technical expertise out into the open. Some hastily drafted laws only lent credence to the NRA argument that restrictions on assault weapons were the first step down the slippery slope to total semi-auto—or even gun—confiscation. This confusion was aided by the sloppy reporting of news outlets that included *The Washington Post, Time* and *NBC Nightly News,* all of whom used the terms assault weapon and semi-automatic interchangeably.

Although pro-gunners attributed such errors to grand conspiracies to confuse the public and exploit the opportunity offered by assault-weapons hysteria, the real cause was simple ignorance.

Desperate to rally hunters and shooters in support of weapons that were identified in the public mind with drug dealers and post-Armageddon psychos, the NRA portrayed attacks against semi-auto assault weapons as a campaign against all semi-automatic firearms. In a modification of the "Master Plan" of the anti-gunners, the NRA warned:

> The national media and organized "gun control" groups have advanced from demanding prohibitions on certain handguns and ammunition, to calls for banning semi-automatic firearms. The pattern is obvious and the strategy has long been clear—isolate certain types of firearms, label them as inherently "evil" or "crime prone," then try to segregate and drive a wedge between firearms owners. All firearms owners should beware. Those who would willingly sacrifice handguns as a compromise, and who may now be willing to sacrifice semi-automatic firearms, will eventually find themselves having to defend their shotguns or any other type of firearm they choose to own.[9]

In legislative terms assault weapons *were* hard to define. Everyone knew what an "assault weapon" was and could tick off common characteristics (usually ending with "and they look real mean"). Crafting laws that would not infringe on legitimate sporting semi-automatics (although most hunters use bolt or lever-action rifles with low-capacity, integral ammunition magazines) while avoiding loopholes for manufacturers to exploit was difficult, perhaps impossible. There would always be gray areas and the need for subjective judgment.

Following the Stockton massacre, a slew of assault weapons bills was introduced in both the U.S. House and Senate. Efforts in the Senate were led by Howard Metzenbaum, who was eventually forced to champion a compromise bill drafted by Arizona Democrat Dennis DeConcini. Like Bush, DeConcini had previously received NRA honors, being named its "Person of the Month" in July 1988. To have him introduce—and forcefully argue in favor of—a bill that actually banned guns sent a chilling message to the NRA.

The DeConcini bill was an assault firearms "greatest hits" list, banning nine specific types of foreign and domestic assault weapons by name, including the UZI, Galil, AR-15, Striker and Street Sweeper, MAC-10 and MAC-11, Steyr AUG and TEC-9. Any additions would require a vote of Congress. Critics were quick to point out—and as "sporterization" proved—that because the bill named specific brands and makes, it could be easily circumvented by companies developing slightly different guns with new names. They also noted that criminals—never known for brand loyalty—could easily switch over to the 40 or 50 other assault firearms still on the market. Because of these factors, the bill would be virtually useless in the long term.

The Senate voted in May 1990. With giant photographs of assault weapons hanging in the back of the chamber, the DeConcini measure was retained as part of the Senate crime bill in a dramatic floor battle. Even though a Metzenbaum amendment expanding the ban to twelve types of guns was easily defeated, the vote was a stinging political loss for the NRA. (After the vote Senator Alan Simpson decried the measure as a misguided attempt to quell crime and offered a far simpler solution: "Let's try 'em and fry 'em.")

If an assault weapons ban was going to pass the House, the fall of 1990 seemed the right time. The previous months had been marked by a series of high-profile assault weapons shootings. Such incidents had become so common that Neal Knox hinted at the presence of a long-running gun control assassination conspiracy. Warning "Gun Control Ghouls . . . can further their aims only by dancing in the blood of innocents," Knox wrote, "I've seen too many perfectly timed 'coincidences' to think it's impossible that evil men, bent on the disarmament of a free citizenry, could never and would never trigger insane acts of insane men to further their cause."

As had been the case in the Senate, the House version of the crime bill contained an assault weapons provision. The measure prohibited production in the United States of any model of assault rifle banned for import by ATF. Made-in-the-USA assault weapons unaffected by the import ban, however, could continue to be manufactured. And new models could be developed and marketed—by foreign and domestic companies—as long as production occurred in the United States.

In October 1990 the measure met a quick and bitter end. Democrat Jolene Unsoeld introduced an amendment that would merely forbid the domestic assembly of banned foreign assault rifles from imported parts. Unlike the original provision, foreign manufacturers would be allowed to license their weapons to U.S. firms for domestic manufacture or establish their own U.S. production facilities. In other words, in a creative protectionist twist, an assault weapon was bad only if it wasn't made in the U.S.A. The Unsoeld amendment was overwhelmingly approved as part of the crime package.

The Senate assault weapons ban was later stripped by House and Senate crime bill conferees and the 101st Congress ended with a familiar ritual. Gun control advocates retreated to lick their wounds and point fingers. Congress heaved a collective sigh of relief, having for the most part avoided the issue. And the NRA, having turned defeat into victory, celebrated.

Endnotes

1. "Bennett Rejects Further Gun Curbs," *Washington Post*, (February 3, 1990).
2. "Temporary Import Suspension May Lessen Semi-Auto Hysteria," *NRAction*, (April 15, 1989).
3. "Import Freeze Expanded," *NRAction*, (April 15, 1989).
4. "NRA, Nation's Gun Owners Honor George Bush," *NRAction*, (January 15, 1989).
5. "Administration Crime Package Urges Increased Spending," *Congressional Quarterly*, (May 20, 1989) at 1211.
6. "Critics on Both Sides Take Aim at Bush Anti-Crime Plan," *Congressional Quarterly*, (May 20, 1989) at 1197.
7. "Gun Makers Take Aim at Ban," *Chicago Tribune*, (October 5, 1989).
8. Letter from ATF Director Stephen Higgins to Patrick Squire, (March 8, 1990).
9. *Semi-Auto Firearms: The Citizen's Choice*, NRA.

Part IV

Decline . . .
and Fall?

Chapter Eleven

Extremism in the Name of . . .

The 1990 assault weapons victory was one of the few bright spots in what had become a series of missteps and failures for the NRA under the leadership of former Institute for Legislative Action head J. Warren Cassidy.

If G. Ray Arnett had been a failed version of former Executive Vice President Harlon Carter, Cassidy, who succeeded Arnett in 1986, was his antithesis. While the membership could easily envision Carter as Patton leading the troops into battle, Cassidy was the desk-bound politician who would remain safely behind the lines. Cassidy, with his TV-evangelist hair and gold jewelry, looked like the former insurance agent that he was. The new EVP represented the "kinder, gentler" NRA that strived to be loved by the American public.

And unlike Arnett, Cassidy was a known quantity that would not threaten Carter's behind-the-scenes power. As a lifetime member of the executive council, Carter's voice was still the one that was always heard. Known as "the old goats," Carter and the other members of the executive council would sit silently in the back row of the board room during policy debates. The discussion would end when Carter rose and offered his pronouncement on the issue.

Following the 1986 Arnett debacle, Carter moved to restore to the board the power he had helped take from it as the result of the 1977 Cincinatti Revolt.

Prior to the 1987 annual meeting in Reno, Nevada, the leadership urged the members to return election of the EVP back to the board. They obediently complied. The only route now left open to dissident factions would be to attain a majority on the 75-member board. In endorsing the shift, Carter abandoned his 1977 promise to the membership that control of the NRA would rest solely with them. Carter now stated:

> The board truly represents the NRA members. [The] executive vice president [must be] directly answerable to a member-elected board of directors. The NRA simply cannot survive an EVP who is out of step with ... [the board].[1]

This shift in power came at a price. With the NRA's leader now serving at the pleasure of the board, the palace intrigue that had previously occurred only at the end of the EVP's five-year term would now be constant.

The NRA inherited by Cassidy in 1986 claimed to have reached three million members. It had also just achieved its greatest victory—McClure-Volkmer—since 1982's Prop 15 in California. Under Cassidy, however, the NRA began a steady decline. His tenure was marked by dramatic drops in membership, respect and even political power. By the time Cassidy resigned in February 1991, the NRA admitted a membership drop to 2.6 million members (*Insider Gun News'* John Aquilino put the figure at 2.4 million), and as the result of its battles against assault weapons restrictions and a seven-day waiting period, it was increasingly seen as representing an extremist, minority segment of gun owners. Talk of a "weakened NRA" was now a standard aspect of any media profile.

The membership—both hard-line and moderate—was quick to blame Cassidy. Compromise may be the nature of politics, but to some it spelled weakness. In his dealings with

Capitol Hill politicians, Cassidy, a former mayor, viewed himself as one of them. His critics charged that he enjoyed being a member of such a special club and feared offending his new friends. Cassidy, they said, seemed more interested in exploiting the NRA's power and his position for personal gain and pleasure than in promoting the pro-gun agenda.

Although Cassidy was an easy target, the NRA's decline was inevitable. Since 1977 it had been driven by the uncompromising Second Amendment positions staked out by Carter and the Federation for NRA. If the NRA's absolutist stance never changed, the world in which it attempted to apply it did. The NRA's "slippery slope" argument was far easier to make when the primary issue was handguns and crime remained relatively static. Amid crack-driven urban violence and a litany of new issues—cop-killer bullets, machine guns, plastic handguns, and assault weapons—an increasing number of Americans, including the NRA's own members, began to question the organization's absolutism. The chance to help the NRA paint itself into an extremist corner was not lost on the gun control movement, which in its public relations attacks was quick to focus on these areas. As for the membership decline, some did leave in protest of the NRA's hard-line stance. A far more realistic answer was that the NRA, like any organization dependent on direct mail for membership, was reeling from the slump that hit that market in the late 1980s coupled with a succession of increases in dues.

If the NRA had been willing to recognize the new dynamics of the gun control debate, Cassidy, with his willingness to compromise, could have been an ideal leader. Recognizing how easily the public—and the gun control movement—could be satisfied, Cassidy viewed the passage of extremely limited gun control measures, such as waiting periods, as giving politicians a chance to satisfy voters' demands while having little real effect on the firearms industry. When Cassidy suggested at a 1988 Orlando board meeting that the NRA should perhaps reconsider its stance against waiting periods, the board didn't view his comment as a political option, but treason. He didn't bring it up again, and denied ever having said it. The NRA stood as a victim of its own rhetoric. It had convinced its members that any control measure was the first step toward total gun confiscation. It couldn't turn back now.

As a result, whoever sat in the EVP's chair was doomed, regardless of his qualifications. To the general public, the NRA was an increasingly reactionary, extreme and dangerous organization. The fundamentalists held Cassidy responsible for this perception, but at the same time vilified him as soft, ignoring the inherent contradiction. Those who felt the NRA was shifting to the extremist right merely failed to renew their memberships. Those who viewed it as softening set their sights on Cassidy.

The Right to Keep and Bear Machine Guns

The most explicit example of this dichotomy followed passage of the McClure-Volkmer bill. A last-minute House amendment banned the future production and sale of machine guns for civilian use. Machine guns already in civilian hands would remain available for sale, possession and use as long as the requirements of the National Firearms Act were fulfilled. Predictably, an uproar followed in the "full-auto community," with claims that they had been sold out. Yet Cassidy didn't defend the machine gun owners—he scolded them. Didn't they understand, he asked, "that in an organization that has fewer than 100,000 machine gun owners in a total of almost three million, something has to give?"[2] This abandonment of a basic NRA principle—that guns, even machine guns, don't kill, people do—and the subsequent dismissal of a segment of gun owners, prompted cries of betrayal.

To pacify these critics, three months after the ban, Institute for Legislative Action head Wayne LaPierre announced that "repealing the machine gun amendment tacked on to the McClure-Volkmer bill will be a high priority." Lobbyist James Jay Baker promised that legislation to repeal the amendment had already been drafted and would soon be introduced.

As a "prelude" to the bill's introduction, the NRA released its newly drafted position on machine guns, stating:

> The National Rifle Association supports the right of law-abiding individuals to choose to own any firearm, including automatic firearms. The individuals who make such a choice, and who are willing to endure the federal requirements necessary prior to obtaining an automatic firearm, deserve, and will receive, the full and active support and backing of the National Rifle Association. The Second Amendment is not limited by its language to the type of arms which the people have a right to own.

The legislation was never introduced. The political and public relations consequences of a machine gun relief bill were just too high. The ban did, however, pose a nagging problem—and it wasn't cranky machine gun fans. It stood as proof that despite the NRA's best Second Amendment arguments, complete categories of firearms could be banned. Moreover, it happened not only on the NRA's watch, but as part of its flagship bill.

Although unwilling to force a political reversal, the NRA was grudgingly amenable to offering its support to a legal challenge. In 1987, J.D. Farmer Jr., a Georgia gun manufacturer—and husband of Linda Farmer, head of the pro-machine gun National Firearms Association—applied to ATF for a license to manufacture a machine gun for his private possession. When denied the application, Farmer sued in federal court, arguing that ATF had misinterpreted federal intent. Under the law, the future production of machine guns was banned except "under the authority of the United States."

ATF allowed the sale of new machine guns only to U.S. military or law enforcement organizations or for export. Farmer argued that because machine guns had previously been regulated by the government under the National Firearms Act, ATF's interpretation was too narrow. In

January 1989 a federal district court ruled in Farmer's favor. The decision was overturned on appeal, with the court noting that the Second Amendment "does not absolutely bar all congressional regulation of firearms." In appealing the decision to the U.S. Supreme Court, NRA lawyer-on-call Stephen Halbrook argued:

> At this time of the bicentennial of the Bill of Rights, this court should not allow . . . a fundamental infringement on the right of the people to keep arms guaranteed by the Second Amendment.

The Court refused to hear the case, letting the lower court ruling—and the ban—stand.

In defense of its position, the NRA's Richard Gardiner stated that "since 1934 no legally owned fully automatic firearms have ever been used in the commision of a violent crime by civilians." Gardiner was wrong. Prior to 1990 ATF had told reporters that agency "old-timers" remembered a few cases, but nothing recent. This story changed that year when ATF acknowledged that instances of misuse did exist and were not uncommon, but that under the National Firearms Act the cases were considered tax information and could therefore not be divulged. Regarding the previous explanation, an ATF staffer acknowledged that the agency had lied.

Tydings' Revenge

If the NRA's stance on machine guns and assault weapons had exacerbated its extremist image, its reputation as the invincible gun lobby came to an end in 1988. Ironically, it happened in Maryland, where the NRA had earned its reputation for merciless retribution with the defeat of Senator Joseph Tydings in 1970. The NRA's Waterloo was the Maryland Saturday Night Special referendum.

The Maryland referendum was the final chapter in an involved series of events that began in 1985 when Olen

Kelley, an employee of a Bethesda Safeway supermarket, was shot during a robbery with an R.G. 14 handgun—the same model handgun used by John Hinckley to shoot President Reagan. Following the shooting, Kelley filed a product liability suit against the handgun's manufacturer, R.G. Industries of Florida.

In his suit, Kelley argued that R.G. Industries knew, or should have known, that the handgun—an inexpensive, low-quality Saturday Night Special—would not be used for any legitimate sporting purpose and was best suited for criminal use. The company, the suit argued, should therefore be held liable for its misuse. The Maryland Court of Appeals, the state's highest court, agreed, ruling on Kelley's behalf. R.G. Industries was soon unable to obtain liability insurance and went out of business. R.G.'s demise and an end to the sale of Saturday Night Specials in Maryland were the short-term effects of the decision. The long-term effects were that any person shot in a criminal act with a Saturday Night Special that had been sold in Maryland could now sue the manufacturer and the case stood as a precedent for similar suits in other states.

In 1986 and 1987 NRA-backed bills were introduced in the Maryland General Assembly to overturn the Kelley decision. Although gun control supporters successfully defeated the proposals, their margin of victory narrowed each year. In 1988 a deal was struck—the Kelley decision would be legislatively overturned if the future sale of Saturday Night Specials was banned in the state. Under the law, a state-appointed panel would use strictly defined criteria, similar to the ATF import standards, to determine which handguns were Saturday Night Specials. The bill was quickly signed into law by Maryland Governor William Donald Schaefer.

Immediately after passage, a local ad hoc pro-gun coalition announced plans to challenge the law on the ballot in November. Although the petition drive had started without the NRA's blessing, the organization soon found itself mired in a referendum battle.

Cassidy reportedly advised against NRA involvement but was overruled by the board, with board member Richard Riley vowing a "gloves off" fight. NRA personnel, however, were forbidden from working on the campaign. By July, the pro-gun petitioners, now named the Maryland Committee Against the Gun Ban, had submitted 51,000 signatures to ensure that the measure would be on the ballot in November. In May the NRA had mailed petitions to its Maryland members and urged them to help gather signatures. Said ILA's LaPierre, "We are confident that the citizens of Maryland will eagerly show their disapproval of the Assembly's vote banning handguns. Their lawmakers should get the message on election day when the law suffers a resounding rejection."[3]

In urging its defeat, the NRA moved quickly to portray the law as a total handgun ban that depended on the (presumably anti-gun) whims of sinister government-appointed bureaucrats. A creatively punctuated ILA fund-raising letter warned:

> The bill railroaded through by anti-gun politicians in the Maryland General Assembly bans the sale and manufacture of all handguns. UNLESS YOU STOP IT, only those handguns approved by a nine member board dominated by anti-gunners and chaired by the Superintendent of the State Police can be manufactured or sold in Maryland.

To ensure victory, the NRA brought in Prop 15 veteran George Young, who proceeded to flood the television and radio airwaves with advertising reminiscent of the California battle. Said Doug Bailey, Young's Prop 15 consulting opponent, "[The NRA has] a very set pattern of creating fear— of the unknown, of crime, of anything. I'm not suggesting that's not perfectly sensible from their point of view. It certainly works."[4]

The unrealistic, "fairy tale" nature of the law was illustrated by ads featuring unicorns, while others decried the "politically appointed" board responsible for determining which handguns could be sold. "They claim it only affects

'Saturday Night Specials,'" warned the committee, "but the words 'Saturday Night Special' never appear in the law." (Pro-control legislators were quick to point out that the term had been removed from the bill at the NRA's request as being too vague; defining characteristics were substituted instead.) One pollster noted of the NRA: "One of the things that is most effective about television is repetition. They've had everyone from a black male to a white woman to a cartoon character making the same point."[5]

The NRA's heavy-handed politicking resulted in attacks from its own members, including Maryland state legislator Richard Rynd. In an op-ed that appeared in *The Baltimore Sun* Rynd wrote, "I'm a member of the NRA, and I'm disgusted with it. [The NRA's Maryland message is] so ridiculous, so totally far-fetched, that it constitutes false advertising." Although the NRA "doesn't trust anyone," he wrote, "Marylanders will not be hoodwinked by the complete distortions and lies in the NRA's campaign. . . . [W]e Marylanders will vote for what is right and what is good for Maryland, not what is good for the NRA."

Citizens for Eliminating Saturday Night Specials, the ad hoc state organization formed by the ban's supporters for the duration of the campaign, benefited from the David and Goliath nature of the battle. And although the organization lacked the money and grass-roots network of the committee, it did have the support of Maryland's political power structure, state police organizations, *The Washington Post* and *The Baltimore Sun*. Governor Schaefer, a popular Democrat, came out in favor of the ban, agreeing to appear in a television commercial supporting it. Schaefer soon received a letter from committee head Fred Griisser, who, citing polling figures that the ban was losing support, warned Schaefer, "Think about these numbers. We certainly want you to be on our side when we win." Replied Schaefer in a handwritten note, "Do not count on me. I want Saturday Night Specials off the street. Incidentally, do you use one when you hunt?"[6]

Having ignored Griisser's warning, Schaefer became the committee's target when it mailed 500,000 copies of the *Free*

State Journal across Maryland. The banner headline of the one-time faux newspaper read: "Governor's Deception on #3 Results in Big Voter Revolt." An "article" in the campaign literature accused Schaefer of having read "seven untruths in eight sentences" in his television ad. Responding to the paper's charge that he was "irritated about the fact that he was not told about all of the flaws in the gun ban measure," Schaefer attacked the "cheap, lousy, deceptive newspapers." Of the NRA, he added, "They're more interested in preserving guns than in helping people."[7]

Both sides recognized that black Baltimore residents could be the swing vote in the election. Knowing the pro-control sympathies of urban blacks, the NRA began, in the words of the local chapter of the NAACP, "literally buying off the community."[8] A key element of the NRA's argument was that banning inexpensive Saturday Night Specials would deprive the urban poor of a means of self-defense available to more affluent, and white, Marylanders. Black canvassers were hired at $6 an hour to increase opposition to the ban in their communities. Initially, the move not only gained the NRA supporters, but engendered goodwill. To many, the issue wasn't guns—but money. "The black community never gets money when these things come around," said one community activist, "and this is the first time anyone has ever valued our work enough to pay us for it."[9]

Others, such as black Washington radio and television personality Cathy Hughes, saw it as just another commercial endorsement. *The Washington Post* assailed the tactics, noting that "one of the lowest of the NRA's low blows in this campaign is the insulting, patronizing pitch being aimed specifically at inner-city blacks." The ban's supporters attempted to counter the NRA's tactics with a radio commercial featuring Jesse Jackson. Attacking the NRA, Jackson asked, "Where were they when we reached out for better housing, education and employment. When have they ever come to the black community for help. The answer is never."[10]

Any inroads the NRA had made were shattered the night before the election, when Baltimore's chief prosecutor served subpoenas at the Committee Against the Gun Ban offices and police removed files under press scrutiny. The raid—decried by the committee as "police state" tactics—followed reports that it was offering inner-city youths $100 to work on election day "get out the vote" activities, a violation of the state's ban on the use of election day "walking-around" money. According to Young, committee polls showed that the raid resulted in a "huge switch" among Baltimore voters.

On November 8, the ban was retained by 58 percent to 42 percent, giving the NRA its first statewide referendum loss, despite their outspending pro-ban forces by more than ten to one. Final tallies for the NRA found that it had spent more than $6 million in the lost cause. Although gun control advocates confidently announced that they would launch similar referenda in other states, they never did. Maryland—with its close proximity to violence-ridden Washington, D.C., the political and population power of Baltimore, and the willingness of a popular governor to lend his support—was unique. After the defeat, committee consultant Young swore, "If this were across the border in Virginia or Pennsylvania we would have killed them."[11]

Contrary to the NRA's dire predictions, and to the disappointment of some gun control advocates, the sale of most handguns continued. As of July 1991, of the more than 1,200 handguns brought before the board for approval, only 18 had been labeled Saturday Night Specials and barred from sale in the state. Another 100 handguns that had been sold prior to the law, and would most likely not have been approved by the board, were never submitted for review.

The value of the Maryland referendum was political perception. No longer was the NRA the omnipotent gun lobby. Faced with this result, the NRA might have recognized its mistake in not heeding Cassidy's advice. Instead, he was blamed for the loss.

Cincinnati Redux

In addition to declining political power, Cassidy's tenure at the NRA was marked by allegations of financial mismanagement, sexual misconduct and incompetency. In addition to the ubiquitous Knox, one of Cassidy's main critics was former public education head John Aquilino. In his *Insider Gun News,* Aquilino faithfully reported NRA travails, with Cassidy as the main villain. This was, presumably, due in no small part to Cassidy's failure to rehire Aquilino after Arnett's ouster in 1986.

A month before the Maryland referendum Aquilino detailed a fall weekend purge attempt by a "select body" of NRA leadership, including Harlon Carter, who were "irate over the bumbling mismanagement style of J. Warren Cassidy that cost the NRA over $4,000,000 in *lost revenues,* wasted $31,000,000 in funds spent for membership promotions, destroyed staff morale, and left NRA staggering under a *$6,000,000 DEFICIT.*"[12] Other irregularities charged by Aquilino included embezzlement—

> The hot, hush hush news at NRA HQ is the revelation that a member of the Treasurer's staff under the NRA comptroller put a tidy $135,000 sum of NRA funds into his own bank account. Three years of audits and internal controls failed to reveal the scam until well after the "nice, young man" left the NRA.[13]

incompetency—

> $250,000 to $300,000 of member dues wasted after the NRA Secretary forgot David Caplan's bio in the board of director candidate roundup [printed in NRA publications].[14]

and sex—

> Rumors of Sex-capades in the Executive Suites: The story goes that a cleaning lady opened the door to one of the

eighth-floor offices and was met with a view of the NRA leadership boosting one female staff member's morale in the buff. Libido fulfillment or interoffice fraternization are not at issue. Exhibiting poor judgment in site selection, bestowing a privileged aura on a sex-partner in the workplace, and cheating on a faithful wife are. Could this be the harbinger of a libertine NRA with satyrs romping around the executive offices? Has the amorous executive quaffed one draft of Potomac water too many?[15]

The in-house intrigue at the NRA inspired Aquilino to images of the proud outdoors. In detailing an alleged attempt by Cassidy to oust ILA lobbyist James Jay Baker, Aquilino characterized Baker as "the mature, heavily antlered buck, graceful and confident protecting the herd and his turf," while Cassidy was "a short-spiked mutant masquerading as the boss stag, attempting to mount any doe in rut, but totally lacking the first clue that he isn't nor ever will be able to perform as a truly 'dominant' male."[16]

Such shortcomings would most likely have been overlooked if the one true measure of NRA power as defined by Harlon Carter—membership—had continued to grow. This was the chief complaint against Cassidy. In spite of increased direct mail attempts, membership continued to fall. To minimize the drop, the NRA abandoned its claim of ever having reached three million members, asserting that membership had peaked at 2.9 million.

Recognizing the growing disenchantment with Cassidy, Knox moved to increase his influence through the only channel left open to him—packing the board with anti-Cassidy, pro-Knox candidates. Prior to the 1991 annual meeting in San Antonio, Texas, Knox launched a bid to have himself returned to the board along with a slate of NRA hard-liners. This time he had a surprising ally—Harlon Carter. In his ads, Knox quoted Carter as stating, "When the board will not make needed changes, then the board must be changed."[17]

In a full-page ad in a January 1991 *Shotgun News*, Knox warned members:

Right now, NRA is going downhill. Membership is sagging toward 2.5 million. And under J. Warren Cassidy's poor management, NRA is headed for bankruptcy—particularly if it doesn't quit paying more to entice new members with expensive premiums and sweepstakes than it receives for each membership.

Urging election of the 21 members of his Second Amendment Action slate (Knox had been forced to abandon the moniker of the Federation for NRA as the result of a 1984 Harlon Carter-directed NRA lawsuit charging copyright infringement), Knox warned that "just as . . . in Cincinnati in 1977, the NRA Board of Directors is split down the middle about whether, and how hard, the NRA Institute should be allowed to fight for our gun rights."

A new battle was brewing, and it was envisioned by some as nothing less than a replay of Cincinnati—the Second Amendment fundamentalists once again seizing control from a leadership grown complacent. Writing in *Gun Week*, editor and Cincinnati co-conspirator Tartaro observed:

> While it might appear that the argument today is between two individuals—formerly allies in the reform movement—Knox and Cassidy, that is not where the main struggle lies. The debate is largely over the directions NRA has been taking, where it will go, and how it will get there. The debate is essentially the same debate that took place fourteen years ago. The factions and philosophies are similar. It is a struggle between hobby shooters who are wary of political activism and a no-compromise stand on the Second Amendment on the one hand, and the social movement gunowners, who see defense of the Second Amendment as the paramount issue for NRA. It is also part of the age-old struggle between people who think that the select few can govern best and who do not trust democracy on the one hand and those who place their trust in the rank and file membership which they want to see informed for thoughtful decision.[18]

The seriousness with which Cassidy viewed the Knox threat was revealed when a full-page "Open Letter to NRA Members" appeared in the January 1991 *Rifleman*. Decrying Knox's attacks as "not necessarily truthful or accurate," Cassidy warned that "the theme of each of these campaigns has been to raise money for advertisements that deceive NRA members into believing NRA is mismanaged, or does not support the rights of law-abiding firearms owners." Knox's "noisy defense of a supposed 'faction' in NRA he claims deserves support," wrote Cassidy, "is in fact to build his own lobbying business and serve his own political ambition." Cassidy's letter did little more than focus members' attention on Knox's charges.

In February 1991 J. Warren Cassidy abruptly ended the battle. Citing personal reasons, Cassidy announced that he would resign as EVP that month and carry on with the organization as a fund-raising consultant. Cassidy's departure was so abrupt that in an NRA members' guide to the organization published in the March edition of the *Rifleman*, a large white space two-thirds of a page wide stood where Cassidy's introduction presumably would have appeared. Cassidy's monthly column in NRA publications also disappeared. No mention of the resignation was made in NRA publications until April 1991, when President Dick Riley explained:

> Warren had decided some time ago not to stand for reelection in April. He said it would have been awkward to remain in a lame duck position for the last few months of his term without announcing his intentions. The executive vice president's position is one of many challenges and immense pressure. Therefore Warren, as he put it in his own words, decided to leave as "a young 60-year-old rather than an older 65."[19]

Others viewed Cassidy's resignation as a calculated ploy by the EVP to obtain a better settlement from the NRA in the face of the upcoming board elections. If Knox's slate won,

Cassidy would most likely be ousted. Riley announced that under the bylaws Gary Anderson, executive director of general operations, would assume the role of executive vice president until the April annual meeting. At the meeting the board would elect a new EVP. That a successor was not named prior to the meeting—an act both Arnett and Cassidy had benefited from—reflected the board's uncertainty as to whom they should select. All was not well in the NRA's wild and woolly domain.

A Man's Organization

Cassidy's sudden trip down the memory hole, however, had little to do with his health or even the NRA's fiscal woes. It was the result of the ghost of Ray Arnett coming back to haunt him. Its messenger was Tracey Attlee.

In December 1988 Marsha Beasley, a ten-year NRA employee and life member who had participated in NRA programs since the age of eleven, was fired by Cassidy for approving the use of an article by Attlee in *InSights* magazine. Attlee's name, Beasley was told, was never again to grace the pages of an NRA publication. Unfortunately, no one had ever told Beasley this. Beasley promptly sued Cassidy and the NRA for sex discrimination.

In the suit Beasley cited examples that confirmed that the NRA, in the words of one of her male co-workers, was still truly a "man's organization." While working in the NRA's education and training division, Beasley was once informed by her supervisior, Wayne Sheets, that she could not attend a show to sell advertising. Such trips, she was told, were reserved for female employees who were willing to dress more femininely and who would flirt with customers. Beasley was encouraged to hire only attractive women for support staff, and when she expressed concerns about the discrepencies between male and female salaries in the organization, it was patiently explained to her that the precise reason the NRA hired female managers was because they worked hard for less money.

In May 1988, Beasley replaced Sheets as head of the division. When Beasley met with Cassidy to discuss the position, the EVP told her that he was scared to death of putting such a "young girl" in such an important position, comparing the 31-year-old Beasley to his 19-year-old daughter. The only good that would come out of it, he noted, was that it would pacify his critics. Although the titular head of the department, Beasley was consistently undercut by Cassidy. The EVP preferred to work with her male assistant, who had been hired by Cassidy after he had told Beasley that such a "young girl" couldn't be trusted to make such an important decision.

Just as in the case of Arnett, the organization that bragged of its willingness to fight virtually any battle chose instead to duck and run. Before the case could come to trial, in November 1990 the NRA reached an out-of-court settlement rumored to total more than half a million dollars. The reasons for settling stemmed less from Beasley's allegations of sex discrimination than her allegation that in the office Cassidy "gave extraordinary access . . . to women who would deal with him on other than a professional basis." According to *Insider Gun News'* Aquilino, in pretrial depositions Cassidy was reportedly forced to give detailed accounts of his sexual liaisons with female staff members. Revelation of such incidents would not do for an NRA that hoped to expand its female membership. In a June 1990 column Cassidy himself had castigated "all NRA critics, especially you cartoonists, who exhaust yourselves portraying us as the epitome of macho chauvinists!" Cassidy fell as much from his indiscriminate taste for women as from his discrimination against them.

Endnotes

1. "Members Vote to Allow Board to Elect NRA Executive V.P.," *Monitor*, (April 30, 1987).
2. *Insider Gun News*, (August 1987).
3. "Marylanders Working to Overturn Handgun-Ban Law," *NRAction*, (June 15, 1988).
4. "Attacking Md.'s Gun Law," *Washington Post*, (October 16, 1988).
5. "Gap Closing in Md. Gun Control Fight," *Washington Post*, (October 27, 1988).
6. "Schaefer Swipes Back at NRA," *Washington Post*, (November 5, 1988).
7. *Ibid.*
8. "Black Leaders in Baltimore Hired by Gun Law Opponents," *Washington Post*, (November 4, 1988).
9. *Ibid.*
10. "For on 3: Battling Big Money," *Washington Post*, (November 5, 1988).
11. "Gun Control Backers Say Maryland Victory Will Spread to Other States," *New York Times*, (November 13, 1988).
12. *Insider Gun News*, (October 1988).
13. *Insider Gun News*, (May 1989).
14. *Insider Gun News*, (April 1988).
15. *Insider Gun News*, (September 1989).
16. *Insider Gun News*, (September/October 1990).
17. *Shotgun News*, (January 1, 1991).
18. "Choosing Sides Within NRA," *Gun Week*, (February 22, 1991) at 11.
19. "When Rights Are Wronged," *American Rifleman*, (April 1991) at 48.

Chapter Twelve

The NRA at the Alamo

On March 29, 1991, Ronald Reagan became a pro-gun quisling. At a ceremony at George Washington University marking the tenth anniversary of the assassination attempt on his life, Reagan announced his endorsement of the Brady bill, a federal seven-day waiting period for handgun sales with optional local background check. Said Reagan, "I am going to say it in clear, unmistakable language: I support the Brady bill and I urge the Congress to enact it without further delay."[1]

After the speech the former president traveled to the White House to urge President Bush to withdraw his opposition to the bill. Reagan's turnabout was characterized by New York Democratic Representative Charles Schumer as akin to "Nixon going to China," while at headquarters an NRA official looked at a picture of the former president on his desk and pleaded, "Don't do this to me."[2]

In a *New York Times* op-ed published that day, Reagan, referring to those injured by Hinckley, wrote, "This nightmare might never have happened if legislation that is before Congress now—the Brady bill—had been law back in 1981."

Three weeks later NRA membership and "official family" met in San Antonio, Texas, for the 120th annual meeting. That the event occurred within sight of the Alamo, the last stand of such "citizen-soldiers" as Jim Bowie and Davy Crockett, was not lost on any of the attendees. Throughout the three-day event, images of the Alamo—*brave men who would rather die than compromise*—were recalled in support of the NRA's gun control battles. (Left unsaid was that the 187 defenders of the Alamo had lost, slaughtered within an hour of the final assault by the 5,000 troops of Mexico's General Santa Anna. Their bodies were later taken to an unknown location and burned in a pyre.)

The NRA annual meetings are reminiscent of 1970s Elvis Presley concerts. Like the King, the NRA has grown fat, bloated and quite wealthy. In San Antonio, its leaders sat on stage reciting to an aging crowd a litany of greatest hits notoriously out of sync with current events. Instead of blue-haired old ladies dominating the event, it was potbellied men with buzz cuts. Sweat-soaked scarves were replaced by pamphlets and flyers—lots of pamphlets and flyers.

Although involved in the firearms debate for eight years, and an NRA member for the past few, this was the first annual meeting I had attended. I soon found that the NRA conventioneers reinforced many stereotypes—and dispelled others. Large bearded members in blue jeans—wearing flannel shirts in spite of the 90-degree heat—joked with leisure-suit-clad men in cowboy hats. Many of them yelled at each other, their hearing destroyed by a lifetime of shooting.

At a formal dinner, three husbands enthusiastically discussed their love of John Wayne movies as their wives patiently looked on. They commiserated over the common problem of getting their spouses to put up with their devoted viewing. "I always say, 'no honey, no honey, we haven't seen this one,' " one member said, laughing. Their conversation was broken up by an energetic, grandfatherly type, a Pennsylvania firearms instructor just back from training South African security forces. He talked cheerfully about the troubles with the "Watusis" in Philadelphia. The racist comments discomfited the John Wayne fans and shocked their wives.

And this actually wasn't too surprising. Although there were some bona fide gun nuts lurking the halls of the annual meeting, most of the attendees weren't evil. They were conservative, patriotic, good Americans—who just happened to love guns. They were also unable to think in the abstract. Their gun experiences were positive. Why should they be forced to pay the price for others' misuse?

Their relationship to the NRA itself is like a golden anniversary marriage. They may grumble and complain, but their devotion is such that they aren't going to leave. "There's that lawyer, the one who kept telling us what we could and couldn't do," a wife said with scorn to her husband as NRA staffer Richard Gardiner rode down an escalator. Another member, dressed in red hunting flannels festooned with sporting patches, a bolo tie at his neck and an orange NRA cap in his lap, told the head of the Connecticut NRA affiliate how the national office took credit for a local program established by his Utah association. This apparent scorn for the NRA's apparatchiks does not, however, translate into criticism of its hard-line goals. Those who attend the annual meeting tend to be the true believers: the leadership's uncompromising stance *does* represent their views.

In the shadow of Desert Storm, the prevailing images of the event were of individual liberty and military might. "War Declared on NRA, Bill of Rights!" warned a special edition of *NRAction* in abundant supply at the meeting. The NRA warned that "as U.S. and allied forces braced for combat operations against Iraqi tyranny overseas, another war was declared in the nation's capital . . . against law-abiding citizens of the United States." The primary weapon of freedom's enemies, warned the NRA, was the Brady bill.

Although former EVP J. Warren Cassidy did not attend the annual meeting, his presence haunted it. (The annual report, printed in advance, contained a message from Cassidy noting his pleasure in serving as NRA head during "these exciting, challenging times.") And while Cassidy's absence confirmed his fall from grace, the meeting marked the triumphant return of Neal Knox to the board of directors and the victory of political hard-line election slates endorsed by Knox and *Soldier of Fortune's* Robert Brown. Of the 26 board positions open, 23 were filled by members of slates offered by

Knox and Brown—including twelve new board members. Knox received nearly 52,000 votes, which placed him 23rd in voting and returned him to the board he had been ousted from in 1984. As usual, voting was light: only 114,000 of the 1.3 million members eligible to vote bothered to mail in their ballots. Following his election, Knox told *The Washington Post*, "What you're seeing now is the NRA on the way back."

The 1991 annual meeting was the first in the NRA's history to center on a theme: the bicentennial of the ratification of the Bill of Rights. All event material proudly announced that the Commission on the Bicentennial of the United States Constitution officially recognized the NRA's theme events as being of "exceptional merit with national significance and substantial educational and historical value." The NRA had, however, played fast and loose with the commission's blessing. Its endorsement had been granted in respect to specific events involving all aspects of the Bill of Rights, most notably a national poster contest for schoolchildren. The NRA quickly turned this into a stamp of approval for itself and its interpretation of the Second Amendment. On the awards banquet program, the commission's seal appeared beneath the statement:

> The NRA takes the bedrock stand that law-abiding Americans are constitutionally entitled to the ownership and legal use of firearms. Therefore, the NRA asks the support of all loyal citizens who believe in the right to "Keep and Bear Arms." Every reputable American who owns or shoots a gun should be a member of the National Rifle Association.

As a result, the centerpiece of the meeting was the Celebration of the Bicentennial of the Bill of Rights. A Las Vegas meets Podunk "patriotic extravaganza," its main attraction was Life Member Charlton Heston. In the convention hall, uniformed Boy Scouts ushered the members to their seats, each chair topped by a flyer decrying the Brady bill. At center stage stood a six-foot Statue of Liberty with gleaming orange torch. It was flanked on both sides by giant red, white and blue NRA logos. Nine-by-twelve-foot video screens stood on either side of the stage, while an orchestra sat in front.

Acting EVP Gary Anderson, playing master of ceremonies, welcomed the full auditorium of NRA members, telling them:

> For 120 years [the NRA has] remained the Bill of Rights' most determined defender. Tonight we honor the vision of our Founding Fathers, we will salute our flag and our brave young men and women who so recently and admirably rose up to defend it. We will pay tribute to our own, the many concerned citizens who have stood firm in support of the Bill of Rights, against what has seemed like overwhelming odds. Yes tonight we celebrate, tomorrow we will prepare for tasks ahead.

The NRA's "heartfelt salute to the Bill of Rights" opened with a high-tech video melange of fighter planes, yellow ribbons, returning troops, "I'm the NRA" ads, flags and loyal Americans. The images raced against a musical backdrop of *Bonanza* cum John Sousa. With flags presented by the University of Texas, San Antonio color guard, the NRA members stood and said the Pledge of Allegiance, their hands held to their hearts. As the national anthem played, they sang, loudly.

After, Institute for Legislative Action head LaPierre addressed the crowd with a forced enthusiasm intended to inspire:

> What a night, for patriots. As I listened to our stirring anthem, and watched all those glorious flags streaming by, words you all know by heart came to mind, a simple yet powerful little slogan so many Americans display with pride: These colors don't run. Now I'd like to take that same slogan, and change it with a word or two, and aim it directly at those who are attempting to trample our precious Bill of Rights. The NRA doesn't run. The Second Amendment is a trust our Founding Fathers placed in a

free nation—rather than a nation of sheep. Those anti-gun shepherds out there can't understand that if you take away the Second Amendment then you and I become the headlines that pour out of an oppressed Eastern Europe [and] . . . someday face the same treachery and torture so commonplace today in the Middle East. We will fight and we will win. Because our cause is the right cause, because we are the *NRA*. We *are* the *NRA*. Ladies and Gentleman, the *NRA* doesn't run.

LaPierre's incantations to the crowd were met with widespread applause and set the stage for the highlight of the evening, a dramatic reading by Charlton Heston. As the music swelled, Heston took the stage. "You thought I was going to sing there for a moment," he joked. After pointed praise for LaPierre and ILA lobbyist James Jay Baker, Heston began his speech. With music rising once again in the background, he talked of the early pioneers who "with their vision . . . changed the land," and reminisced about his Michigan boyhood and an innocent, rural past that he, like many NRA members, seemed to long for:

When I was a boy . . . this idea of disarming the people, never even crossed my mind, or the minds of the good solid people who lived there. One day an old Civil War veteran who lived near let me heft his campaign rifle. And suddenly the bond between past and present . . . touched my hand. The war came, I was called away. I've still got my service .45. I keep it out of pride *and* precaution. I don't plan to fire that .45. Ever. But I have a right to that gun, guaranteed in the Bill of Rights. If I give it up, I break my bond with every American who ever rode into the west wind and died for freedom. The breathing, living spirit of Concord Ridge . . . Hamburger Hill. They call to us. They've come with a message for us. We've fought a good fight, they say. Now it's your turn. You stand tall for freedom, ya hear. The Bill of Rights, don't you back down from this now. We didn't. Take this pledge. For the sake of all those who come after us. It just may be the most important thing you ever do.

The Heston speech held the NRA crowd in rapture. An elderly woman took her husband's hand, tears welling in her eyes. The evening ended with the crowd joining in a rendition of the '80s GOP campaign anthem, Lee Greenwood's "God Bless the USA." Everyone waved miniature, Boy Scout-provided American flags.

Following the event, Heston and LaPierre met with reporters from NBC network news, *The Washington Post*, and French television. Conversation centered on the Brady bill, and Ronald Reagan's recent endorsement of it. Heston dismissed the Brady bill, arguing that "people seem to regard the Brady bill the way people recommend chicken soup if you have a cold. . . . 'Vat vould it hoit? Vat vould it hoit?'"

Heston attributed Reagan's change of heart to Nancy, noting that "I know that my wife would've been pretty upset if I'd been shot." He didn't, however, have firsthand proof, adding, "As Kitty Kelley said, I wasn't behind the bedroom door. I have heard how strongly Nancy feels about firearms." Realizing how his comments might sound in print, he later added, "If you print that Chuck Heston says Nancy made him do it . . ." To Heston, the Second Amendment stood as nothing less than the Ten Commandments, to the point where he interchanged the two, stating that the amendments to the Constitution "are carved in the same size letters in the same block of marble. People have indeed suggested," he added, "that the Second Amendment may be the most crucial, because it is the only one that anyone ever questions seriously."

Heston continued:

> I was raised in a town in Michigan where there were maybe a hundred people in the whole town. There must have been 500 guns in that town, almost all of them used for hunting. The Beltway, Los Angeles, San Francisco are kind of special. They make the laws, they set the fashions, they make the movies, television and books. You've

heard the phrase I'm sure, the rest of the country they call flyover country. But that's really the spine of the country.

Heston the actor was at ease during the press briefing, shifting between heartfelt devotion and disarming humor. ILA head LaPierre, the front runner to replace Cassidy, was sputtering and nervous, and often lapsed into rehearsed responses. At one point, when LaPierre was asked about waiting periods, an NRA press flak, unseen by the reporters, held up a piece of paper with "Gaineseville" written across it. LaPierre immediately launched into a set speech on the 1990 Gainesville, Florida, college murders and how a seven-day wait would have prevented the women from obtaining handguns.

The next day was the actual "meeting of members," the yearly conclave that had in its past glory brought Harlon Carter to power and democracy to the NRA. With power now returned to the board, the meeting has become little more than a forum for members to vent their frustrations or beliefs through the adoption of empty resolutions. Members are granted the illusion of participation when they are, in fact, powerless. Not surprisingly, some board members skip the daylong event to avoid, as the wife of one board member put it, the members' "haranguing."

The twin plagues to be excoriated at the meeting were the news media and the Brady bill. Lesser evils included lawyers, liberals and bureaucrats. Since many NRA leaders are lawyers, self-deprecating acknowledgment of this fault was required. Addressing the meeting, First Vice President Wayne Anthony Ross (whose personal stationery features a half-tone handgun and his initials—WAR) noted that after arriving in the Texas heat from Alaska he now knew what, as a lawyer, his afterlife would be like. Ross then explained the difference between Alaska and the rest of the country:

> The East Coast liberal is someone who wants to take away the right to own guns. And the conservative is someone who wants to keep the right to own guns. In Alaska, a

liberal is someone who carries a 9mm, a .357 or something small like that. And a conservative is someone who carries a .41, .44 or .45.

That morning, Ross noted, a Texan asked him if he knew what the difference between a liberal and a conservative was in the Lone Star state. A conservative, Ross was told, was a citizen. A liberal was a politician.

The members that day were, above all, looking for reassurance. They wanted a denial that the gun control issue was changing and a list of scapegoats to be pilloried. Second Vice President Robert Corbin, a former Arizona attorney general, gave them what they wanted. Asked Corbin:

> What would the media do today if we went to them and said you can't do your job until we make you wait seven days so that we can check you out and make sure your facts are correct . . . ? What if there had been a Brady bill in those days [at the Alamo], when those people wanted to come and fight for freedom? What if they had to wait seven days to get that rifle to come to the Alamo to fight? Where would they be?

(*Alive* was one answer that most likely didn't occur to any of those listening.)

The importance of the NRA's media conspiracy was illustrated when acting Executive Vice President Anderson admitted that the bad press was having an effect. Voicing his support of "General LaPierre and his troops," Anderson warned:

> Many, unfortunately among our own members, see the NRA as somehow declining, losing clout. Our attackers say our membership is going down, and that this somehow shows that our members have lost faith in us. The public is told that internal dissension demonstrates how the NRA is weakening. Our challenges today are greater than ever before, but no one should ever count the NRA out.

This acknowledgment of an embattled NRA was countered by a newly unveiled theme song that filled the hall as members filed out at the meeting's conclusion. The anthem, "I'm the NRA," was sung in a Lee Greenwood-esque voice and sounded like an outtake from the singer's most famous record. The beginning of the song promised that:

I come in every shape and size,
  Every color, sex and creed.
You'll see me walkin' every street in
  this land of the free.

The sing-along chorus boasted:

Yes, I'm Proud to Say
  I'm the NRA.
Born in America,
  And this is where I plan to stay.

Yes I'm the NRA.
  Ask me why, and I'll say
It's a God-Given freedom
  a God-Given right
A God-Given duty . . .
  AND WORTH THE FIGHT.
I'm the NRA.
I'm the NRA.

(Contrary to the song's promise, diversity was not a common trait of the meeting attendees. For the most part their colors were white, off-white, lily-white and other pale shades. Their sizes ran to large and extra-large.)

That night at the Members Banquet (steak—no substitutions) Texas Representative Jack Brooks, chair of the House Judiciary Committee, joined Corbin in railing against the Brady bill and offered his dedication to that "most maligned" of the Constitution's amendments. The Second Amendment, warned Brooks, was at risk "by those who would propose to reinterpret it. The Founding Fathers' insistence on the right to keep and bear arms was the essence of individual liberty."

Among those who sat onstage at the head table were Harlon Carter, who had been rumored to be dying of cancer. Earlier in the day, Carter had been introduced at the meeting of members as "one of us, who has been ill, but is now on the mend and doing great, and is here hale and hearty, Mr. Second Amendment himself . . ." Carter did not, however, address the audience at either event.

The meetings, receptions and ceremonies of the annual meeting all occurred against a backdrop of guns, guns, guns. The major draw of the annual meeting was the huge firearms trade show that accompanied it. With more than 150 commercial exhibits, virtually every main-line gun manufacturer was represented. Beyond a sign warning visitors not to bring any personally owned firearms into the area was a panoply of handguns, shotguns, rifles and ammunition, as well as displays touting other firearms-related endeavors. *Soldier of Fortune* magazine offered bull's-eyes with Saddam Hussein caricatures that allowed "NRA conventioneers" a chance to "take your best shot at Saddam Insane!" The Second Amendment Foundation booth offered free matchbooks with the warning that "Registering Guns to Prevent Crime is Like Registering Matches to Prevent Fire."

The majority of attendees passed over these and other less deadly product displays—outdoor clothing, brass tumblers, collectibles—for a chance to handle a Colt AR-15 assault rifle or a Smith & Wesson handgun. At a display for Sturm, Ruger & Co., an eight-year-old boy, his blond hair in a bowl cut, played with one of the brushed metal semi-automatic 9mm handguns on display. "Don't touch it. Don't touch it," said the boy's mother with a note of concern—for the gun. "You'll scratch it," she admonished. The boy's father eventually had him hold up the handgun, as he took his son's picture. The pistol, tethered to the table by a retracting cable, was difficult for the child to hold. "Hold it steady," said the father, getting angry as he snapped the photo. "Stop fooling around." While his parents admired other weapons, the boy moved on to a snub-nosed revolver, grimacing as he struggled to pull the trigger. Two minutes later he had put the handgun down.

"He's learned his lesson," said Mom. "He caught his finger in the hammer."

At the display for Derringer handguns, Lady Derringer herself, Elizabeth Saunders, a large-breasted woman in a very low cut dress, signed copies of her revealing Lady Derringer poster. She ended each personalized inscription with "Love, Lady Derringer." But if Lady Derringer represented the politically incorrect view of women and guns (Mrs. Saunders' cleavage had been featured in a critical note in *Women & Guns* magazine), Sturm, Ruger & Co. held the female high ground. At its display, Kelly Glenn, an attractive, conservatively dressed, suburban-mom type signed posters of herself in tasteful shooting clothes with a Ruger shotgun on her lap. Unlike the free affections of Lady Derringer, Ms. Glenn signed her posters "Best wishes."

For those who wished to venture beyond the convention center, chartered, air-conditioned bus tours were available. The "American Pride Tour" offered three hours of local air force bases, Fort Sam Houston and, of course, the Alamo. The "Solemente San Antonio" tour viewed San Antonio's major attractions, including the Buckhorn Hall of Horns, the largest private collection of horns, bird, fish and other animal trophies in the world. Located on the grounds of the Lone Star Brewery, visitors could drink free Lone Star beer as they toured the Halls of Horns, Feathers and Fins. Once back in their hotel rooms, NRA members could watch the NRA television commercials featuring Charlton Heston, Paul Sorvino and Linda Howard that ran continuously on the convention hotel's in-house cable system.

While the membership returned home after three days, two days of board meetings remained for the NRA's "official family." On the fourth day the board of directors met to elect the new executive vice president. A single name was submitted by the nominating committee, ILA head Wayne LaPierre. LaPierre, 41, had begun his career with the NRA in 1978 as a lobbyist in ILA's state and local affairs division, rising to head ILA in 1986. Although expected, LaPierre was in many ways a surprising choice.

The new NRA head lacked the charisma of Carter, or even Cassidy. According to NRA members and former staff, La-Pierre often appeared distracted, playing the role of the lost boy. LaPierre had a reputation for avoiding conflict with his fellow NRA staffers, often telling them what they wanted to hear. This sometimes backfired on him. As a result, LaPierre would walk around NRA headquarters with his shoulders slumped, asking of his co-workers, "Why does everybody hate me?" One fellow lobbyist had an easy answer for him: "Because you lie to them, Wayne."

LaPierre's distractions had sometimes humorous results, such as the time he overslept for a golf date with Vice President Dan Quayle. However, LaPierre was a hard-liner, and elevation of the ILA head by the board would reassure the membership of the NRA's dedication to battling gun controls. LaPierre's assistant at ILA, James Jay Baker, was moved up to head the NRA's lobbying arm. The only somewhat unexpected move at the board meeting came when First Vice President Wayne Anthony Ross was unseated. But Ross' ouster was surprising only to those with short memories. Ross, a Cassidy supporter, had introduced the motion to have Knox removed from the board in 1984. The newly conquering army had claimed its first victim.

Endnotes

1. "Bush May Compromise on Gun Bill," *Washington Post,* (March 29, 1991).
2. "Gun Control Bill Backed by Reagan in Appeal to Bush," *New York Times,* (March 29, 1991).

Chapter Thirteen

Beyond Myth

The National Rifle Association's success in battling gun controls has been due in large part to the political ineptitude of gun control organizations, the apathy of their supporters, politicians' fear of NRA retaliation and many Americans' misplaced faith in firearms as effective self-defense tools.

The violence of the past decade, however, has begun to alter the dynamics of the debate as it becomes increasingly clear that the NRA's idealized view of guns is badly out of sync with today's bloody reality. And if, as expected, gun violence increases and moves from the cities to the suburbs, the drug market reinvents itself in response to increased enforcement, and new, more powerful, technically advanced weapons continue to sweep onto the market, then things aren't going to get any easier for the NRA.

The NRA is, above all, a victim of its own success. The violence of today is the predictable result of the ready availability of a broad range of firearms and an unfettered gun industry. It's been a century-long free ride for the NRA and the manufacturers it protects, and the bill is coming due. But it's not one the NRA is yet prepared to pay.

The NRA hungers for the glory days of Prop 15 and McClure-Volkmer. The ascension of Wayne LaPierre and the resurrection of Neal Knox as a response to its slide in power indicate that the world may change, but the NRA won't. In his June 1991 inaugural column to the membership, titled "Standing Guard," LaPierre affirmed:

> Critics in the media have referred to me as a "hardliner," probably not realizing that I accept their words as a compliment. What they refer to as a hard line is in fact my bottom line. I do not intend to waver from my belief that the rights of law-abiding American citizens must be protected, no matter the cost. This belief is set in stone, and it will serve as the foundation of every policy that originates from this office.

The NRA views the gun control battle as a literal war. The organization will accept nothing less than its total destruction as proof of loss, and views the slightest ideological softening as tantamount to unconditional surrender. With the likelihood of a "born again" NRA unlikely and gun violence showing no signs of abating, the 1990s could prove to be an insecure and unhappy time for America's pre-eminent gun apologists.

Unfortunately, even if the NRA is humbled, this in no way means that laws will be enacted that reduce firearms violence. If the NRA has nothing constructive to offer on this issue, its opponents are equally threadbare in their thinking. This is because the NRA's greatest success in battling gun control has not been its legislative victories, but its ability to define the parameters of the debate and shift its focus to the organization itself. The NRA has successfully controlled the vocabulary and terms of the debate, most particularly in its ability to define firearms violence solely as a crime issue. The most notable victim of the NRA's semantic noose is America's leading gun control organization, Handgun Control, Inc. (HCI).

The Opposition

HCI was founded in 1974 by Mark Borinsky, who, after being robbed at gunpoint as a college student looked for a gun control organization to join upon his arrival in Washington, D.C. Finding that none existed, he founded the National Council to Control Handguns (NCCH). Borinsky was soon joined by Nelson T. "Pete" Shields, a marketing manager with E. I. du Pont de Nemours and Company, whose son had been murdered with a handgun in San Francisco's 1974 Zebra killings. At approximately the same time, the Board of Church and Society of the Methodist Church established the National Coalition to Ban Handguns (NCBH), a coalition of more than 30 national religious, labor and non-profit organizations, including NCCH. NCCH soon left the coalition, renaming itself Handgun Control, Inc. (HCI). It now dominates the gun control movement, to the point where it is equated in the public mind with the movement itself. HCI today is a high-profile, non-profit corporation with an annual budget of $7 million. NCBH, renamed the Coalition to Stop Gun Violence in 1990, continues to labor in the shadow of its former partner.

HCI's public relations strategy focused on the tragedy of Shields' loss and his belief that "sensible" handgun controls would have prevented his son's death. This "victim's strategy" dictates HCI's outlook and activities to this day. In 1985 Sarah Brady, wife of injured White House Press Secretary James Brady, joined the organization as its primary spokesperson and in 1989 succeeded Shields as chairperson. Brady's Republican ties only aided the organization's "reasonable"—i.e., non-liberal—image. She quickly became the preeminent media figure in the gun control debate. In 1989 James Brady joined his wife in battling for the HCI flagship bill named in his honor—a seven-day waiting period for retail handgun sales with optional local background check.

Although in its early days HCI avoided direct attacks on the NRA, since the early 1980s it has presented itself as the

NRA's blood enemy and successfully used its opponent's size and reputation as a tool to win members and dollars. In HCI literature the NRA is a thuggish giant that it alone can bring down. Ever thin-skinned, the NRA has responded in kind, finding in Sarah Brady and HCI the face of the enemy it both fears and needs.

Both HCI and the NRA demonize one another in their direct mail and publications. The envelope of a famous HCI direct-mail piece promises the recipient that enclosed is "your first real chance to tell the National Rifle Association to go to hell!" Inside the reader is warned that "if you've ever doubted that the National Rifle Association is thumbing its nose at you just consider these frightening facts. . . ." After a litany of firearms violence and NRA political goals the letter asks, "Just who the hell is running this country . . . Congress or the National Rifle Association?"

In NRA publications, HCI has been pictured as a giant vulture, presumably feasting off the carcasses of handgun victims. A January 1991 article in *NRAction* headlined "Baseless, Personal Attacks From A Vicious Lobby" offered Washington Representative Jolene Unsoeld's characterization of Sarah Brady and her husband as "Unprofessional. Threatening. Fanatics who 'shrieked in my face.'"

Ironically, despite the genuine hatred that each organization feels for the other, HCI and the NRA share a similar view of the nature of gun violence. Neither sees the handgun itself as inherently the problem, but views violence as stemming from the weapons being in the "wrong" hands. The NRA states its case with the familiar bumper sticker slogan: "Guns Don't Kill, People Do." HCI's catchphrase, "Working to Keep Handguns Out of the Wrong Hands," clarifies the NRA's argument into "Guns Don't Kill, *Bad* People Do."

HCI defines the "wrong hands" as minors, criminals, drunks, drug users and the mentally incompetent. Yet this universe, by its own definition, is small. Those who die in alcohol-fueled shootings aren't necessarily drunks, and people who put a gun to their head aren't by definition mentally incompetent. Such an approach implies that it's somehow possible to separate "good" handguns (those in our hands for self-defense) from "bad" handguns (those in the hands of criminals). This view fails to acknowledge the inherently dangerous nature of handguns.

Like the NRA, HCI is quick to paint handgun violence as a "crime" issue and promises that its legislative remedies will make it harder for these "wrong hands" to hold a handgun. HCI argues that the problem of handgun violence can be solved through the passage of a national handgun waiting period with background check, a ban on the manufacture of snub-nosed handguns (handguns with barrels of three inches or less), a ban on the sale of assault weapons, establishing standards for secondary handgun sales and the reporting of handgun theft; mandatory safety training and use of trigger locks; and restrictions on multiple handgun sales.

By framing the issue in terms of "crime," HCI and the NRA have created a situation where, no matter which organization eventually triumphs, little will be accomplished to end the killing. Although drug-related violence has recently escalated, it isn't criminals who are killing most of the 22,000 people who die each year from handguns. Crime is merely the most publicized aspect of the widespread public health problem created by the easy availability of handguns.

The vast majority of handgun deaths are suicides—about 12,000 per year. And although one out of ten who attempt suicide will kill themselves no matter what, for most the will to die lasts briefly. The success or failure of an attempt rests primarily on the lethality of the means employed. Pills and razor blades are inefficient and allow for second thoughts. Handguns do the job to near perfection. The importance of lethality of means in suicide attempts is illustrated by the fact that although women try to kill themselves four times as often as men, men succeed three to four times as often. Women use pills or other less lethal means, and often survive. Men use handguns. (As more women buy handguns, increases are also being seen in their suicide success rates.)

In 1989, more than 9,000 Americans died in handgun murders. For all murder victims, more than half knew their killers. Fifteen percent occurred between family members, while 39 percent involved acquaintances. Most murders were the result of arguments. Only 21 percent were felony-related. This is not to suggest that all of the perpetrators were model citizens driven to kill by the mere presence of a handgun; violence may have already been a component of their lives. Yet handguns allowed them to kill at will, in the home or on the street, with the unique efficiency that only these weapons can offer. As the FBI has noted in its *Uniform Crime Reports,* "Murder is a societal problem over which law enforcement has little or no control." It is also a problem "common sense" gun control measures will have little or no effect upon. Most of these people would have no problem obtaining a handgun under any control scheme proposed by HCI. As an extension of their "wrong hands" thesis, HCI and the NRA both defend the right of citizens to own handguns for protection of their homes—even though the vast majority of handguns used in suicides and murders were originally purchased for just that purpose. According to federal statistics, for every time a citizen uses a handgun to kill a criminal, 118 innocent lives are ended in handgun murders, suicides and accidents. In other words, whenever handguns are around, the "right hands" have a nasty tendency to turn into the "wrong hands."

The Straw Man

In spite of this evidence, Handgun Control, Inc. clings to its "wrong hands" argument. This is because its agenda has been driven less by research and analysis than by what people will accept—as reflected in public opinion polls. In his 1981 book, *Guns Don't Die—People Do,* Shields points out that the majority of Americans don't favor a ban on handguns. (The percentage of the American population that favors banning handguns holds at about 40 percent, with higher percentages in urban areas and among women and blacks.) "What they do want," says Shields "is a set of strict laws to control the easy access to handguns by the criminal and the violence-prone—as long as those controls don't jeopardize the perceived right of law-abiding citizens to buy and own handguns for self-defense."

This wasn't always the organization's stand. Shields originally labeled a ban on private handgun possession the "most effective" solution to reducing violent crime. In a 1976 *New Yorker* article he expounded on this:

> Our ultimate goal—total control of handguns in the United States—is going to take time. My estimate is from seven to ten years. The first problem is to slow down the increasing number of handguns being produced and sold in this country. The second problem is to get handguns registered. And the final problem is to make the possession of *all* handguns and *all* handgun ammunition—except for the military, policemen, licensed security guards, licensed sporting clubs, and licensed gun collectors—totally illegal.

This position was abandoned when Shields got his "first hard lesson in the political facts of life." Handgun bans, he was told, weren't a legislative reality. As a result, by 1985 Shields was on Capitol Hill attesting to his firm belief "in the right of law-abiding citizens to possess handguns . . . for legitimate purposes."

Most of the credit for HCI's shift, however, belongs to a 1981 poll it commissioned from Washington's Peter Hart Research Associates, Inc. The Hart poll showed that people were more likely to favor immediately limited forms of handgun controls such as licensing and waiting periods as opposed to outright banning. The poll quickly became a virtual holy text for HCI, continually cited to its critics in the gun control movement as justification for its legislative proposals.

That the organization redefined its legislative approach in light of political realities is not surprising. What critics of HCI have questioned is the organization's tendency to recast the reality of gun violence in the mold of its political tactics. Once it is granted that handguns have a utilitarian purpose, the

NRA has won half the battle. This approach reinforces NRA myths and helps forestall the day when it's acknowledged that the country's handgun problem stems from the weapons themselves. That HCI suffers from institutional schizophrenia is illustrated by the fact that the organization and its foundation, the Center to Prevent Handgun Violence, consistently acknowledge the damage done by legal handgun possession and their uselessness as self-defense tools, yet are unwilling to endorse handgun banning. Like the NRA, the Center to Prevent Handgun Violence even offers a pamphlet with easy guidelines for the safe storage and use of handguns. The implication is that with proper care and feeding, a handgun can be made as safe as any other household tool. Unfortunately, a handgun isn't a blender.

Admittedly, in terms of dollars and publicity, HCI's approach has made it one of the great success stories in the history of public interest politics. But HCI's "wrong hands" philosophy has also created the ultimate straw man for the NRA to knock down. As the NRA correctly points out, criminals will be the last segment of society to obey gun control laws, no matter how limited or severe. They are, after all, criminals.

In addition, less than 20 percent of criminals buy their guns in gun stores. Most buy, rent or trade them second-hand on the street, or steal them from people who own them for self-defense. Virtually all gun control proposals ignore the numerous ways—legal and illegal—that guns can be siphoned from the vast American firearms pool of 200 million guns, 50 million to 70 million of which are handguns. In fact, anyone who wants a gun can get one. The "black market"—the world beyond the gun store counter—is now merely an alternative, far more convenient, showcase.

The disturbing conclusion is that America is long past the point where licensing, registration, safety training, waiting periods or mandatory sentencing are going to have much effect. Such measures may save a few lives and catch some criminals, but they will have little effect on most handgun suicides and murders. After all, a "controlled" handgun kills just as effectively as an "uncontrolled" one.

Giving the People What They Want

The Brady bill is a case study in the limitations of control measures and the risks they represent to the long-term success of the movement to reduce gun violence.

The Brady bill was unveiled by HCI in 1987 as its flagship measure. By 1991 momentum was gaining for passage. The NRA, mirroring its past political tactics, offered a last-minute compromise: an "instant check" for handgun purchases that would allow dealers to check buyers' names against a national data base to block those with criminal records from purchasing firearms. Critics labeled the measure a gun control "Star Wars," arguing that development of such an information base would take years, cost hundreds of millions of dollars and be of limited accuracy.

NRA efforts in the House of Representatives were too little, too late. The Brady bill passed in May 1991 by 239 to 186, a greater margin of victory than gun control activists had expected.

Building on the momentum of the House vote, a month later the U.S. Senate approved a hybrid bill that combined Brady with the NRA's instant-check proposal. On June 28 the Senate voted 67 to 32 to approve a national five-day waiting period as part of an omnibus crime bill. (The crime bill also contained an assault weapons ban similar to that passed in 1990.) Under the bill, local police would be required to use any resources available to them to conduct a background check on possible handgun purchasers. At the same time, federal money would be allocated to aid in the development of the computer data bases necessary for the instant check. The waiting period itself would be repealed in two and a half years as the instant-check system went on line. Records would need be only 80 percent complete for the previous five years. States that failed to develop the system would be forced to retain the five-day waiting period.

The Senate version of the bill was generally acknowledged to be the version that would leave Congress for presidential signature. And although stronger than the House version of the Brady bill, it was in fact little more than a phased-in version of the NRA's instant-check compromise. Even if signed into law, the NRA's primary goal—that law-abiding citizens shouldn't have to wait for handguns under federal law—could eventually be achieved.

Nonetheless, congressional passage of the Brady bill was a great political victory for the gun control movement and was hailed as marking the end of the NRA's dominance of Congress. Charles Schumer, chair of the House Subcommittee on Crime, promised after the House vote that "the stranglehold of the NRA on Congress is now broken. They had this aura of invincibility, that they couldn't be beaten. They were beaten handsomely and handily."

Schumer was right in that Congress' voting for anything labeled "gun control" can only weaken the NRA's influence and ease the passage of future measures. Yet passage of the bill was not a substantive victory. In battling for passage, the bill's advocates talked mostly of the public's support—more than 90 percent—not what the measure would do. This was not surprising, since waiting periods and background checks are of limited value. California has a 15-day waiting period for all guns with a mandatory background check. In 1990, less than one percent of all applicants were denied firearms—2,400 of more than 330,000 applications. Of these 2,400, most of whom who were merely told they couldn't have the gun, no one knows how many instead bought their guns second-hand, stole them or had someone else purchase the gun for them.

Even the most celebrated example cited in support of the Brady bill—John Hinckley—would most likely not have been stopped by its restrictions. Hinckley used a valid state I.D. in a Texas pawn shop to purchase the handgun with which he shot Ronald Reagan and James Brady. Under the bill, nothing in his criminal or psychiatric history would have raised a red flag. And the seven-day wait would have had no effect. Hinckley had the handgun five months before he tried to kill the president.

A waiting period will stop those few people who run out to a gun store to buy a handgun on impulse to kill themselves or someone else, and force criminals foolish enough to buy their handguns retail to turn to other sources. It might also push up the price of illegal street guns by placing one more hurdle in the way of gun traffickers. Finally, it could also act as a disincentive for legal handgun purchases. Americans hate to wait, even for handguns.

Faced with its limitations, Brady bill supporters unfailingly fell back on the gun control argument of last resort—"if it saves one life." Of course, saving even one life is good. Distorting the realities of gun violence, however, assures that the number will never grow much beyond this.

Prior to the House and Senate votes, expectations for the Brady bill—built up by the news media and the gun control movement—far outweighed anything it could possibly do. This point was acknowledged by the bill's House sponsor, Ohio Democrat Edward Feighan, who told *The Washington Post*:

> We've had to invest an enormous amount of political capital in order to get to this point of near passage, of a very moderate, common-sense bill like the Brady bill. In the process, many of us have been forced to overstate what we can get from the Brady bill.

Overstatement had reached the point where the Brady bill had become equated with gun control itself. The danger of this is that enactment of a national waiting period could result in Congress, the press and the public viewing the problem as solved, leaving the issue of gun control to founder for the near future—probably for years. And as firearms violence continues unchecked, the bill will then serve as just another NRA example of how "gun control" doesn't work. While the press and public have rallied around the Brady bill as a virtual motherhood issue, it is unlikely that the limited handgun control measures being trumpeted by HCI for the '90s—such as bans on multiple handgun sales and mandatory trigger locks—will have the same appeal. And even if they do, their effect on gun violence will be negligible.

From the NRA's perspective, passage will not only remove one of the gun control lobby's most powerful weapons against it, but will stand as proof that it has not been crying wolf to American gun owners. It can, with a newfound credibility, point to the Brady bill as the first step down the slippery slope of the oft-cited gun grabbers' "Master Plan" to disarm America. Historically, NRA membership rises in the wake of significant gun control legislation.

Why then was so much political capital spent for a bill that really doesn't do much? The easy answer is politics. The Brady bill is the only measure HCI thinks it can get passed. It is a legislative Last of the Mohicans, the sole remnant of Kennedy-Rodino, HCI's grand omnibus gun control bill of the late 1970s and early 1980s. Kennedy-Rodino would have required a national 21-day waiting period with background check for all retail and private handgun sales; held handgun sellers civilly liable for the misuse of an illegally sold handgun; banned the future sale of short-barreled handguns; raised dealer licensing fees; required record keeping of all secondary handgun transfers; and required handgun manufacturers, dealers and owners to report the theft of handguns. Its paucity of support in Congress quickly became a bitter joke among gun control advocates. HCI has never won a national fight on any of its key issues as defined by Kennedy-Rodino and badly needed a victory. In short, gun control had to shake its loser image.

At times it seems as if the effectiveness of HCI's proposals doesn't matter to the organization anymore. The purpose for which the movement was created—saving lives—has been superseded by a new goal: beating the NRA. The thrust of the news stories following House passage of the Brady bill focused not on the measure itself, but the NRA's loss. The gun control movement must decide. If it chooses to refocus on its original mission of ending gun violence, it must abandon the cliché-ridden dicta that have dominated the debate for the past two decades and examine the issue with a hard-edged objectivity that seeks solutions that will work, not just slogans that will sell.

The Final Challenge

Passage of the Brady bill represents the first major hurdle for the modern handgun control movement—showing that the NRA can be beaten on a core issue. The second challenge is for the movement to acknowledge the realities of firearms violence and establish long-term goals that address them.

Since its inception, the gun control movement has been reactive, developing legislation to meet challenges posed by the firearms industry. All too often the effectiveness of legislative solutions has been reduced by the compromising nature of politics. In addition, the industry is adept at following the letter but not the intent of the law. With burgeoning new technology and the perpetual need to resell the market, such industry challenges will continue well into the 21st century. To approach each new issue as an individual problem can only fail in the long term. There must be a unified plan, the first step of which would be to remove the firearms industry's most unique characteristic: its virtually total lack of regulation.

The turning point will come when handgun violence is recognized for what it is: a broad-based public health problem stemming from the widespread and virtually unregulated distribution of a hazardous consumer product, a problem that cannot be solved until the product is taken off the market. Handguns and other firearms enjoy a unique niche in the consumer marketplace. Virtually all products sold in America come under the regulatory power of specific federal agencies to ensure their safety. Guns are one of the notable exceptions.

The ultimate solution to America's firearms crisis lies in implementing a comprehensive regulatory scheme that gives a federal agency real power to control the design, manufacture, distribution and sale of firearms and ammunition. Each category of firearm and type of ammunition would be subjected to a risk/benefit analysis to weed out those products whose potential harm outweighs any possible benefits. Manufacture and distribution would be tightly controlled, with compliance actively monitored. And the number of licensed manufacturers, dealers and importers would be severely curtailed. The implementation of such standards would most likely result in an immediate ban on the future production and sale of handguns and assault weapons because of their limited utility and high risk. The granting of federal regulatory power would also act as a check on the industry from developing products it knows it would never be allowed to market. Such an approach is the NRA's and the industry's worst nightmare and would require a long-term willingness on the part of the gun control movement to tell the American public some unpleasant truths about gun violence. Such clearly defined and effective goals would, however, give intermediate measures such as the Brady bill new significance.

The political will for such an approach doesn't exist even in the gun control movement, let alone Congress. Yet as violence increases, it stands as the only solution left. The NRA's power and influence may well diminish throughout the 1990s. Yet if the gun control movement fails to acknowledge the realities of firearms violence for fear of offending an American public enchanted with the NRA's 120-year-old myths, this will stand as the NRA's greatest victory.

Appendix One

No Right to Keep and Bear Arms

by Kristen Rand

[Kristen Rand is Of Counsel to the Firearms Policy Project of the Violence Policy Center.]

The National Rifle Association is the only lobbying organization in America with half of a constitutional amendment emblazoned across the front of its headquarters. When citing the Second Amendment, the NRA systematically deletes the phrase "A well regulated militia, being necessary to the security of a free state," from the oft-quoted second half of the amendment, "the right of the people to keep and bear arms, shall not be infringed."

Primarily as the result of the NRA's efforts, the Second Amendment is the most misunderstood provision contained in the Bill of Rights. The purpose of the Second Amendment is to guarantee the states' ability to maintain independent militias composed of state residents available to be called upon to defend the country should its security be threatened. The Founding Fathers' reliance on state militias to perform this military task stemmed from their deep distrust of a standing federal army. The NRA and other members of America's gun lobby neatly ignore the legal history surrounding the amendment, choosing instead to propagate the myth that it guarantees an individual right to keep and bear arms.

The U.S. Supreme Court, the ultimate arbiter of the amendment's intent, has addressed its meaning in several cases. In 1886, the Court ruled in *Presser v. Illinois* that the Second Amendment functions only as a check on the power of the federal government—preventing it from interfering with a state's ability to maintain a militia—and in no way limits the states' powers to regulate firearms.

States, therefore, are not prohibited by the Second Amendment from controlling private ownership of handguns and other categories of firearms in virtually any way they see fit. The question then becomes to what extent may the federal government regulate the ownership of firearms by citizens?

The U.S. Supreme Court dealt directly with this question in a 1939 decision, *United States v. Miller*. In *Miller* the Court upheld a federal law making it a crime to ship a sawed-off shotgun in interstate commerce. Refusing to strike down the law on Second Amendment grounds absent any evidence that a sawed-off shotgun had "some reasonable relationship to the preservation or efficiency of a well regulated militia," the Court held that the Second Amendment "must be interpreted and applied" only in the context of safeguarding the continuation and effectiveness of the state militias.

Yet perhaps the most significant case is the 1980 decision in *Lewis v. United States*. The majority opinion, joined by then Chief Justice Warren Burger and current Chief Justice William Rehnquist, ruled that restrictions contained in the Gun Control Act of 1968 prohibiting felons from owning firearms were constitutional. In its analysis, the Court applied a "rational basis" standard, which requires that the remedy need merely be "rationally related to a legitimate purpose." The application of this standard is revealing. When determining whether a statute meets equal protection requirements, statutes that impinge on fundamental, individual rights—such as freedom of speech or the right to counsel—are judged by the more rigorous "strict scrutiny" standard. In *Lewis*, the Court stated, "These legislative restrictions on the use of firearms do not trench upon any constitutionally protected liberties." The opinion listed voting, the practice of medicine, and even holding office in labor organizations as "activities far more fundamental than the possession of a firearm."

In 1972 Justice William O. Douglas warned that one aspect of the damage wrought by the popular misinterpretation of the Second Amendment is a diminution of Fourth Amendment protections against search and seizure. In a powerful dissent to a decision extending the ability of police to stop and frisk suspects, Douglas argued, "The police problem is an acute one not because of the Fourth Amendment, but because of the ease with which anyone can acquire a pistol. A powerful lobby dins into the ears of our citizenry that these gun purchases are constitutional rights protected by the Second Amendment. . . . There is no reason why all pistols should not be barred to everyone except the police."

And in January 1991 the U.S. Supreme Court refused to hear a challenge to the 1986 congressional ban on the manufacture of new machine guns. The Court let stand a ruling by the Eleventh Circuit Court of Appeals in *Farmer v. Higgens* that denying the plaintiff a license to manufacture a new machine gun was not unconstitutional.

The Eleventh Circuit's ruling was not surprising. The federal courts, in accordance with Supreme Court precedents, have consistently held that there is no individual right to own a gun.

In *United States v. Warin,* the Sixth Circuit Court of Appeals in 1976 expressed exasperation with the misguided arguments made by the defendant in attempting to persuade the court that the federal law prohibiting possession of an unregistered machine gun violated his Second Amendment rights. Upholding the defendant's conviction, the court stated, "It would unduly extend this opinion to attempt to deal with every argument made by defendant . . . all of which are based on the erroneous supposition that the Second Amendment is concerned with the rights of individuals rather than those of the states."

In a decision upholding a 1981 ban on the possession and sale of handguns in Morton Grove, Illinois, the Seventh Circuit Court of Appeals stated flatly that "possession of handguns by individuals is not part of the right to keep and bear arms." The U.S. Supreme Court refused to review the decision.

In 1984 the same court upheld a two-year-old ordinance that froze the number of handguns in Chicago. In allowing the law to stand, the court noted that it did "not impinge upon the exercise of a fundamental personal right."

In short, the federal courts have consistently given the Second Amendment a collective, militia interpretation. Moreover, no gun control measure has ever been struck down as unconstitutional under the Second Amendment. The federal government is clearly free to regulate the possession and transfer of specific categories of firearms in order to promote public safety.

Yet despite the volume of evidence to the contrary, many Americans believe the Second Amendment protects individual rights. A Hearst poll conducted in the mid-1980s found that half of those surveyed believed that the Constitution guarantees their right to own a handgun.

The primary reason for this confusion is the National Rifle Association. In its advertising, direct-mail and public appearances the NRA plays upon the public's fear of big government and crime, offering private firearm—specifically handgun—ownership as the last bulwark against criminal and governmental takeover. The NRA has successfully transformed the public's perception of firearms ownership from a privilege to an inalienable constitutional right.

Contrary to the rhetoric, however, the issue has long been settled. The Second Amendment in no way guarantees an individual right to keep and bear arms.

Appendix Two

Toward a Better NRA

by Ted and Françoise Gianoutsos

[The authors are life and benefactor members of the National Rifle Association.]

National Rifle Association members currently face twin realities: record firearms violence in the United States and growing discord in their organization. As Americans and NRA members, we understand the deadly harm that can result from firearms misuse. We believe, however, in self-control, not gun control, as a solution to firearms violence. Self-control is best learned by example, reinforced by firearms laws that allow its practice.

The National Rifle Association must place protection of the Second Amendment second to the ethical, responsible, accountable and safe use of firearms. The best way for the NRA and its members to ensure that their right to own guns remains intact is to demonstrate and promote respect for firearms while acknowledging their dangers.

Ethical firearms use can only be promoted by example. NRA members should be the leaders in agreeing to a code of basic ethical standards regarding the ownership, trade and use of all firearms. Federal, state and local laws regarding hunting and personal firearms use should always be adhered to and respected. Because the leadership of the NRA sets the example not only for the members of our association but for all gun owners, they should adhere to the most strict of ethical standards in their personal and professional lives, armed or unarmed.

Responsible firearms use requires the development of a set of accepted high standards regarding firearms ownership and use and a dedication on the part of gun owners to help enforce such standards. In addition, the NRA leadership should publicly condemn, and work to reduce, the glorification of firearms and gratuitous depictions of firearms violence on television and in movies. The development of such standards would require the establishment of comprehensive national laws including: standardized firearms licensing laws, background checks for firearms purchases and strict laws regulating the transportation of firearms. Minimum possession standards should require that firearms owners obtain use-specific licenses for their guns and that they demonstrate competency and proficiency through completion of a mandatory, national firearms training program. In some European nations compulsory firearms training for hunters is more than 100 hours of weekend instruction over months. So should it be here.

Accountable firearms use requires stricter, standardized laws to punish those who misuse firearms. The NRA should lead in the development of such laws and actively work to aid in the improvement of the criminal justice system.

Safe use of firearms use requires training. The NRA is the acknowledged leader in this field. The NRA should now develop realistic curricula for personal certification, licensing and youth safety.

Members and money are the heart and lifeblood of any organization. The future of the NRA lies in direct member participation and the responsible use of each member's contribution. To this end:

- Annual NRA dues should be set at $100 per member per year. Although such an amount may seem high, many members give close to this amount each year in the wake of special fundraising mailings conducted by the organization. Of this annual contribution, $50 should be placed in an NRA endowment fund invested in long-term U.S. Treasury securities. The fund would be used to help establish firearms training and shooting facilities throughout the nation. The remaining $50 would be used to finance the operations of the NRA.

- All members should be enfranchised to vote by mail ballot for directors and officers of the NRA. The board of directors should be reduced from its current level of 75 to 15. The executive council should be abolished.

- Each year the NRA should release to the members a detailed financial report on its income and expenses identical to the tax returns filed with the federal government.

- Member magazines should be free of industry advertising to ensure their impartiality in firearms reviews. In addition, space should be made available for unedited commentary from membership regarding member concerns and NRA policy.

- Critical policy decisions facing the National Rifle Association should be placed before the membership via referenda. Such votes can be undertaken via mail balloting through the NRA's publications.

- The NRA's lobbying arm, the Institute for Legislative Action, and its political action committee, the Political Victory Fund, should be abolished. In their place, NRA leadership should put in place programs to encourage and promote direct member participation in local, state and federal legislative activities.

We want to see an NRA with honest, courageous and exemplary leadership. Our vision is of an NRA that earns the respect of all Americans, especially the majority of citizens who do not own or use firearms. Our firearms rights and privileges rest on the respect and tolerance of our fellow citizens. Recognizing this, the NRA should encourage a more diverse membership with respect to sex, age and race.

We also look to the day when we will see an end to the hyperbole and emotional rhetoric that now defines the tone of the NRA as the result of its fund-raising efforts. There should be an end to the vilification of citizens legitimately concerned about firearms violence. Such people are not the enemy. It is absurd to consider them a threat to our welfare. After all, we are the ones who are armed.